HOW WE'D TALK
If the English had WON in 1066

David Cowley

Bright Pen

Visit us online at www.authorsonline.co.uk

A Bright Pen Book

Copyright © David Cowley 2009

Cover design by David Cowley ©

All rights reserved. No part of this publication may be reproduced, stored in a retrieval system, or transmitted in any form or by any means, electronic, mechanical, photocopy, recording or otherwise, without prior written permission of the copyright owner. Nor can it be circulated in any form of binding or cover other than that in which it is published and without similar condition including this condition being imposed on a subsequent purchaser.

ISBN 978 07552 1167 8

Authors OnLine Ltd
19 The Cinques
Gamlingay, Sandy
Bedfordshire SG19 3NU
England

This book is also available in e-book format, details of which are available at www.authorsonline.co.uk

A thief in the dark ate up noble speech, and its steadfastness

(Adaptation, after part of Old English Riddle 47 in the Exeter Book)

... sette ... swa swa he hit sweotolost and andgitfullicast gereccan mihte ...

... set ... as he could reckon it in the clearest and ongetfullest way
(= most perceptive way)

(King Alfred the Great, from foreword to one of his translations into Old English, Author's translation.)

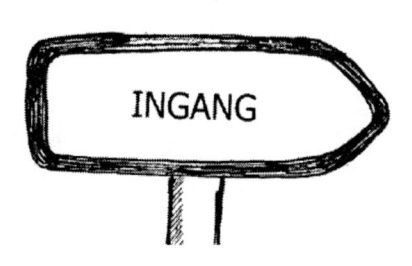

> Feel free to look:
> No boundness to buy!

Acknowledgements: To my kinsfolk at home, for bearing with the writing of 'daddy's book'. Sincere thanks to Prof. David Crystal for some heartening advice and comments at a critical stage. Also to Hindrik Sijens of the Fryske Akademy, Ljouwert, for Frisian translations (p. 18). Also for comments/ advice from Joseph Biddulph, Tony Linsell and Martin Cutts. Steven Jones - technical input with cover. And in the past, to those who gave helpful words here and there, which can go a long way when one is working on this kind of 'big' idea over many years, not forgetting Steve Cowley - 'ta, youth'.

Layout, all illustrations (including handwritten copy in Foreword) and idea for cover layout - by author.

The Author
A former teacher of English as a foreign language, David Cowley is from the East Midlands and lives in North Wales, working in an advisory role in local government. Having an early interest in languages, he became fluent in Welsh and studied Old English, Scottish Gaelic, Greek, and other languages. A qualified teacher, he taught in a Welsh-medium school for some years, later taking CELTA before teaching English in Moscow. He is the author of a short forerunner to the present work, *Eldsay English* (1999).

INSIDE

Foreword	6
Aims, Background and Why	8
Outline of Book, with Notes	11
Booklist	20

PART 1: FIVE STEPS TO HOW WE'D TALK

Lead-in: Some Choices in English	23
Step 1: Ready and Clear	28
Step 2: That Sounds Right	40
Step 3: I Think I get that	61
Step 4: What's that Mean Exactly?	78
Step 5: Weird and Wonderful	104
Further Examples and Tests	134
Answers to Tests	141

PART 2: REFERENCE WORD LISTS

I. Words from Steps 1 - 5, with Old English Sources	152
II. Thesaurus in Order of Loanwords	211
Endword	265

Foreword

The Parker version of the Anglo-Saxon Chronicle for 1066 includes this stark statement:

𐑎 hep cō pillelm 7 geþann œngla land.

= And her com Willelm and gewann ængla land

= And here came William and won England

One could ask the question 'what if things had been different?' about many aspects of history. So, why especially *this* big 'what if?' The main reason is the undisputed fact that the Norman Conquest was a key time of change in English history which led to the English language taking on many words from French and Latin in the long run. Many happenings in England, Britain and elsewhere – including many aspects of European and world history, were also coloured by the conquest. With the English language itself bound up in history, and such a familiar and strong force in the world today, it is especially fascinating to see how we could be talking now had Hastings gone the other way. And that *could* so easily have happened. The armies at Hastings had been so evenly matched that they had (unusually for the time) fought most of the day before King Harold was killed and it was clear which side had won. In our cover scenario, the arrow has hit a little higher, and broken on his helmet. There were many other things about 1066 which, if only very slightly different, could have led to an outcome other than a Norman king on the throne by the end of that year ...

The book fills a gap, because (to my knowledge), there hasn't before been such a study showing how so many words from Old English might look today, had 'we' won in 1066. It seeks to do this in a format which will be understandable and entertaining for most folk (and with the Old English source words given in part of a reference section, for those who want to see the evidence). I hope you'll find it fun, interesting and **fremeful** (useful)!

The English-speaking world is a many-hued world, and there has never been such a variety of folk on earth who have shared the same speech. I hope that this book can offer something of helpful use for all. English has gained much by borrowing form other tongues, but there are important insights to be had from considering what had been lost too. Not least, I feel we should spare a thought for the many languages which are today being influenced, changed, and sometimes dying out under the weight of modern English.

One more thing: when you've been through the five Steps, give some thought as to whether something of this wealth of words could find its way back to that many-hued tongue that we know as today's English.

Aims, Background and Why

The main aim of this book is to get an insight into how English might have looked had there been no Norman Conquest, based on updates of known words from the English of and around that time. I have tried to do this in a way that lets those who have little or no knowledge of grammar follow with ease, whilst also giving the *main* basic grammatical terms (and the original Old English source words) in the appropriate places, for reference. The book runs from the very easy in Step 1, through to the 'weird and wonderful' in Step 5. Though the way in which words are presented varies a little to reflect this progression, I have always sought to group words under suitable common themes to make for a smooth learning process, which will hopefully be fun too!

The book also aims to shed a little light into ways in which languages can change. I hope that it will be clear from the early chapters that the gaining of foreign loans may not always bring a gain in clarity (see what *you* think on this). We shall see that quite a few words - especially many in Steps 1 to 3 - are actually meaningful in today's spelling. In that light the book has a further aim to bring these into the public eye and mind, for potential use once more.

A quick history lesson will help explain how the need for this book arose. The earliest English we have written down in any quantity (usually known as Old English or Anglo-Saxon) comes from the time around and a little before a thousand years ago. Whilst a few loanwords from Latin and Greek found their way into English at this time, the writers and poets that made up/ set down work in English, or translated *to* English - did so mainly using the basic wordstock of Old English. Then, in and after 1066, many of the most powerful and influential English speakers were swept away by the Norman Conquest and its aftermath. French came to be much used as a spoken tongue in higher circles, and Latin tended to replace English in many of the written contexts where it had been used before. Over the next few hundred years many French and Latin words replaced earlier English ones, though far from all, because many of our most everyday words are from Old English. English has gone on taking on more and more words from other languages, often to great effectiveness. But there has been little thought as to whether there may have been more appropriate alternatives from the wordstock of early English.

Why? - Ten Reasons for this Book

Linked to the aims above, here are some key reasons for spending time on this subject:

1. It's fascinating and fun to consider how English could look today, had history been different.

Many of the words themselves are very interesting because they ...

2. ... can sometimes say things that we have no one exact word for today: *He **yearnfully** watched the **middaily** rush, **misthinking** they were better off than him.*

3. ... can sometimes make more sense than the word currently used for the same idea: *An **upness** of 20 degrees* (elevation of 20 degrees). *A king with no **afterfollower*** (no successor).

4. ... are often like familiar everyday words, which can make them sound more friendly, less pretentious/ less overawing: *Guilty of **oathbreach*** (perjury). *She was **forebusied**, and **onbeloaded** with work* (... preoccupied and had had work inflicted upon her). *A five week old **birther*** (instead of cold medical-speak *foetus*).

5. ... are expressive and colourful: *Through **beholdness**, they saw the **behideness** of gold* (through observation, they saw the concealment of gold). ***Sayness anewed!*** (expression renewed!).

And, furthermore...

6. Having borrowed so much from Latin, French and other languages, is it not time to look back to the roots of English itself?

7. Leaning about how English changed can help us understand how fragile languages can be in the face of might.

8. It can also help us learn more broadly about how languages change.

9. The study can foster an interest in language and how words are used for expression.

10. The loss of many words, in the wake of 1066 and its long aftermath, is a wrong that should be righted - it is time to think about claiming some of our words back!

Forthfroming Room
Departure Room

Outline of Book, with Notes

The book is in two parts. Following background material, Part 1 is made up of five Steps, each of which covers a range of words with origins in early English, with some examples of use. These take you from the easy and clear, through to harder, and sometimes strange-looking words that really would give English a very different feel if still in use.
Outline of Steps:

> Step 1 - Use of a first set of words modernised from Old English. These are readily understandable, and cover ideas for which there are sometimes no obvious exact alternatives in current English.
> Step 2 - More words updated from Old English, but generally these have alternatives today which are foreign-derived loanwords. The updated words often sound 'right', and meaningful to modern English speakers.
> Step 3 - Builds further on the kinds of words covered in Step 2. Words are still often quite clear and understandable to readers.
> Step 4 - Words modernised from Old English which need more thought and/ or explanation of their updated forms for today's English.
> Step 5 - A fascinating look at some of the words which have utterly died out of use, but which were once at the heart of English. Here, more than anywhere, we get some insight into just how different English might have looked today, had the Norman Conquest never taken place.

Each step starts with some test examples for the reader to think about and work out. There are also tests at the end of each step, and some further examples and tests after Step 5. Answers to all tests are given at the end of Part 1. The tests are broadly geared to the Step in which they are found, but there is an element of revision, and also surprise, as every now and then forms from other steps are given to stretch you! You should be able to start to get your head round likely meanings of many words you have not yet met, as you become more used to the way in which they are built up from more than one 'bit'. You'll be building on a language you already speak, rather than learning a new one.

Part 2 is made up mainly of two reference lists; the first of these gives all of the words covered in Steps 1 – 5 (and some more) with the Old English words upon which these are based. The last reference list gives all of the words covered in Steps 1 - 5 *the other way round* (loanwords first). This list also includes many current, more English alternatives to foreign-derived loans (of the kind looked at briefly in the Lead-in to Part 1). Following this is an Endword, which links back to some key questions which had been asked at the start.

Abbreviations:
a.s.f. (and so forth) = *etc.* (et cetera).
f.e. (for example) = e.g.

Some Key Notes

1. Authenticity - *Does the book make up new words?*
The answer is no - it rather *updates* known words from English around the time of 1066. All of the words presented in Part A sections of Steps 1 - 5, and in the Reference section, List I are updates of authentic Old English examples. In the Part B sections of Steps 1 – 5 (showing words in use) there are some updated forms used which have been given very normal endings along the lines of the following example: Take the word *enoughful*, which has the following entry in Reference List I:

engoughful *a.* abundant *genyhtful*

Although it seems that the form *'genyhtfulic'* - which gives **enoughfully** when updated - may not be known in any Old English writings that have survived, it is highly likely to have existed, and would have been completely natural. Likewise, ***frimdy*** means *curious*, so ***frimdily*** would be *curiously*. These kinds of words are found in some examples of updated words in use in the Part B sections. Other than such slight 'exceptions', all of the words given as updates in this book are based on known forms (which are given for reference in Part 2, List I).

Where updated words are related to words in current English, their meanings have been worked out to reflect modern meanings. This means that meanings of updates can be different from what the Old English source-word meant (see Part 2, List I *Further Notes* ii), on p. 152).

I have left the possibility of coining *brand new* words open, though the Old English themselves had no qualms about doing that, and would have been likely to have gone on doing so to great effect. The coining of new words and phrases from what were Old English words still happens (take *world wide web*). We'd have had many more though, had the English won in 1066. The poet William Barnes in the 1800s made a number of suggestions for coining more English-based words. Some of these – such as *foreword* and *handbook* - are now common. Skillful use of words could doubtless yield many new and useful ways of saying things, but this book focuses on *updating* what the Old English themselves used.

This said, I *have* given examples of what some modern things would be, but *based on straight translation of individual words* (for example: **Stowly Onwield** for Local Authority).

2. Range of Words Covered and Method for Working out Updates

a) Range of Words Covered

The book gives a sample only of updated words from the wealth of Old English. A glance at Clark Hall (see Booklist) shows how broad this wordhoard was. How have the updated words here been chosen? Firstly, for convenience, we can classify words in Old English into three kinds, as follows:

1. Words which have lasted into Modern English.
2. Words which, though not in Modern English, when updated, are close to forms that are.
3. Words which are not in Modern English, and which look unfamiliar and unusual in updated forms.

Words of the first kind are ones we use in everyday speech now. But note that in cases where these compete with loanwords today, they have an important background role in the book. This is explained in the Lead-in to the five Steps (see p. 23; also, many such words are listed in Part 2, List II). Many words of kind 2 above have been covered in Steps 1 – 3 in particular. Step 4 is more of a crossover between words like these and the kind 3. These are covered particularly in Step 5.

Overall, words were chosen for their most likely potential appeal to readers, in terms of one or more of the following: a) being easy to work with/ learn; b) expressing concepts that would be most likely to be familiar (so usually avoiding detailed technical terms); and c) things that would be eye-catching for examples of use (in headlines, signs and suchlike).

b) Working out Updated Words

The updating of Old English forms of words is normally fairly straightforward. Based on a knowledge of how *current* words which are from Old English have changed, updates can often readily be made along similar lines. For example, Old English *muðhrof* is made up of the words *muð* and *hrof*, which developed into *mouth* and *roof* in today's spelling. So the updated form works out as **mouthroof** (meaning *palate*). In some cases, it was not so straightforward to work out an updated form. Take Old English *andwlita*, which is found in English of a later time in the form *anleth*. Here, a loss of *d* can be seen (as in a number of other words), but the use of *th* instead of *t* is more unexpected. Where I came across later forms, I tried to take them into account in working out updates, because they reflect continuity and can sometimes be closer to modern spelling anyway. But words which lasted to be recorded in Middle English are sometimes written in dialects not so close to the South Western forms in which much of Old English is written, which adds another angle to the working out of updates to fit modern English spelling.

3. Some Key Differences between Old English and Modern English

This topic can be studied in detail elsewhere, but at a basic level, we can summarise three key differences:

i). Old English was inflected, meaning it had a system of case-endings which were used in different grammatical situations. Latin, Greek, and

modern Russian all have case-endings, and a few are still to be found in English (such as the *s* in *my friend's hat*).
ii). Pronunciation, including that of vowels, was often quite different.
iii). Many words were different, and were not normally based on Latin loans.
This book focuses on key difference iii) - the words - rather than any questions about how i) and ii) might have developed without the Norman Conquest. I would however point out that case-endings are known to have been weakening in English from well before 1066, especially in the North. Pronunciation could have gone various ways. For updated words here we follow modern English, for your normal accent - wherever you're from in the English-speaking world.

4. How English lost Ground after 1066 - Bare Facts
Of course, Old English did not die at Hastings nor in the few years it took the Normans to get their vice-like hold on England. But as a direct outcome of Hastings, English took a very different path to that which it had been on until that time. It borrowed many more words from French and Latin - quite often at the cost of words already in English. Here are some of the main, key dates/ timespans to help understand what happened:
1066 - England is a strong state with organised central, and grass-roots local government. Normans win at Hastings, killing King Harold II. Large numbers of English ruling class die at Hastings, but also at Stamford Bridge and Fullford (earlier battles in 1066 against the Norwegians).
1066 - 1070s - various English uprisings, which are dealt with one after another. English elite further weakened and replaced by Normans and their followers.
1066 - mid 1100s - fresh Old English texts known to have been written, but use in official contexts lessens quite swiftly after the Conquest.
1066 - early 1200s - Copies still being made of Old English texts until end of this time. It seems that large numbers of English elite leave and never come back. Known to have gone to places such as Denmark, Scotland and Byzantium (the last lands of the Roman Empire, where, settling in the

capital Constantinople, some become Emperors' elite guards, a tradition which lasted until at least the 1204 fall and sack of the city).

1100s - 1200s and beyond - ever-greater amount of French and Latin words find their way into English, which is for a long time largely sidelined in high circles. With the loss of case-endings and later changes in pronunciation, Old English becomes less and less understandable to what have now become Middle English speakers.

5. Spelling and Fonts

Words are given in line with modern (British) English convention, without changing spelling in any way. This is to let readers focus on the words and their sounds, rather than burden them with an unneeded layer of unfamiliarity. But spelling would very likely have developed differently had there been no Hastings. As a taster of what *might* have been, try to read this:

> Hwen you ðinc haw Englisc coud luc wið anoðer speling, it can teic a hwail to get seteld wið it.

If one thing about Old English spelling *could* be brought back, we could argue for use of the letter Ð/ ð ('eth') for the '*th*' sound in *the*, *these*, *this* and so forth. Ðe sound comes up so often ðat using it would be likely to save raðer a lot of paper! It is in fact used in phonemic spelling internationally, as well as in Icelandic and some North Frisian. But, ðat said, let's leave spelling ðere for now!

The shapes of the letters used in writing Old English (the font) was also somewhat unlike that used today. After 1066 there was a shift to use of more continental forms, with a loss of the distinctive script used for writing Old English. The older style might well have stayed in use had the English won, and the drawing below shows how the title of *How We'd Talk* would look (to be read the same as the actual cover) but with both different spelling and font.

6. Scots

It's a point of interest that a few updated words from Old English in this book happen to be like some words still found in Scots. These include *eme* (uncle), *lith* (joint) and *thole* (to suffer, endure). Scots not only kept some words such as these, but also some features of pronunciation that were lost in England. These include rolling *rs*, guttural *ch*, and vowel-sounds which are sometimes closer to Old English. The well-known *'Bricht, moonlicht nicht'* is a good example showing some of these features. They are, by the way, one of the reasons not to belittle Scots pronunciation! Their survival in Scotland is a result of the differing histories of the two countries. Speakers of early English at various times found themselves in Scotland. Some key reasons for this were: i) border changes (part of the old Northumbria went to Scotland in the 900s), ii) coming as refugees (straight after 1066 and from the brutal harrying of the North in 1069), and iii) coming as traders/settlers under Scottish King David I in the 1100s. This king was himself a son of an important branch of old English kingly stock which had wed into the Scottish line soon after 1066. Consideration of how some of these events would have been different (or rather not happened) had the English won in 1066 would be a key part of trying to answer question v) in Note 8 below.

7. Closeness to Other Languages

Some readers will spot that *some* words covered in How We'd Talk are closer to some words in other European languages, such as Dutch, Danish and German. Though this book is based wholly on words updated from Old English, this likeness is not surprising, given that Old English grew from the speech of settlers from the North Sea coast. They came from a stretch of that sea rim roughly from the west coast of what is today Denmark, south and westwards to what is today the Netherlands. Its a little-known fact that the closest language to English today is Frisian, which is spoken along parts of this coast, mainly in West Friesland (part of the Netherlands) and North Frisland (the far North Western part of Germany). A few words in Frisian show how close this can be:

Ik tink dat it hijr better foar him is = *I think that it is better for him here*

And:

Wat as de Ingelsken it wûn hienen yn 1066? Ingelsk en Frysk soenen tichter byinoar bleaun wêze.

Which means:

What if the English had won in 1066? English and Frisian would have stayed closer to one another.

So, if you've never heard of it before, bear in mind that 'Frisian' applies to more than the well known cows - its the nearest speech to English!

8. Interesting and 'fun', Yes - But what difference would keeping a more English, less French/ Latin kind of English have made anyway?

This question is hard to give clear answers to (harder than the actual working out of updated forms of words from Old English!). So, let's keep an open mind and come back to this at the end of the book (Endword).

But here for now are some questions in a little more detail on this, to begin to think about as you read through the book.
i) Would less educated people have felt such a gap between their own speech and that of the ruling classes right down to today?
ii) Would there have been less social friction and stress as a result?
iii) Might England have had a less class-ridden history, and generally been a fairer place to those who might appear to be underlings?
iv) Could the history of fighting, colonial conquest and invasion, which ran through many aspects of England's dealings with the rest of Britain, Europe and the world - could this have been different?
v) In light of question iv), how would 'we' talk in Wales, Scotland, Ireland and elsewhere if the English had won in 1066?

9. Use of Loanwords in Examples in Steps 1 – 5.
Some readers will spot that example sentences themselves sometimes use loanwords. The point here is not to deny that there would have been *some* loans and we shouldn't go over the top to avoid them. Its an accepted fact that languages tend to take on some loans. Old English itself did, but on a relatively small scale (for example, for some churchly terms). After 1066, though, loans under Norman/ French influence would eventually come in thick and fast, often at the cost of older English words. This was another level of borrowing altogether. Follow the book to learn something about what was lost!

10. Summary Key Assumptions for Updated Words
1. Basic structure, spelling and font style follow today's standard English.
2. Where related to words still in use, updated words are based on what would make sense to the modern ear. Thus, **lessness** is *minority*, though the Old English word upon which it is based had other meanings. For such cases, it has been taken that today's understandings would still apply.

Booklist

Old English words used as starting points for updated words and given for reference in Part 2 List I are from original texts. Standard listing of these is in:
A Concise Anglo-Saxon Dictionary, J.R. Clark Hall, 1894. Spellings have been checked to be in line with listings from 4th Ed. 1960, in 1996 reprint, University of Toronto Press.

Further reference made to: **Eldsay English**, David Cowley. Joseph Biddulph publ., 1999. Old English forms used here were checked partly against Clark Hall and especially:
Wordcraft. Concise Dictionary and Thesaurus, Modern English-Old English, Stephen Pollington. Anglo-Saxon Books 1993 (Pollington himself also used Clark Hall as a check for his listings).

Further Reference/ background books:
The Pocket Oxford Dictionary, Oxford University Press, 7th Ed., 1990 reprint.
The Plain English Guide, Martin Cutts. OUP, 1996
The Rebirth of England and English; The Vision of William Barnes, Fr Andrew Phillips. Anglo-Saxon Books, 1996
First Steps in Old English, Stephen Pollington. Anglo-Saxon Books, 1997, rev. 1999
From Old English to Standard English, Dennis Freeborn. Palgrave, 1998 (Gives a lot of detail of how the language changed, based on many actual texts).
A Guide to Late Anglo-Saxon England, Donald Henson. Anglo-Saxon Books, 1998/ 2002
An Invitation to Old English and Anglo-Saxon England, Bruce Mitchel. Blackwell, 1995/ 2001
Old and Middle English An Anthology, Elaine Treharne (Ed.). Blackwell, 2000

PART 1: FIVE STEPS TO HOW WE'D TALK

Key *to grammatical abbreviations in Part 1*

a. = adjective (describes a noun: 'big' in big house)
adv. = adverb (shows way in which something is done: fast, happily)
n. = noun (normally things and ideas: car, bird, freedom)
neg. = negative (such as in words starting with 'un')
v. = verb (doing words like to run, to write, to sing)

These terms are given after words covered, but a knowledge of grammar is not needed to understand the meanings.

(Some words can be both adverbs and adjectives. Listings seek to define what use sounds most natural to today's ear, but should not always be considered hard and fast.)

Other abbreviations:

a.s.f. (and so forth) = *etc.* (et cetera).
f.e. (for example) = e.g.

Angsome?
In Woemoodness?
Call our
Helpline on
(0123) 456 789

Lead-in: Some Choices in English - What would these be like without 1066?

Before the main Steps, and the listing of updated words from Old English, the first point to note is that, had the Normans lost in 1066, many words still alive today would in fact be used more, because loanword alternatives would not have come into English. So, of *sight* (English), and *vision* (French), only the former would be in use. Here, we shall look at a few similar words. This sheds light on how competition between words meant that many Old English words lost ground and fell out of use altogether.

In the 1800s, Dorset poet and linguist William Barnes noticed that children brought up to say things in certain ways, would be taught differently at school. A few examples (quoted by Philips) show the point. The more English versions are in **bold**:

you can take that two ways	that is ambiguous
I can't bear it	this is intolerable
you can't get away from it	this is inevitable
he may well come	he will probably arrive

Barnes argued that the more straightforward English was to be preferred over the loanword versions being foisted on the children. The process is still going on - how many readers, for example, have been drilled to write *I* ***received*** *your letter*, rather than ***had*** or ***got***? (Martin Cutts, in the Oxford *Plain English Guide,* is right to point out how uncalled-for and unreasonable this is.)

It would be possible to write a whole book on choices between older English words and loanword alternatives in today's English, and many such examples are included in Part 2, II. Here are a few examples.

1. Some 'high-sounding' words and phrases (more English alternatives for these in **bold**):

accordingly - **so, thus, therefore**
as a consequence of - **through, thanks to**
ascend - **go up**
ascertain - **find out**
consequently - **so, thus, therefore**
constitute - **make up**
deduct - **take away, take off**
dissuade - **put off**
due to the fact that - **as, for, through**
employment - **work**
for the duration of - **while, as long as**
for the purpose of - **to, so as to**
if this is the case - **if so**
impose - **put upon**
in accordance with - **in line with**
in addition to - **also, as well as, on top of, furthermore**
in conjunction with - **with, together with**
in lieu of - **instead of**
in receipt of - **get, have**
in regard to - **about, on**
in the event of - **if, when**
in view of the fact that - **as**
on the contrary - **its the other way, there again**
prior to - **before**
proceed to - **go on to**
profound - **deep, heartfelt**
proprietor - **owner**
pursuant to - **under**
refer to - **talking about, meaning**
reside - **live, stay, dwell**
verbose - **wordy**
with reference/ regard to - **about, on**
with respect to - **for, about**

2. A few other Examples of Loanword/ Older English Choices:

different - **unlike**
difficult - **hard**
direction - **way, path**
incorrect - **wrong, not right**
insensitive - **unfeeling**
liberty - **freedom**
manner - **way**
perhaps - **maybe**
perverse - **warped**
predict - **foretell**
succumb - **fall to**
suffering - **hardship**
suitable - **fitting**
translate - **put into**
zero - **nought, nothing** (there seems to be an over-use of zero in schools – lets use out good old nought more!)

3. Phrases and Instructions Still in Latin
Suggested alternatives, some with more English-based shortened forms.

e.g. (exempli gratia) - **such as, like, for *example*** (why not use f.e.?)
etc (et cetera) - **and so forth a.s.f., and so on, and suchlike**
i.e. (id est) - **that is** (why not use t.i.?)
per annum - **yearly, a year**
per capita - **a head, each**
per person - **each, a head**
per diem/ per day - **daily, a day**
pp (per procurationem) - **on behalf of, for**
per se - **as such, by or in itself**
pro - **for**
sic - **so spelled!/ said!, thus spelled!/ said!**
via - **go through/ by way of**
versus/ vs - **against, playing**

4. Some examples in use. More English forms in **bold**:

Choose right settings needed for work in hand. Select correct settings required for current working.
Let brake off before backing. Disengage brake prior to reversing.
Inside leaks likely to stay unseen. Internal leaks probably remain invisible.
Outwardly much like kinds made before 1970s. Externally very similar to types manufactured pre-1970s.
It is hard to see talks starting straight away. It is difficult to envisage negotiations commencing immediately.
One in four buyers came back yearly. One quarter of purchasers returned annually.
If address is wrong, fill in slip over and send to... or call us on... If address is incorrect complete slip on reverse and return to... alternatively phone us on...
Overseeing handout of... Supervising distribution of...

Plain, Straightforward English
The recent move towards plainer English in official documents and some other areas aims at clearer ways of saying things, and avoiding terms that may look pompous. Although not aimed at promoting more English words as such, this often means use of older English words. Indeed, many of the examples listed above would sit happily in guides for plain English.

What's the Upshot of this?
From this Lead-in, the **first lesson** in how English would look without 1066 is that the older, more English words could well have been the only ones in use today (so we'd say *sight* and not a mixture of *sight* and *vision*). There would have been a greater consistency between use of words in various spheres of life. Example sentences given later in the book will also take this background fact on board. Needless to say, I would urge, along with William Barnes, that the more English choices are used when there is a straight choice.

We have also touched on the fact that the use of different words in higher contexts was one of the main reasons that many Old English words fell out of use after 1066, and learned that there is *still* a kind of competition between the native forms and loanwords - which can basically be traced to that time.

Last Point: Keep Some Less Used Words Alive
Here are a few words which are current, but could be used more:

> blithe, doughty, gainsay, harry (*v.*), overweening, rue (*v.*), winsome

Step 1
Ready and Clear
- Some of the most straightforward words

To Think About ... Have a look at the examples below – they should all be clear without any helps!

Our teachers misteach
us - day in, day out - ha!

                                      What a craftless mess!

... but that's unlaughterworthy,
    thinking about it ...

                          If you misdo your work, I'll be unblithe!

Where's the rhyme that Lee wrote
so lovesomely to Laura?

                          Look in the underneathmost drawer

Now open the door for me!

                          Yes - UNGLADY!

Your unrightdeed means you're
guilty of lawbreach!

We begin with the easiest kinds of words which would very likely be around still, had the English won in 1066. These first lists are very clearly related to well-known current words. In fact, of all the updated words covered in this book, these are the ones which could fit most easily into use today.

Part A: Breakdown of Words by Type

Note 1: Words covered here often lack obvious One-word Equivalents in Today's English.
2: You'll know the words in normal lettering; updates of words from Old English which are related to these are in **bold** (Part 2, I gives actual Old English source examples for these).
3: As it was not possible to check all current English dictionaries, the fact that some of these words could sometimes be deemed current anyway cannot be ruled out.

1.1.1 Adjectives (sometimes adverbs) of familiar nouns:
awe: **awely**
bliss: **blissy**
blossom: **blossomy**
cliff: **cliffy**
craft: **craftly**
earl: **earlish**
evil: **evilful, evily**
fake: **fakely**
fen: **fenny**
field: **fieldly**
flood: **floodly**
frost: **frostly**
grim: **grimful**
guest: **guesty**
harvest: **harvestly**
kin: **kinly**

laughter: **laughterful**
lore: **lorely, loresome**
love: **lovesome, lovesomely**
midday: **middaily**
mind: **mindily, mindy**
mood: **moodful**
qualm: **qualmful**
room: **roomly**
sin: **sinny**
tear (n.): **teary** (a.)
wife: **wifely**
wonder: **wonderly**
wrath: **wrathly**
youth: **youthly**

1.1.2   Adjectives/ adverbs of familiar verbs:
bear: **wellborn**
deal: **dealtly**
do: **ondoing** (like 'ongoing')
forgive: **forgivenly**
scathe: **scathingly**
wish: **wishingly**

1.1.3   Two familiar nouns giving one word:
book + lore: **booklore**
fake + deed: **fakedeed**
friend + lore: **friendlore**
hand + tame: **handtame**
heavy + mood: **heavymood**
law + breach: **lawbreach**
lore + writer: **lorewriter**
mood + sick: **moodsick**
mood + sickness: **moodsickness**
mood + thought: **moodthought**
right + willing: **rightwilling**
song + craft: **songcraft**

sorry + mood: **sorrymood**
stark + mood: **starkmood**
womb + addle: **wombaddle**
womb + hoard: **wombhoard**

1.1.4 Adjectives/ adverbs of familiar adjectives:
groundless: **groundlessly**
late: **latemost, latesome**
manifold: **manifoldly**
old: **oldly**
overseas: **overseaish**
rough: **roughful**
uncouth: **uncouthly**
unsound: **unsoundly**
untamed: **untamedly**
upland: **uplandish**
winsome: **winsomely**
worse: **worsely**

1.1.5 Familiar word(s) + *ness* to give a noun
careful: **carefulness**
Christian: **Christianness**
deathly: **deathliness**
end: **endlessness**
forlorn: **forlornness**
grim: **grimness**
hard + mood: **hardmoodness**
little: **littleness**
mild + heart: **mildheartness**
mood + sick: **moodsickness**
narrow: **narrowness**
nought: **noughtness**
offset: **offsetness**
qualm: **qualmness**
qualm + bear: **qualmbearness**
tight: **tightness**

uncouth: **uncouthness**
unstill: **unstillness**
unwise: **unwiseness**
weak + mood: **weakmoodness**
wise: **wiseness**
wished: **wishedness**
witless: **witlessness**
witty: **wittyness**

1.1.6   With other ending + *ness*:
awe + less: **awelessness**
inland + ish: **inlandishness**
love + some: **lovesomeness**
will + some: **wilsomness**
lust + ful: **lustfulness**

1.1.7   Familiar word + other ending to give a noun
dizzy: **dizzydom**
fiend: **fiendship**
lore: **loredom**
towards: **towardness**
wife: **wifehood**

1.1.8   Familiar word + *less*:
awe: **aweless**
craft: **craftless**
good: **goodless**
hue: **hueless**
loathe: **loathless**
man: **manless**
meat: **meatless**
mood: **moodless**
sorrow: **sorrowless**
way: **wayless**

1.1.9   *Over* + familiar word:
drink: **overdrink**
set: **overset**
show: **overshow**
speak: **overspeak**
speech: **overspeech**

1.1.10   *Under* + familiar word:
do: **underdo**
set: **underset**

1.1.11   *Fore* + familiar word:
seek: **foreseek**
token: **foretoken**

1.2   Negatives with familiar words

1.2.1   With *mis:*
birth: **misbirth**
do: **misdo**
hold: **mishold**
live: **mislive**
speak: **misspeak**
shrink: **misshrunk,**
teach: **misteach**
think: **misthink**
write: **miswrite**

1.2.2   With *un:*
bearing: **unbearing**
binding: **unbindingly**
blithe: **unblithe**
cleansed: **uncleansed**
craft: **uncraft,**
crafty: **uncrafty**
deadly: **undeadly**

ended: **unended**
glad: **unglad**
gladly: **ungladly**
gladness: **ungladness**
good: **ungood**
health: **unhealth**
heed: **unheedy**
little: **unlittle**
marred: **unmarred**
might: **unmight**
mightily: **unmightily**
mightiness: **unmightiness**
mighty: **unmighty**
shrunken: **unshrunken**
speaking: **unspeaking**
trim: **untrim, untrimly, untrimness**
truly: **untruly**
whole: **unwhole**
wittily: **unwittily**
witty: **unwitty**
wrought: **unwrought**

1.2.3 Others beginning with *un-*:
deadly: **undeadliness**
heed: **unheedly**
laughter: **unlaughterworthy**
lust: **unrightlust**
mood: **unmoodiness**
right: **unrightdeed**
shameful: **unshamefulness**

1.3 Others

1.3.1 Showing movement/ position:
hither: **hithercome, hitherward**

nether: **netherward**
thence: **thenceward**
towards: **towardly**
underneath: **underneathmost**
up + spring: **upspring**

1.3.2 To show position/ size:
here: **hereonamong**
less: **lessly**
much: **muchly**
small: **smally**

1.3.3 A few more:
glad: **glading**
many + hue: **manyhuely**
in + wise: **inwise**
like + worth: **likeworthily, likeworthiness**
liking: **likingly**
little + heed: **littleheedy**
qualm + bear: **qualmbearingly**
thus: **thusly**

Step 1, Part B: Words in Use

Look at the examples below, reading the sentences and thinking about the meanings. Because the meanings of these Step 1 examples are so clear and simple, they should all be understandable on their own (note, unlike Steps 2 – 5, this step does not have tests)

Adverts and Signs:

- For guesthouse or hotel: Homely with guestly feel
- a laughterful evening of glee and wittiness
- a bay with sandy beach and cliffy background
- Fitness workouts: Don't underdo it, don't overdo it!
- Show Carefulness at all times
- Warning: Do not mishold tools

Welcome to a Laughterful Evening of Glee!

Headlines:

- Theft case: Man groundlessly hounded
- Health warnings: many littleheedy
- More greenfield land lost to townly spread
- Crash down to narrowness of road
- Meatless diets: going too far?
- Stabbing: Guilty man 'well-known for harmheartness'
- Grimness of northern towns now 'mostly gone'
- GB's 'forsakeness' of islander's rights

- Cuts mean caring lessly for 'most needy'
- End to overtime 'foretoken of coming cutbacks'
- Partygoers: unshamefulness 'shocking'
- Undeadliness makes new stun gun a winner
- Some towns 'in deep forlornness'
- Newly drafted update to oldly made law
- Man fakely dressed as fire fighter
- X's songcraft only smally shown in his youth
- Leaders said to be sorrowless over cuts
- Horse's tiredness 'from being overshown'
- Unwiseness 'at work in both Houses'
- Study shows rising feelessness for others
- X shown to be most manless town!
- Would-be thieves' plan 'evilful'
- Builder's work 'craftless'
- 'Bad lad' forgivenly brought back onto front bench
- Many in 50s and 60s foreseeking advice to deal with elderliness
- Townly Plan 'unsoundly written'
- Wifely life is 'bliss and weariness'
- New food rules 'unrightful'
- Leader's speech scathingly slams banks
- Flood warnings: Townsfolk 'unheedy'
- Loathingness against 'backhanders' grows
- Teachers: 'onbeloaded with paperwork'
- New health setup 'unworkly'

Snippets from Articles, Textbooks and suchlike:

- Of all her books of the last few years, the latemost was the best
- … had wilfully written out the work again, but worsely
- … teething problems down to the newness of the setup …
- One thing offset the other, and that offsetness won the day …
- Unmoodiness made x a steadfast worker
- Right now, needwise, clean water is top of our list …
- Houses are farly sited from road

- The Bight Stream (Gulfstream) heads northeastlong

- The Azores: at the endmostness of Europe

- Winter brings storms and floodly rains
- ... late summer bringing dry, harvestly weather
- ... for this island's homesteads, and those who live hereonamong
- ... most come by car or train, by car being the mostlyest.
- England's kings in the 600s - made shift from heathendom to Chrisendom, from heathenness to Christianness
- Roof frame is underset with breezeblocks

Bookly bits:

- We can't foresay what the outcome will be, but they misthink if they write anyone off now
- ... a dish which smells beckoningly good!
- ... all the children started in year one as evenlings ...
- ... x is forethankful to you for your time ...
- ... rows of blossomy apple trees in spring
- ... grimful grey walls with a hueless townly backdrop
- ... best to be really forethinkful on this one ...

- ... a hardworking, likeworthy learner ...
- Wild weather brought seaupwarp onto the shore ...
- ... an open door for those who wish to go selfwillingly ...
- Shetland breed is well known for its littleness
- Her middaily work was feeding the 20 children
- A teary love film
- ...a cold stare of deathliness
- ...to stay on the rails and not mislive life
- ... a book full of blissy tales of island life
- ... your first time to have your say, so don't misspeak
- ... often miswrites from lack of care
- ... looked back at his youthly go at writing a blockbuster ...
- X tends to be latesome
- an unstill mind in a mood of wishedness
- Seeking gold from unbearing stones
- ... a lustfulness for gold fed by these old, overseaish tales
- T.V.: ... and now the lightmoodness goes on with ...

SLEEPFULNESS KILLS!
Have a Break

What about? Try slipping some of these words into e-mails, or when talking – do they get noticed or are they so natural-sounding that this doesn't happen much?

Step 2
That Sounds Right
– Words which are quite clear in today's spellings

To Think About ... Have a look at the examples below – Test i) What do you think they mean? Think and read on - you can check answers on p. 141

You speak well - what wordcraft!

I'm wordful in two tongues

He was wifeless, she was manless

And together they found matchness!

One is ongetful, one ongetless
- but both need steerness!

He's into idlebliss!

He should forlet it for worthwhile bliss

I'd be forethankful for any help

This chapter covers updated words for which there are generally loanword alternatives current in today's English. Being based on familiar and commonly used English elements, the updates are logical and expressive of their meanings.

Part A: Breakdown of Words by Type

Note: 1. Current words in normal lettering, updated words from Old English in **bold** (Old English sources are listed in Part 2, List I).

2.1 Words which are made up of from elements which can be clearly seen in current words:

after + follow = **afterfollow** *v.* to succeed
bone + breach = **bonebreach** *n.* bone fracture
bone + break = **bonebreak** *n.* bone fracture
book + hoard = **bookhoard** *n.* book collection
book + house = **bookhouse** *n.* library
borrow + breach = **borrowbreach** *n.* failure to repay loan/ surety
borrow + sorrow = **borrowsorrow** *n.* loaning/ security trouble
brother + slaying = **brotherslaying** *n.* fratricide
cleansing + drink = **cleansingdrink** *n.* purgative
dear + worth = **dearworth** *a.* precious
earth + tilth = **earthtilth** *n.* horticulture, agriculture
end + speak = **endspeak** *n.* epilogue
even + born = **evenborn** *a.* of equal birth
even + night = **evennight** *n.* equinox
fire + hot = **firehot** *a.* ardent
folk + free = **folkfree** *a.* uninhabited
hipbone + ache = **hipboneache** *n.* sciatica
hunger + bitten = **hungerbitten** *a.* famished, starving
idle + bliss = **idlebliss** *n.* vain joy
laughter + smith = **laughtersmith** *n.* comedian

41

oath + breach = **oathbreach** *n.* perjury
steep + high = **steephigh** *a.* acute
wonder + work = **wonderwork** *n.* impressive work/ action, deed, miracle
word + hoard = **wordhoard** *n.* vocabulary
word + craft = **wordcraft** *n.* eloquence
work + worthy = **workworthy** *a.* able-bodied

2.2 Currently used word with currently used ending, giving 'new' (but really *updated*) form:

2.2.1 Word + *ful*:
almsful *a.* charitable
engoughful *a.* abundant
fakeful *a.* deceitful
mightful *a.* powerful
scatheful *n.* injurious
soundful *a.* in good condition, prosperous
wifeless *a.* unmarried
wordful *a.* fluent, verbose
workful *a.* active, industrious
yearnful *a.* desirous

2.2.2 Word + *fully*:
soundfully *a.* prosperously

2.2.3 Word(s) + *ish*:
folkish *a.* common, popular, of the people
inlandish *a.* native, indigenous
ourlandish *a.* of our country, native

2.2.4 Word + *less*:
fakeless *a.* without deceit, guileless
haveless *a.* destitute
steerless *a.* profligate, out of control

trueless *a.* false, deceitful, treacherous
weaponless *a.* unarmed

2.2.5 Word + *less* + *ly*:
steerlessly *adv.* profligately

2.2.6 Word + *less* + *ness*:
endlessness *n.* infinity, eternity
truelessness *n.* falsehood, deceit, treachery

2.2.7 Word + *ly*:
beckoningly *a.* enticingly
bookly *a.* literary
bridely *a.* bridal
churchly *a.* ecclesiastical
enoughly *a., adv.* abundantly
everly *a.* perpetually, in perpetuity
fleetly *a.* nautical, naval
folkly *a.* public, popular, common
footly *a.* pedestrian
fourfoldly *adv.* quadruply
gatheringly *a.* collectively
guestly *a.* hospitable
headly *a.* principal, capital
hearingly *a.* audibly
houndly *a.* canine
mightly *a.* possible
moonly *a.* lunar
needly *a.* necessary
sealy *a.* marine, maritime
sorrowly *a.* miserable
streamly *a.* riparian
sunly *a.* solar
waterly *a.* aquatic

2.2.8 Word + *ness*:
almightiness *n.* omnipotence
beholdness *n.* observation
blitheness *n.* joy, pleasure
boundness *n.* obligation
broadness *n.* extent, surface, liberality
deepness *n.* profundity, mystery
drenchness *n.* immersion
fakeness *n.* deceitfulness
farness *n.* distance
feedness *n.* nourishment
fewness *n.* paucity
filledness *n.* fulfillment, completion
fleshliness *n.* carnality
fleshness *n.* incarnation
gripness *n.* seizure
growness *n.* development, prosperity
hinderness *n.* restraint, hindrance
hueness *n.* colouration
lessness *n.* minority
matchness *n.* compatibility
midness *n.* centrality, mediocrity
muchness *n.* size, abundance
needness *n.* necessity
newness *n.* novelty
onsetness *n.* constitution, establishment
rueness *n.* regret
sayness *n.* expression
scatheness *n.* injury
shapeness *n.* formation, creation
shieldness *n.* protection, defence
soberness *n.* sobriety
steerness *n.* guidance, discipline
suchness *n.* nature, quality
threatness *n.* affliction, tribulation
wetness *n.* moisture

workness *n.* workability, operation

2.2.9 Word + *liness*:
evenliness *n.* equality
mindiliness *n.* remembrance

2.2.10 Word + *ship*:
eldership *n.* seniority

2.2.11 Word + *some* (compare *lonesome*)
enoughsome *a.* abundant, abounding, satisfactory
enoughsomeness *n.* sufficiency, abundance
holdsome *a.* economical, frugal
holdsomeness *n.* economy, restraint, custody, preservation, observance, devotion
longsome *a.* tedious, protracted
longsomely *adv.* tediously, protractedly
longsomeness *n.* tediousness, patience
unwilsomely *a.* involuntarily

2.2.12 Word + *er*, to give a noun showing doer of an action and suchlike
afterfollower *n.* successor
comer *n.* visitor
earthtiller *n.* horticulturist, farmer
evenlotter *n.* equal sharer, partaker
inlander *n.* native
scather *n.* injurious person, antagonist
selfmurderer *n.* one who commits suicide
shielder *n.* protector, defender
steerer *n.* pilot, director
unhaver *n.* poor person

2.3 Currently used word with currently used beginning, giving 'new' (updated) form:

2.3.1 *Be* + word:
befasten *v.* establish, put safe, utilise
belaugh *v.* deride
beride *v.* ride round
berow *v.* row round
beshow *v.* exhibit, demonstrate, display
beshower *n.* exhibitor, demonstrator, guide
beshowing *n.* demonstration, exhibition
besmear *v.* disgrace, reproach, defile
besmear *n.* disgrace, reproach, defilement
bewarp *v.* pervert
beweapon *v.* disarm
beweep *v.* mourn

2.3.2 *For* + word (note, most have kind of a negative meaning, though *forspeaker does not*):
forcome *v.* prevent, surpass, surprise
fordim *v.* obscure
fordo *v.* ruin, destroy
forflee *v.* evade
forlet *v.* abandon, relinquish
forsaking *n.* denial
forspeaker *n.* sponsor, advocate (= *speaker for*)
forspend *v.* squander

2.3.3 *Fore* + word:
forebody *n.* thorax, chest
forebusy *v.* preoccupy
forechoose *v.* prefer in preference
forecome *v.* block, prevent move/ action, prevent
foredeem *v.* prejudge
forego *v.* precede
forelook *v.* preview

foresay *v.* predict
foreset *v.* propose, place before
foreshow *v.* give a preview
foreshower *n.* one showing previews
foreshowing *n.* preview (showing of)
forestep *v.* anticipate, prevent, precede
forestepping *n.* anticipation, precedence
forethankful *a.* grateful in advance

2.3.4 *Forth* + word (compare *forthright*):
forthfare *v.* depart
forthsay *v.* proclaim, announce

2.3.5 *Mis* + word
misbirth *n.* miscarriage
misborn *a.* degenerate
misfare *v.* 'mis'-travel

2.3.6 *On* + word
onbeload *v.* inflict upon
onget, anget *v.* perceive, recognise, distinguish (compare to '*I get that*')
ongetful *a.* perceptive
ongetfully *adv.* perceptively
ongetless *a.* lacking perception

2.3.7 *Over* + word:
overdrinker *n.* alcoholic
overdrunkeness *n.* alcoholism
overfill *n.* excess, surfeit
overfillness *n.* excess, surfeit
overmuchness *n.* excess

2.3.8 Negative, with *un* + word:
unbliss *n.* affliction
unbold *a.* timid
undrunk *a.* sober

unright *a.* incorrect
unrightful *a.* unjust
unrightly *adv.* incorrectly
unseldom *adv.* infrequent
unstiring unmoving
unweary *a.* indefatigable
unwinsome *a.* unpleasant
unwisdom *n.* ignorance, stupidity

2.3.9 *Well* + word:
wellwilling *a.* benevolent
wellwillingly *adv.* benevolently
wellwillingness *n.* benevolence

2.4 Currently used word with both currently used beginning *and* ending:

2.4.1 *Be* + word + *less*
besmearless *a.* unrepproached

2.4.2 *Be* + word + *ly*:
beheadly *a.* of capital punishment
beshowingly *adv.* demonstratively
besmearly *a.* disgraceful, reproachful, defiling
beweepingly *adv.* lamentably

2.4.3 *Be* + word + *ness*
behideness *n.* concealment
besmearness *n.* contemptibility

2.4.4 *For* + word + *ness*
forletness *n.* abandonment, relinquishment
forsakeness *n.* rejection, denial, abandonment

2.4.5 *Fore* + word + *ness*
foresaidness *n.* prediction
foresetness *n.* proposition, purpose
foreshieldness *n.* protection

2.5 Current word used in another way:
anew *v.* renew
anewed renewed
anewing *n.* renewal, restoration
onset *v.* impose (as a verb, broadens use of current word *onset*, which is a noun with basic meaning *start*)
scathing *n.* injury, damage (note: as a noun, broadening use of the word)
upping *n.* increase, accumulation

2.6 Related to/ somewhat like currently used word:

2.6.1 **alease** *v.* release, redeem, save (Compare *release*)

Updated words which are related to currently used word(s) with currently used ending:

2.6.2 Word + *ly*:
aleasingly *adv.* redeemingly

2.6.3 Word(s) + *ness*:
afterfollowedness *n.* sequel
afterfollowingness *n.* succession
aftergoingness *n.* posterity
afterwardness *n.* posterity
aleasedness *n.* redemption, remission, release
ongetness *n.* comprehension, perception, recognition
outleadness *n.* abduction
rightness *n.* correction, rectitude
rightsetness *n.* rightful establishment/ appointment/ office

rightwiseness *n.* justice, righteousness
scathiness *n.* injury, damage
slackerness *n.* laziness
sleepfulness *n.* lethargy
soundfulness *n.* prosperity
unmightliness *n.* inability, impossibility
unrightness *n.* error, injustice
unrightwiseness *n.* injustice, iniquity
well-likeworthness *n.* likeability
woemoodness *n.* depression
yearnfullness *n.* desire

2.6.4 Word + *liness*:
smalliness *n.* subtlety

2.7 Related to currently used word with currently used beginning, and/ or ending, giving 'new' form:

2.7.1 *Be* + word:
behavedness *n.* behaviour, restraint, temperance

2.7.2 *For* + word:
forbearingly *adv.* tolerably

2.7.3 *Fore* + word:
foregearing *n.* preparation

2.7.4 *Over* + word:
overeattle *a.* gluttonous
overeattleness *n.* gluttony

2.7.5 *Un* + word:
unmightly *a.* not possible, impossible
unshapen unformed, uncreated
unstiringly *adv.* unmovingly, motionlessly, immovably

untellingly *a.* indescribably
unwatery *a.* desiccated, dehydrated
unweaponed unarmed
unweened unexpected
unweenedly *a.* unexpectedly

2.7.6 *Well* + word:
well-likeworthy *a.* very likeable
wellbeshowed *a.* well demonstrated

2.8 Grouping of words which have common elements

2.8.1 With *bear* and related forms to show a quality (compare *forbearing*):
deathbearly *a.* lethally
deathbearness *n.* lethalness
unbearingly *a.* unbearably

2.8.2 With *fire*:
fireburn *n.* conflagration
firefood *n.* fuel
firehot *a.* ardent

2.8.3 With *folk,* showing *public/ common*:
folkland *n.* common land, public land
folkmoot *n.* public meeting
folkneed *n.* common need, basic need

2.8.4 With *right,* to show sense of justice:
righting *n.* correction, reproof
rightwise *n.* just, in a correct way
rightwise *v.* justify
rightwisely *adv.* justifiably
rightwising *n.* justification
unrightwise *a.* unjust

51

2.8.5 Words using *worth* and related forms to show value (compare *newsworthy*):
dearworthly *adv.* preciously
dearworthness *n.* preciousness
likeworth *a.* pleasing, likeable
likeworthly *adv.* pleasingly, likeably
likeworthness *n.* likeability
likeworthy *a.* acceptable, nice, likeable
mindworth *a.* worth remembering/ minding/ mentioning
unthankworthily *a.* (from unthankworthy)
unthankworthy *a.* undeserving of gratitude
worthfullness *n.* dignity, honour
worthfully *a.* with dignity, honourably

2.8.6 Using *yearn* and related forms to show quality of desire:
lustyearnness *n.* concupiscence
unyearnful *a.* indifferent
yearnfully *a.* desirously

2.8.7 With ending -*le* to make an adjective (compare *brittle*)
laughle *a.* inclined to laugh
sleeple *a.* lethargic, somnolent

2.9 Made up of what are current forms together to show feelings, quality and suchlike:

evilwilling *a.* malevolent
evilwillingness *n.* malice
fleshbesmittenness *n.* carnal attraction (compare *smitten*)
hotheartness *n.* zeal, rage, mania
idlelust *n.* vain desire
lightmoodness *n.* frivolity
needhood *n.* necessity
unbecraved *a.* not desired
unbefought *a.* unopposed, uncontested

unbethought *a.* not considered, not expected
unbowingly *a.* inflexibly
unsteadful *a.* unstable
unsteadfulness *n.* instability

2.10 Mixture of further forms:

2.10.1 Nouns:
elddom *n.* age
elderborough *n.* metropolis
endmostness *n.* extremity
fareing *n.* journey
faring *n.* removal
hueing *n.* colouration
infleshness *n.* incarnation
oldness *n.*, **eldness** *n.* old age
seaupwarp *n.* marine deposits on shore
selfdom *n.* independence
selflike *n.* egotism, vanity
selfmurdering *n.* suicide
shielding *n.* protection, defence
throughlooking *n.* perusal, review, summary

2.10.2 Adjectives:
erebethought *a.* premeditated
evennightly *a.* equinoxual
guesty *a.* of guest
honeysweet *a.* mellifluous
midmost *a.* most central
ruey *a.* regretful
scathy *a.* injurious
truefast *a.* reliable, trusty

2.10.3 Verbs:
offdo *v.* eliminate

2.10.4   Others:
rueing regretting
mostlyest   most particularly, most especially
togetherward   towards unity

Step 2, Part B: Words in Use and Tests

(Some of these should be clear enough without any explanation; where needed, explanation is in *italics*.) For answers to tests, see p 141.

Adverts and Signs:

- SLEEPFULNESS KILLS! Have a Break
- Wanted: Workworthy Folk! - for ...

- Art Beshowing this Way ...

- Wanted: Beshowers - Workful folk to beshow cookers - *Demonstraters - Active people to demonstrate cookers*
- Sun Cream: Foreshieldness for up to six hours ... *protection for up to ...*
- Warning: Stolen Goods; Beware of Fakeness

Test ii). *Do you understand the following five examples?*

1. Free Forelook at New Film
2. Feel Free to Look around; No Boundness to Buy!
3. Waterly and sealy gear
4. Unnamed Overdrinkers
5. Beholdness Room

Film Forelook

Headlines:

- Health cutbacks 'righwisely made' - ... *'justifiably made'*
- Formerly 'steerless' teen heads own business - *Previously 'out of control' teen manages own business*
- Sacked overseer showed a 'trueless selflike' - ... *displayed a 'false egotism'*
- Housing safety outlines 'beshowingly backward' - ... *plans 'demonstratively backward'*
- Unsteadfulness may lead to uprising in x - ... *Instability may ...*
- New road 'deathbearly narrow' ... *'lethally narrow'*
- Shire seat to go unbefought - *County (Council) Seat to go unopposed*
- Laughtersmith deemed 'Unlaughterworthy' - *Comedian judged to 'lack comedy'*

- Small lessness still smoking - *Small minority still smoking*

> **News Weekly**
> Only small lessness still smoking
> Just a small minority still smoking

- Old English had words for Credit Crunch!: 'borrowsorrow'

> **Daily News**
> Credit Crunch 'down to borrow-sorrow'

Test iii). *What do the following mean?*

1. Rise in overseaish holidaymakers
2. Early election 'mightly'
3. Hothearness for cosmetic surgery lessens
4. Deemer asks: was killing erebethought?
5. Hungerbitten flee drought

Snippets from Textbooks, Articles and suchlike:

- ... why did **oathbreach** lose out to such an outlandinsh word as *perjury*, which even now is not understood by many folk?
- ... an enoughsome supply of oranges all year round - ... *an abundant supply*
- Sand dunes: suchness is to be unsteadful, shifted by the wind - ... *nature is to be unstable ...*
- giving sayness by raising and lowering speech loudness - *giving expression by intonation*
- From form: ... any kinly history of the following illnesses ... - ... *any family history of ...*
- Bought mostly by women from 16 - 30, but mostlyest those in the early 20s - ... *most particularly/ especially ...*
- The team was unwilsomely held back by heavy rain - ... *involuntarily ...*
- ... no matchness between the laptop and the older printer - ... *no compatibility*
- ... it was then a more manish world in politics ...
- ... said to be the midmost point on the island ...
- ... with sharp houndly teeth - ... *canine teeth*
- ... would onset new laws to deal with that unrightwiseness - ... *would impose new ... with that injustice*
- ... the steerer foreset that they needed first to get better feedness for the small children - ... *the director proposed that ... better nourishment ...*
- ... had been taken ill, and it was thought to be some kind of gripness - ... *some kind of seizure*
- ... a land shaped by ickly flows and waterwash - ... *a land shaped by glacial flows and alluvium*

- ... that the unwisdom of those days has now gone and that folk have evenliness there, whatever their hue - ... *the ignorance of those days ... have equality there ...*
- ... would be the faring of these mightful fleetly ships - ... *the removal of these powerful naval ships*
- ... well known that we cannot make anything which would work everly - ... *would work perpetually ...*

Test iv). *What do you think these mean?*

1. Steerness for house buying
2. Sunly fire bursts
3. Selfenoughsomeness
4. England: Unoverwon after the late 1000s
5. ... where green meadows were formerly enoughful

Bookly bits:

- ... had a sound house, sound friends and a sound working life; with such a soundful life, why leave? - ... *with such a prosperous life ...*
- ... in those first two months together they'd known an endlessness of new feelings, and felt the bliss of being enoughly happy - ... *of being abundantly happy*
- ... saw that they had together gatheringly done this great thing - ... *had together collectively done ...*
- A moodful maid might make Mike mad ...
- Summer was beweepingly short - *Summer was lamentably brief*
- They thought back to their early days together; what hotheartness! what fleshbesmittenness! ... *What mania!, what carnal attraction!*
- ... had himself called his work that year 'forbearingly middling' - ... *'tolerably mediocre'*
- ... put her mind to good works in her oldness - ...*in her old age*
- ... felt that forsakeness of all that would be wrong and that they should show some holdsomeness - ... *felt that rejection (denial/ abandonment) of all that ... show some restraint*

- ... that fareing took him out of her life, but brought an unweened unsteadfulness - ... *that journey took him ... an unexpected instability*
- ... and mindiliness of the worthfullness of that deed brought a feeling of well-being - *and remembrance of the dignity/ honour* ...
- ... there were the wealthy ones and then there were the unhavers - ... *were the poor people*
- ... the overmuchness of those times showed no smalliness, so that afterwardness would barely believe how selfish they'd been - ... *the excess of those times showed no subtlety, so that posterity would* ...

What about? Try using some of these words – which are the most useful?

Step 3
I Think I get that
- More words that make sense in updated form

To Think About ... Test i) What do you think the examples below mean? Think and read on - you can check answers on p. 142.

Tell me a shiply yarn

Ah - how I overfared the seas! ...

Oh - I underget what's going on!

Don't let wealth forlead you!

It wasn't outly mightly, my friend!

Sorry, I felt an underdriveness to say that

You're moodful and steadless!

We'll do a selfwilling seekness into the eviladdle

Building on Step 2, here are more words which are quite clear.

Part A: Breakdown of Words by Type

3.1 Words, clearly based on elements which developed into currently used words:

3.1.1 Made up of what came to be two or more current words:
again + come = **againcome** *v.* return (compare *overcome*)
bit + meal = **bitmeal** *adv.* (compare *piecemeal*)
earth + kin = **earthkin** *n.* human race
errand + speech = **errandspeech** *n.* message
eye + seen = **eyeseen** *a.* visible (compare *unseen*)
fall + sick = **fallsick** *a.* epileptic
harm + speech = **harmspeech** *n.* calumny
high + work = **highwork** *n.* excellent work
high + berg = **highberg** *n.* mountain (compare *iceberg*)
high + bliss = **highbliss** *n.* exultation
hot + hearten = **hothearten** *v.* become zealous, become enraged/angry
house + breach = **housebreach** *n.* burglary
land + folk = **landfolk** *n.* natives
law + right = **lawright** *n.* legal right
learning + house = **learninghouse** *n.* educational establishment, university, college, school
lore + craft = **lorecraft** *n.* erudition
month + sick = **monthsick** *a.* menstruous
month + sickness = **monthsickness** *n.* menstruation
moon + sick = **moonsick** *a.* lunatic
mouth + roof = **mouthroof** *n.* palate
out + fare = **outfare** *n.* outward passage
out + shove = **outshove** *v.* exclude
over + fare = **overfare** *v.* travel over
over + fare = **overfare** *v.* traverse

62

over + go = **overgo** *v.* traverse, transgress
over + go = **overwork** *n.* superstructure
over + work = **overwrit** *n.* superscription
right + doing = **rightdoing** *a.* just
roof + fast = **rootfast** *a.* firmly established (compare *held fast, steadfast*)
sea + berg = **seaberg** *n.* coastal cliff
self + willing = **selfwilling** *a.* voluntary
ship + fight = **shipfight** *n.* naval battle
speech + house = **speechhouse** *n.* auditorium
steer + speech = **steerspeech** *n.* reproof
stench + bringing = **stenchbringing** *a.* odiferous
stone + berg = **stoneberg** *n.* rocky hill/ crag, mountain
stove + bath = **stovebath** *n.* sauna
water + wash = **waterwash** *n.* alluvium
wed + breach = **wedbreach** *n.* divorce, adultery
wide + going = **widegoing** *a.* itinerant, widely traveled (compare *seagoing*)
woe + token = **woetoken** *n.* portent, sign of misfortune
wonder + token = **wondertoken** *n.* miracle
word + lock = **wordlock** *n.* logic (compare *wedlock*)
word + lore = **wordlore** *n.* etymology
word + mark = **wordmark** *n.* definition
word + winsome = **wordwinsome** *a.* affable
word + wrestle = **wordwrestle** *v.* debate, argue, discuss
work + craft = **workcraft** *n.* mechanics
work + deed = **workdeed** *n.* action, operation
world + kind = **worldkind** *a.* secular

3.2 Of currently used word(s) with currently used ending:

3.2.1 Word + *fast* (compare *steadfast*)
hearthfast *a.* having a stable, settled home
holdfast *a.* safe, secure
homefast *a.* resident, established (in a home)
housefast *a.* occupying/ established in a house
rooffast *a.* with a solid, firm roof

shamefast *a.* modest
wifefast *a.* happily married
wordfast *a.* reliable

3.2.2 Word + *ful*:
speakful *a.* talkative
teamful *a.* prolific (compare *teeming*)
toungeful *a.* talkative
trueful *a.* reliably, trusty
worthful *a.* valuable, dignified, honourable

3.2.3 Word + *ing* to make a noun (compare *baking, skating*)
asundering *n.* division
bettering *n.* improvement
gearing *n.* preparation
highting *n.* climax, exultation
littling *n.* diminution
mooting *n.* discussion, conversation (as a noun, broadens current use of the word)
nethering *n.* abasement, condemnation
minding *n.* remembrance, memorandum
overing *n.* delay, excess
shoting *n.* missile
smalling *n.* reduction, atrophy
thoughting *n.* consideration, advice, consultation
timbering *n.* edification, structure
weaponing *n.* armour
wiving *n.* marrying (a wife)
worthing honour, honouring, valuing

3.2.4 Word + *ish*:
mannish *a.* male, masculine

3.2.5 Word + *less*:
goodless *a.* evil
steadless *a.* unstable

3.2.6 Word + *ly*:
ally *a.* universal
almsly *a.* charitable
deedly *a.* active
doly *a.* possible, doable
eatly *a.* edible, eatable
fallenly *a.* unstable, perishable, transient
fingerly *a.* digital
goodly *a.* excellent
hately *a.* hostile, horrible
heldly *a.* safe, secure
herdly *a.* pastoral
kinly *a.* pertaining to family
lawly *a.* legal
loathly *a.* horrible
loftly *a.* aerial
matchly *a.* conjugal
minely *a.* in my manner
missly *adv.* inaccurately, erratically
netherly *a.* inferior
noughtly *a.* of no avail, without result
outly *a.* remotely
plightly *a.* dangerous, perilous
seedly *a.* seminal
seenly *adv.* visibly, evidently
seldly *a.* rare, strange
shiply *a.* nautical
smithly *adv.* dexterously
threely *adv.* triply
twofoldly *adv.* doubly
unfilledly *adv.* insatiably
unreadly *adv.* illiterately
uply *a.* high quality
winly *a., adv.* positively
workly *a.* operationally, practically

worthly *a.* important, valuable, distinguished
woundly *a.* wound inflicting, dangerous

3.2.7 Word + *ness*:
awaydriveness *n.* dismissal, expulsion
awayleadness *n.* removal
blowness *n.* inflation
bringness *n.* donation, support
Christianness *n.* of Christian
crippleness *n.* severe disability
eatness *n.* edibility
fallness *n.* ruin, offence
fallsickness *n.* epilepsy
furtheringness *n.* promotion
gatheredness *n.* abscess
gearingness *n.* preparation
healness *n.* recovery, salvation
hearness *n.* report, obedience
holdness *n.* observance
letness *n.* remission, parole
loathingness *n.* hostility
netherness *n.* inferiority
overflowness *n.* excess, superfluity
ownness *n.* property
rearness *n.* disturbance, commotion (compare *to rear up*)
seekness *n.* inquiry
shineness *n.* radiance
sightness *n.* vision
standness *n.* status, existence
stirness *n.* movement, power of motion, disturbance, commotion, tumult
toungeness *n.* eloquence, fluency
twofoldness *n.* duplicity, duplication
understandness *n.* comprehension
unreadness *n.* illiteracy
upness *n.* elevation
warpness *n.* perversion

wasteness/ wastedness *n.* desolation, destruction
winsomeness *n.* pleasure, delight
worthness *n.* value, importance, estimation

3.2.7 Word + *liness*:
worthliness *n.* importance, value, estimation

3.2.8 Word + *ship* (compare *hardship*):
holdship *n.* loyalty, allegiance
manship *n.* maleness, masculinity
matchship *n.* compatibility

3.3 Of currently used word with currently used beginning, giving 'new' (really *updated*) form:

3.3.1 *Be* + word:
bebid *v.* instruct, command
bebid *n.* command, order
bechide *v.* to complain
beclose *v.* confine, imprison
befare *v.* traverse, surround
befold *v.* envelop
bego *v.* traverse, perform
belean *v.* dissuade, prevent
besee *v.* provide for, have regard for
besit *v.* occupy, posses
besorrow *v.i.* to have compassion
besorrowing *n.* compassion
bethink *v.* consider
betoken *v.* designate
betrap *v.* entrap
beward *v.* protect, guard
bewind *v.* entwine, envelop, encircle
bework *v.* construct, adorn, insert

3.3.2 *For* + word (a kind of wayward/ negative meaning, compare *forget, forsake*):
forbow *v.* decline
forbreak break in pieces
forburn to be consumed by fire
fordeem *v.* prejudge, prejudice, prematurely judge
forfare *v.* obstruct, intercept
forharry *v.* ravage
forharrying *n.* devastation, raid
forhave *v.* restrain
forlead *v.* seduce
forlearning *n.* wrong/ incorrect education
forletting *n.* intermission
forlie *v.* commit adultery or fornication
forlose *v.* abandon
formelt *v.* dissolve
forolding *n.* old age
forride *v.* intercept with vehicle/ horse a.s.f.
forshape *v.* transform
forspeak *v.* denounce (not the same use of *for* here as seen in Step 2 in *forspeaker = advocate*)
forspill *v.* destroy
forstand *v.* prevent, resist, oppose, obstruct, block
forthink *v.* despair, despise, mistrust
forthought despaired of
forworth *v.* deteriorate
foryield *v.* recompense, requite

3.3.3 *Fore* + word (compare *foresee*):
foresit *v.* preside
forespeech *n.* preamble
forestand *v.* excel, prevail
forethink *v.* premeditate, consider
forewriteness *n.* prescription

3.3.4 *Over* + word:
overbecome *v.* supervene
overlive *v.* survive
overmarking *n.* superscription
oversend *v.* transmit

3.3.5 Negative, with *un* + word(s):
unbeshowed *a.* not displayed, not demonstrated
unbewedded *a.* unmarried
unbreakingly *a.* inextricably
unhold *a.* disloyal, unreliable
unlikeworthy *a.* displeasing
unmenishly *adv.* unmasculinely
unoverwon *a.* unconquered
unrightcrafting *n.* poor quality
unriped *a.* immature
unsayingly *a.* indescribably, unspeakably, ineffably
unscathedness *n.* not suffering injury
unscatheful *a.* not causing suffering injury
unscathefulness *n.* lack of capacity/ inability to injure
unscathily *a.* not dangerously, not injuriously
unscathy *a.* not dangerous, not injurious
unseenly *adv.* invisibly
unset *v.* destabilise
unshamely *a.* immodest
unsinny *a.* innocent
unthank *n.* ingratitude
untime *n.* unseasonableness
unthroughfare/ unthoroughfare *n.* cul de sac
untrimness *n.* infirmity, state of not being trim
untwofold *a.* without duplicity
unwitful *a.* senseless
unwitfulness *n.* senselessness
unwork *v.* deconstruct
unworkly *a.* impractical, redundant

3.3.6 *Under* + word:
underbear   support, endure (compare *underpin*)
underbegin *v.* purpose, design, intend
underborough *n.* suburb
underdriveness *n.* subjection, compulsion
underget *v.* perceive, notice (compare *understand,* also to *get* something)
underreeve *n.* deputy governor
underseek *v.* examine, investigate, scrutinise
underthink *v.* consider, meditate

3.3.7 *Well* + *word*:
welldeed *n.* beneficial act

3.4   Of currently used word with both beginning and ending:

3.4.1 *Be* + word + *ness*
begengness *n.* application

3.5   More words, listed by topic:

3.5.1 To do with condition, opinion and suchlike:
maidhood *n.* virginity
sameheart *a.* unanimous
sorrowword *n.* lamentation
soundy *a.* favourable
steerworth *a.* reprehensible
stepmeal *adv.* by degrees, gradually
thankworthy *a.* acceptable, pleasing
thickfold *a.* dense
thoughtingly *adv.* deliberatively
thrithely *a.* excellent
wive *v.*   to marry (a wife)

3.5.2 Medical Conditions a.s.f.:

addlebearing *a.* disease/ trouble bearing
addly *a.* spoiled, diseased
angbreast *n.* asthma
bladderwark *n.* pain in the bladder
breastwark *n.* pain in chest
heartwark *n.* pain in heart
inaddle *n.* internal disease
liveraddle *n.* liver complaint
liversickness *n.* disease of liver
liverwark *n.* pain in liver
shoulderwark *n.* pain in shoulder
sideaddle *n.* pleurisy
sidewark *n.* pain in the side
slitness *n.* laceration
spewdrink *n.* liquid emetic
wateraddle *n.* dropsy
waterfrightness *n.* hydrophobia
woundswathe *n.* scar
waterful *a.* dropsical
yellowaddle *n.* jaundice

3.5.3 Specialist terms for building and suchlike:

earthbegoingness *n.* habitation
floodward *n.* flood barrier protection (compare *to ward off evil*)
groundstone *n.* foundation stone
groundwall *n.* foundation
groundwall *v.* lay/ build foundations
housestead *n.* site of a house (compare name *Housesteads*, were Roman groundwalls and ruins are to be seen)
smithcraft *n.* manual art
stonetimber *n.* masonry
wallthread *n.* plumb line
wallwork *n.* masonry

Step 3, Part B: Words in Use and Tests

Answers to tests on p 142/3.

Adverts and Signs:

- Get our Holdship card - *Get our Loyalty card*
- Earthtilth Learninghouse - *Horticultural College*

Headlines:

- Worthliness of mild workouts shown - *Importance of gentle workouts demonstrated*
- Leader clashes with headbold party - *... with confident party*
- Mankind's early African homelands: Onlightness from new finds - *... illumination ...*
- Shakeup to driving fallness scores mooted - *... to driving offence scores debated*
- 'Seedly' talk 'seenly plightly' - *'Seminal' talk 'evidently dangerous'*
- Bankers 'back to overing' - *back to excess*

- Better health from deedly life - ... *from active life*
- Worldwide Warming forecasts: heading for eviladdle - ... *Global Warming heading for disastrous situation*

```
TV 24-7
10·14    Newsworld
Breaking
News:
Worldwide Warming:
Heading for 'Eviladdle'
```

Test ii). *Do you understand the following?*

1. Businessman did not bename bringness
2. Rise in alcohol forhaveness
3. Many yearnful to forshape lifestyles
4. Laughtersmith's wittiness wellbeshowed
5. Lessness of ourlandish goods show unrightcrafting

Snippets from Speeches, Articles, Textbooks and suchlike:

- ... the need to be seen to be themselves rightdoing - ... *themselves just*
- ... a manifoldly hard thing to underthink the meaning of ... - ... *to consider/ meditate the meaning of ...*
- Outcome of stowly talks is unbreakingly linked to things in the wider world - ... *of local talks ... inextricably linked ...*

- ... through the hard times ahead, we can forestand, come what may - ... *we can prevail ...*
- We have set down how we shall bework a new, better deal for all ... - *we shall construct a new, better ...*
- ... need to see the begengness of this in daily life - ... *the application*
- ... meaning less twofoldness of work - ... *less duplication*
- ... for a greater understandness of what needs doing - ... *for a greater comprehension of ...*
- ... leading to better teaching in some learninghouses - ... *educational establishments*
- The Kingly Fleet won many shipfights - *The Royal Navy won many naval battles*
- From cookbook: ... formelt the sugar in warm water - ... *dissolve the sugar in warm water*
- Underbearing the children and in full-time work - *Supporting the children and in full-time employment*
- Owness Rights - *Property Rights*
- ... muchness of wealth going down yearly - ... *abundance of wealth declining annually*
- *Instruction:* Build model again if misdone - *Reconstruct model if incorrectly assembled*
- *Lawly term:* Evilwillingness aforethought - *Legal term: Malice aforethought*
- ... aleaseness of sins - ... *remission of sins*
- An upness of 32 degrees - *an elevation of 32 degrees*
- ...a time of hardliness - ...*a period of austerity*
- England's highbergs are not so high! - ... *mountains are not ...*

Last Boat Forthfares: 18·00

Test iii). *What do the following mean?*

1. Doctor's Forewriteness

2. The kingly afterfollowingness

3. ... the furtheringness of a wordhoard from early English ...
4. Last boat to x forthfares
5. Can be workly run

Bookly bits:

- Unhealth and unmight went hand in hand
- Wisely working with the wordhoard - ... the vocabulary
- A bewarped foresetness - *an indecent proposition*
- ... saw that if he went that way they would forride him before the stream - *would intercept him* ...
- ... should forget that and forhave the yearning to stay longer - *...and restrain the yearning* ...
- ... giving 'help' that was unthankworthy in his eyes – *giving 'help' that was unacceptable/ not deserving of thanks in his eyes*
- Thoughts of a mum to be: Grow well, little birther, brightness-bringing burden!
- ... learned to swim late, and still felt somewhat held back by waterfrightness - *...held back by hydrophobia...*
- ... a loathingness of old friends stemming from feelings of netherness - *... a hostility to ... from feelings of inferiority*
- ... felt a need to forethink before giving an answer to that ... - *... to premeditate/ consider ...*

Test iv). *What do you think these mean?*

1. ... too speakful and longsome ...
2. ... put it to them that they had gone out with evilwillingness that night
3. 'Oneness in Mislikeness ...'
4. Looking for Healness ...
5. Seating set by eldership ...

What about? Use some of the words in talks, e-mails and reports. If someone says they're not in the dictionary, tell them politely that they were written down longer ago than the dictionaries we've been using, and that the word(s) you said are actually more English than the ones you're using them instead of!

> Come and See...
>
> Highbergs,
> Meres,
> Wealds...
> England's far North

Step 4
What's that Mean Exactly?
– Words which make one think more about meaning

To Think About ... Test i) What do you think the examples below mean? Think and read on - you can check answers on p. 143.

I aqueath this new setness building open!

From toletness to eftnewing - wonderful!

Now, is there a guestly bed and breakfast nearby?

- there's good comelitheness at one two doors down

I ween that'll be alright then

Are you under the fortruing that I love you?!

WIELD YOURSELF!

You're not so bad ... but not unharmyearn either!!

Words from here on tend to be less clear than those looked at so far, falling somewhere in between those in Steps 3 and 5 in terms of hardness.

Part A: Breakdown of Words by Type

4.1 Less-familiar Sounding, but usually linked/ related to Current Words

4.1.1 Same as/ related to/ sounds something like current word:
acover *v.* recover
afear *v.* terrify, make afraid
anget *n.* intellect
aqueath *v.* declare, express (compare: *bequeath, quote*)
ascruten *v.* investigate, examine
awayen *v.* repudiate (compare: *to do away* (with))
lave *n.* remnant, legacy (compare *leavings*)
mothren *a.* maternal
neb, nib *n.* beak, face
scruten *v.* examine, scrutinise
sot *a.* stupid (compare *besotted*)
thole *v.* endure, suffer (current use - boats: *thole pins* = pegs acting as rowlocks)
wrack *n.* vengeance, revenge
ween *v.* hope, expect, imagine
ween *n.* hope, opinion, expectation, supposition
whelm *n.* surge, fervour
wield *v.* control (current in narrower sense, as in: *to wield power*)
wield *n.* control

4.1.2 Same as/ related to/ something like more than one current word together (sometimes with current ending):
againwardly *adv.* adversely (compare *against*)
breastwhelm *n.* emotion, grief
comelithe *a.* hospitable
endbirth *n.* order
eviladdle *n.* disastrous situation

friendhold *a.* amiable
friendholdly *adv.* amiably
greenhuen *a.* green coloured (other would be likewise, a.s.f.)
handweald *n.* personal power
handwhile *n.* instant
mindday *n.* anniversary
scathedeed *n.* injurious deed/ crime
seafare *n.* sea voyage
seldseen *a.* rare, extraordinary
sleepbear *a.* soporific
waterleet *n.* aqueduct
waterthrough *n.* conduit
wayleet *n.* junction (compare *mill leet*)
wedfasten *v.* pledge
wreckness *n.* vengeance, revenge
yondfare *v.* travel to a place away, traverse, pervade
yondsee *v.* examine

4.2 Same as/ related to/ something like current word + current ending, giving 'new' (updated) form:

4.2.1 Word + *ful*:
angetful *a.* intelligent (compare *to 'get' something*, with the meaning *understand*)
bismearful *a.* ignominious
shandful *a.* disgraceful, scandalous

4.2.2 Word + *ing* to make a noun (compare *following, quickening* - as nouns)
beseening *n.* example, pattern
likebusning *n.* imitation
readthoughting *n.* considering literature
samening *n.* union, unification
tholing *n.* endurance, suffering, passion
tighting *n.* incitement, instigation, exhortation
weening *n.* expectation (compare *overweening*)

Note also:
whiling *a.* passing, transitory, temporary

4.2.3 Word + *ly*:
adreadingly *a., adv.* terribly
bebidingly *adv.* imperatively
endbirthly *a.* in order, in succession, orderly manner
ickly *a.* glacial (compare *iceicle*)
missenly *a.* various
leavedly *a.* permissible
mannishly *adv.* masculinely
selfwieldly *adv.* arbitrarily
selfwillingly *adv.* voluntarily, arbitrarily
shandly *adv.* disgracefully, scandalously
sidely *a.* discrete (compare *on the side*)
wiseheedly *a.* sagacious

4.2.4 Word + *ness*:
acknowness *n.* acknowledgement
afoundness *n.* invention, device, discovery
arearness *n.* elevation
bearingness *n.* fertility, fecundity
betingness *n.* amendment (compare *better*)
betness *n.* reparation, atonement
comelitheness *n.* hospitality
endbirthness *n.* order, series, succession, arrangement, degree
havedness *n.* continence
heartsoreness *n.* grief
highmoodness *n.* pride
mannishliness *n.* masculinity
mannishness *n.* masculinity
onemoodness *n.* unanimity
roomheartness *n.* liberality
setness *n.* institute, foundation, position, institution, construction, record
shandliness *n.* disgrace, scandal
timberness *n.* edification

4.2.5 Word + *liness*:
hapliness *n.* convenience
hardliness *n.* austerity
missenliness *n.* variety, diversity
tideliness *n.* opportunity

4.2.6 Word + *ship*:
fareship *n.* community, retinue, society, companionship
sotship *n.* stupidity

4.3 With more unusual, but recognisable, ending

4.3.1 Adjectives ending in *-le* (compare *brittle, fickle*):
fasthavle *a.* retentive, tenacious
forethinkle *a.* prudent
givle *a.* generous
hattle *a.* hostile, odious
hatethinkle *a.* with hostile intentions
housebreachle *a.* burglarious
overspeakle *a.* over talkative
roomgivle *a.* bountiful
speakle *a.* talkative
unhavle *a.* destitute

4.3.2 Related forms from ending in *-le* + other endings (compare *brittleness*):
fasthavleness *n.* retentiveness, stinginess, economy, tenacity
forethinkleness *n.* prudence
forgetelness *n.* oblivion
givleness *n.* generosity, liberality
hattleness *n.* hostility
overspeakleness *n.* overtalkitiveness
roomgivleness *n.* liberality, bountifulness
sleepleness *n.* lethargy, somnolence
speakleness *n.* loquacity
unhavleness *n.* destitution

4.4 Same as/ related to/ something like current word with current beginning, giving 'new' (updated) form

4.4.1 *Be* + word:
beclip *v.* embrace, encompass
bedidder *v.* deceive (compare: *diddle*, which *may* be related)
behovely *a.* necessary (current word *behove* = be a duty/ fitting)
bereaver *n.* despoiler (compare: reevers were a kind of robber-criminal)
beruesing *n.* repentance (compare: *rueful* = *regretful*)
beshear *v.* deprive (compare: *shear* menaing *cut*)
beshearedness *n.* deprivation
betweenforletness *n.* intermission

4.4.2 *For* + word (compare *forget, forsake*):
forbode *n.* prohibition
forburnedness *n.* consumption by fire
fordeemedly *a.* in prejudicial way
fordeemedness *n.* prejudice
forgoedness *n.* abstention, deprivation
forhavand/ forhaver *n.* one who is abstinent
forhavedness *n.* temperance, self restraint, abstinence
forhaveness *n.* abstinence
forhavingly *adv.* with temperance
forlayness *n.* fornication
forspilledness *n.* destruction
forswornness *n.* perjury
fortrueing *n.* presumption
forwedded pledged
forworthness *n.* devaluation, deterioration

4.4.3 *Fore* + word:
foregang *v.* precede
foresteppand *n.* precursor
forewrit *n.* prologue

4.4.4 *In-* + word (compare *inside, insight*):
inbewind *v.* enwrap, enfold
inblow *v.* inspire - see also onblowness - these call for some thought about what the words imply and how they are used
indrench *v.* saturate
infare *v.* enter, incursion
infare *n.* admission
infind *v.* discover
ingang/ ingo *v.* enter
ingang *n.* entrance, access (compare: *gangway, gangplank*)
inheaten *v.* inflame
inheed *n.* sense, conscience
inheedness *n.* consciousness
inlead *v.* introduce
inlightand *n.* illuminator
inlighten *v.* illuminate, enlighten
inlightness *n.* illumination, enlightenment
inly *a.* internal, interior
inning *n.* contents
inset *v.* institute
insetness *n.* institution, regulation
insetted inserted
inshowing *n.* demonstration, inspection
instand *v.* to be present
instandingly *a.* in way of being present
inthink *n.* intention
inthought *n.* intention
inwark *n.* internal pain
inwise in terms of what is popular/ 'in'
inwitness *n.* consciousness, conscience
inwriter *n.* secretary
inwriting *n.* inscription

4.4.5 *Mis* + word:
misholdsomeness *n.* incompetence
mislikeness *n.* variety, diversity, dissimilarity, difference

4.4.6 *Over* + word:
overfoundness *n.* trial, experiment

4.4.7 *Un* (negative) + word:
unanewingly *a.* unrenewingly
uncomelithe *a.* inhospitable
unforbowingly *a.* unavoidably
unforcouth *a.* reputable, honourable
unforrotedly *adv.* incorruptedly
unforrotingly *a.* incorruptibly
unforthought *a.* not considered, not expected
unharmyearn *a.* inoffensive
unhearsome *a.* disobedient
unhearsomeness *n.* disobedience
unholdsome *a.* incontinent
unholdsomeness *n.* incontinence
unlievedly *a.* incredibly
unlieveful *a.* incredible
unlievefully *a.* incredibly
unlievefulness *n.* incredulity
unrightyetsing *n.* avarice
unshearingly *adv.* inseparably
unsunderedly *a.* inseparably
unthroughshotingly *a.* impenetrably
untidely *a.* unseasonable
untodealed *a.* undivided
untruefast *a.* inconstant, unreliable
unwinsomeness *n.* unpleasantness
unwitherward *a.* not contrary, not discordant
unwitherwardly *a.* not contrarily, not discordantly
unworthing *n.* dishonour
unworthly *adv.* dishonourably

4.5 With beginings, some of which are not currently used:

4.5.1 *Eft-* to show 're'/ doing again (related to *after*):
eftleasing *n.* redemption
eftmind *v.* remember
eftmindy remembering
eftnewing *n.* restoration
These might have developed to have *aft* instead of *eft*, giving *aftleasing* a.s.f.

4.5.2 *Ang-* to show trouble, stress (compare *anger, anguish*):
angmood *n.* distressed/ frustrated mood
angmoodness *n.* distress, frustration
angness *n.* anxiety, trouble
angset *n.* eruption
angsome *a.* troublesome, distressing
angsomely *adv.* troublesomely, distressingly
angsomeness *n.* distress, trouble, pain

4.5.3 *At-*:
atgo *v.* approach
atsake *v.* deny, renounce
atstandand *n.* attendant

4.5.4 *Betwix-* (meaning *between*, as in: '*and so betwix the two of them*'):
betwixalayedness *n.* interjection
betwixgoing separating
betwixset interposed

4.5.5 *Even-* to show ideas of equality and/ or similarity:
evenlatch *v.* imitate
evenlatcher *n.* imitator
evenlatching *n.* imitation
evenmoodly *adv.* with equanimity
evenold *a.* contemporary
evensorrow *v.i.* commiserate
evensorrowing *n.* compassion, sympathy

evensorry *a.* compassionate

4.5.6 *from-* to show movement away:
fromfare *n.* departure
fromship *n.* exercise, action, progress
fromward *adv.* departing, about to depart

4.5.7 *Forth-* often showing movement (physical or otherwise):
forthbear *v.* produce
forthbuilding *n.* encouragement
forthfatheren *a.* paternal
forthfroming *n.* departure
forthgang *v.* progress, advance
forthing *n.* advancement
forthlet *v.* emit
forthly *a.* advanced
forthseen *a.* conspicuous
forthsetness *n.* proposition, proposal, motion
forthshaft *n.* future
forthship *n.* progress
forthspell *n.* declaration
forthstep *v.* advance
forthstepping *n.* advance
forthward *a.* advanced, progressive
forthwardness *n.* progress
forthyearn *v.* to be impetuous

4.5.8 *Full-* to show completion/ muchness:-
fullfasten *v.* ratify/ apply fully
fullgo *v.t.* accomplish, complete, fully perform
fullholden *a.* totally responsible
fullsomeness *n.* abundance
fullwork *v.* complete

4.5.9 *Head-* to show high/ top position/ strength (compare *headstrong*) a.s.f.:
headbold *a.* confident, impudent
headguilt *n.* capital offence
headstead *n.* chief place
headward *n.* chief protector

4.5.10 *Need-* to show compulsion:
needbehove *a.* necessary (compare *behove* = ought/ should)
needbehovedly *a.* necessarily
needbehovedness *n.* necessity
needbehovely *a.* necessary
needbehoveness *n.* requisite
needright *n.* duty
needwise *adv.* in terms of need
needwiseness *n.* necessity

4.5.11 *Off-* to show removal or negativity (compare *offcut*):
offcarve *n.* section, amputation
offlike to be displeasing, displease
offthink *v.* displease

4.5.12 *On-* to show movement, passing, getting a.s.f.:
onbeshowing *n.* inspection, examination
onblowness *n.* inspiration - see also *inblow*, and note, p. 84
onfind *v.* perceive, notice
onfoundleness *n.* experience
onfoundness *n.* explanation, experiment, experience, trial
onlighten/ onlight *v.* illuminate
onlighting *n.* illumination, enlightenment
onlightness *n.* illumination
onlikeness *n.* parable, allegory, form, pattern
onseen *n.* face
onsend *v.* transmit
onshot *n.* attack (f.e. by shooting, also spoken)
onsow *v.* introduce into, implant

onstir *v.* move, disturb, agitate, excite
onstiredness *n.* movement
onwield *n.* authority, command
onwieldness *n.* power, authority

4.5.13 *Out-* to show movement from (compare the noun *out-take*):
outgang *n.* departure, exit
outgoing *n.* exit, exodus
outkind *a.* extraneous, external, foreign

4.5.14 *Right-* to show correctness/ straightness:
rightfathrenkin *n.* direct paternal descent/ pedigree
rightlithely *a.* articulate
rightset *a.* properly appointed/ established
rightsetedness *n.* proper ordinance/ appointment
rightwittly *a.* rational
rightworth *a.* proper

4.5.15 *Same* showing unification/ joining:
samed *a.* unified, absorbed, merged
samedfast *a.* joined, merged, united, unified
samedworking *a.* cooperating

4.5.16 *sunder-* to show separation:
sunderborn *a.* born of disparate parents
sundercraft *n.* special skill
sunderliness *n.* separation, seclusion, separateness, singularity
sunderly *a.* separate, special, private, singular

4.5.17 *Through-* to show movement, passing along and suchlike:
throughdrench *v.* saturate
throughfasten *v.* transfix
throughgo *v.* penetrate
throughholed *a.* pierced, holed
throughsee *v.* examine, study, scrutinise
throughseek *v.* inquire, research

throughwatch *v.* to keep vigilant, alert, keep vigil

4.5.18 *To-* (compare *together, towards*):
todrivedness *n.* dispersal
toknowness *n.* discernment
toletness *n.* despondency, decline
toseekening *n.* pursuit
toseekness *n.* pursuit
tosetedness *n.* disposition
towarpedness *n.* perversion
towarpness *n.* perversion
towriteness *n.* description (written)

4.5.19 *Up-* to show movement upwards (physical of otherwise):
upariseness *n.* resurrection
upcome *n.* source, origin   compare *outcome*
uphavely *adv.* presumptuously, arrogantly
uphaveness *n.* presumption, arrogance

4.5.20 *Well-* to show benefit:
welldoness *n.* benefit, beneficial action (well-do-ness)
wellfremeness *n.* benefit, beneficial planning
wellroomly *a.* spacious, spaciously

4.5.21 *With-* and *wither-* to show turning away and related ideas (compare *withhold, withdraw, withstand*)
withchoose *v.* reject
witherward *a.* contrary, adverse
witherwardly *adv.* contrarily, adversely
witherwardness *n.* opposition, adversity
withlead *v.* abduct
withleadness *n.* abduction
withsaking *n.* denial, rejection
withsetness *n.* opposition
withshove *v.* repel, refute

4.6 Further combinations, variations and use of words to give noteworthy meanings:

4.6.1 *Couth* showing certainty/ familiarity (compare *uncouth*):
couth *a.* manifest, certain, familiar
couthly *a., adv.* manifestly, certainly, familiarly, evidently
couthness *n.* acquaintance, familiarity
seldcouth *a.* unusual, rare, strange (compare *seldom*)
widecouth a. commonly known/ common knowledge

4.6.2 From *dare*:
daresty *a.* venturesome, presumptuous

4.6.3 *Elder*:
elderdom *n.* authority, dominion, seniority, pre-eminence
elderdomliness *n.* pre-eminence, authoritativeness
elderdomly *a., adv.* authoritative, pre-eminently
elding *n.* ageing (process)
eldright *n.* ancient right, tradition
eldsay *n.* tradition

4.6.4 *Ere* (meaning before):
ereworld *n.* ancient world

4.6.5 *Far*:
farsibb *a.* distantly related (compare *sibling*)

4.6.6 *Find*:
findle *n.* invention, device (compare: *thinble, spindle*)

4.6.7 Use of *folk* to show public:
folkcouth *a.* publicly known
folkright *n.* human/ common right, generally accepted, people's right
folkship *n.* population, nation, people
folkstowe *n.* public place

4.6.8 *Gain-* for *again*:
gainwrit *n.* rewriting

4.6.9 *Hear* + *some* to show obedience:
hearsome *a.* obedient, attentive
hearsome *v.* obey
hearsomely *adv.* obediently
hearsomeness *n.* obedience, attentiveness

4.6.10 *One* to show simplicity:
onefold *a.* simple, single, unique, sincere
onefoldness *n.* simplicity

4.6.11 With *shed*, meaing *distinction, separation, discretion*. Can still be found in *watershed* (= unseen line on higher ground, either side of which rain drains different ways). The word is related to *shade/ shadow*.
beshed *n.* distinction
beshed *v.* discriminate
shedwise *a.* discrete
shedwiseness *n.* discretion
unshedwise *a.* indiscriminate, indiscrete, irrational
unshedwisely *adv.* indiscriminately, indiscreetly, irrationally
unshedwiseness *n.* indiscretion, irrationalality
These might have developed to have *shade* instead of *shed*, giving *beshade* a.s.f.

4.6.12 *Stowe* and *stead* to show place/ location:
deathstead *n.* place of death
mootstow *n.* forum
showingstowe *n.* place of demonstration
stead *n.* place, position, location, station (compare *instead, steadfast, steady*)
stowe, stow *n.* site, position, locality, station (compare *stowaway*, also verb *stow*)
stowly *a.* local

4.6.13 Use of *yearn* and *yet* to show desire/ want:
evilyearness *n.* malice
feeyearn *a.* covetous, greedy
feeyetsing *n.* avarice
idleyearn *v.* to be indolent
yetsing *n.* avarice, covetousness, desire
yetsingly *adv.* avariciously, insatiably
yetsingness *n.* avarice

4.7 Lists of words by certain topics:
4.7.1 – 4.7.6 Nouns showing qualities/ doers of things:
4.7.1 Ending in *-and*. This ending, from *-and* and *-end* in Old English, has effectively been ousted in today's English, though still *may be* in brig*and*. Other endings to show functions/ qualities of people in Old English included *-a, -er, -ere* and *-or*. These have tended to become *er* in today's English. There are examples in Old English of the same word with more than one of the above forms, for example: *forlicgend* and *forliger*, both meaning *adulterer, fornicator*. The updated forms from these are *forlieand* and *forlier (for* here having a wayward/ negative meaning). Clearly, the *–er* ending looks the most familiar in today's English, though *-and* is not so unlike the *ant* forms found in some common loanwords (such as: *entrant, occupant* and *participant*).

The following are updated from Old English forms ending in *-and* and *–end*. A choice of forms ending in *-and* and *–er* have been offered for most:
aleasand/ aleaser *n.* deliverer, redeemer, liberator
bebidand/ bebider *n.* commander
foresingand/ foresinger *n.* precentor
forlieand/ forlier *n.* adulterer, fornicator
freeand/ free-er *n.* liberator
furtherand/ further-er *n.* promoter
healand *n.* saviour
holdand/ holder *n.* protector, guardian, ruler
middliand/ middlier *n.* mediator
onfindand/ onfinder *n.* discoverer
onlightand/ onlighter *n.* enlightener
shepand *n.* creator

wastand *n.* devastator
witherspeakand/ witherspeaker *n.* adversary (in speech), contradictor

4.7.2 Ending in *-er.:*
birther *n.* embryo/ foetus - and don't forget that *unborn child* is from Old English words
deemer/ deemster a judge (Manx law has deemsters)
earthbeganger *n.* inhabitant
eatgiver *n.* host at a meal
feeyetser *n.* miser
fleshmonger *n.* butcher
foreganger *n.* predecessor
forlier *n.* adulterer, fornicator
highelder *n.* ruler, prime minister
ingenger/ ingoer *n.* entrant, visitor
inshower *n.* demonstrator
ownslayer *n.* one who commits suicide
readthoughter *n.* literary commentator
scrutner *n.* examiner
shipsteerer *n.* pilot
thoughter *n.* adviser
unrightdeemer *n.* unjust judge/ critic
witter *n.* sage, philosopher

4.7.3 Ending in *-ling* (compare *earthling*):
evenling *n.* equal person
hinderling *n.* conspirator, betrayer
witherling *n.* opponent, adversary

4.7.4 Ending in *-ward,* with the idea of *guarding* (compare *steward*, also *warden, warder*)
hoardward *n.* guardian of treasure
lifeward *n.* lifeguard
seaward *n.* coast guard
shipward *n.* ship master

4.7.5 Ending in -*man*:
boroughman *n.* town citizen
highshireman *n.* county council leader
overalderman *n.* chief officer
shireman *n.* county council official

Note: Some folk avoid using forms ending in -*man*. There would though, be the choice to adopt endings in -*woman*, or *person* (though the latter is not from Old English) or maybe *were* (see 5.1.17).

4.7.6 Other forms:
highreeve *n.* chief officer *reeve* can refer to a king of official in the Middle Ages. The basic form is also found in *sheriff*, which is from 'shire-reeve'.
withersake *n.* advesary, enemy Compare *namesake*
workreeve *n.* manager

4.7.7 Kith and Kin:
eldfather *n.* grandfather
eldmother *n.* grandmother
third, fourth eldfather *n.* great, (and) great great grandfather; likewise, third eldmother would be great grand mother and so on.

4.7.8 To do with position, area and suchlike:
beck(o)nand *n.* indicator, discloser, index
boroughshire *n.* city/ town administrative area
eastlong *adv.* extending east
farlen *a.* remote
fitherdealt *a.* quartered
landmark *n.* boundary, border
loften *a.* aerial
nethergo *v.* descend
sheeringly *adv.* in way that mark/ cuts off
southright due south
westnorthlong extending NW

Step 4, Part B: Words in Use and Tests

Answers to tests on p 143.

Adverts and Signs:

- Searim Shieldness - *Coastal Defences*

[Sign: Searim Shieldness]

- Mootstow for the Forthshaft - *Forum for the Future*
- OUTGANG - *ENTRANCE*
- INGANG - *EXIT*
- Stowly Health Onwield - *Local Health Authority*

- Footly Ingang - *Pedestrian Access*

- Town Showingstowe - *Town Exhibition Centre*

Test ii). *Do you understand the following?*
1. The Women's Setness
2. Folkly Hapliness
3. Forthfroming Room
4. Holdfast Webstead
5. Body: Forehaveness Fellowship

Headlines:

- 'Forthship' in fight against beshearedness - *'Progress' …against deprivation'*
- Felled tree had sunderly dearworthness - ... *had special preciousness/ value*
- Hidden weapons deal now folkcouth - ... *now publicly known*
- Shire forsets new deal for business - *County proposes new deal ...*
- The Welfare State: how givle now? - ...*how generous now?*
- Losses down to worker misholdsomeness - *Losses caused by staff incompetence*
- Former homeless now stowly homefast - *Previously homeless now residing locally*
- Insetness Body: steerworth behaviour 'widespread' – *Regulatory Body: reprehensible conduct 'widespread'*
- Onefold answer to being overweight? - *Simple solution ...*
- Withsetness: health cutback 'warpness' - *Opposition: health cutback 'perversion'*
- Need for new ring road 'unbeshowed' - ...*'not proven'*
- Seekness yields unbethought outcome - *Inquiry yields unexpected result*
- Angsome throng sidestepped weaponless guards - *Frustrated crowd evaded unarmed guards*
- House ownership by unbewedded twosomes rises - ...*by unmarried couples increases*

- First Thane - Inthought to stand down? - *P.M. - Intention to resign?*

Test iii). *What do the following mean?*
1. Out of work forecasts found to be untruefast
2. Many Scots said to forechoose selfdom
3. Thief forflees being caught
4. Fans showed 'lack of holdsomeness'
5. One fourth of stowly folk deem selves unhavers

Snipetts from Articles, Textbooks and suchlike:

- ... begengness of wordhoard is down to folk - ...*application of vocabulary depends on people*
- Folkly unhearsomeness - *Civil disobedience*
- ... standness of life on other worlds thought to be likely - ... *existence of life on other worlds thought to be likely*
- Overall Throughlooking - *General Summary*
- ... a breakdown of soil bearingness - ... *an analysis of soil fertility*
- Playgound and field have a betwixgoing wall - ... *a separating wall*
- Leaflet: How to Spend without Forspending - *How to Spend without Squandering*
- Mindliness Sunday - *Remembrance Sunday*
- ... that such hinderlings should be caught straight away - ... *such conspirators*
- ... town has about 200,000 overeseas ingoers (or ingengers) yearly - ... *visitors*
- ... a need to throughseek more illnesses - ... *to research* ...
- ... with a new rightset Stowly Onwield - ... *properly appointed/ established Local Authority*
- ... had to show that rightsetedness had been made - ... *that proper appointment* ...

- ... the need for rightwittly thinking had overcome withsetness in those talks - ... *for rational thinking had overcome opposition ...*
- ... was guilty of weeing in a folkstowe - ... *of urinating in a public place*
- ... which is couthly acknowledged the elderdomly work in this field - ... *certainly acknowledged the authoritative work ...*
- ... that they would stop witherwardly wending in such a forthseen way - ... *stop contrarily changing in such a conspicuous way*
- ... would need to show toknowness in choosing the best - ... *to show discernment*
- ... but fromship would not needbehovedly be made that way - ... *but progress would not necessarily be made ...*
- ... could ween a folky onbeshowing at any time - ... *could expect a public inspection ...*
- ... want forthship in the forthshaft on this - *want progress in the future ...*
- ... the two works shown here being evenold - ... *being contemporary*
- ... said that nearly all eftmind something about '1066 and all that' - ... *nearly all remember ...*
- Wildlife missenliness - *Biodiversity*
- ... giving alms for unhavle children - ... *aid for destitute ...*
- ... is a great tideliness to eftnew words - ... *a great opportunity to restore words*

Bookly and other bits:

- To give careful thoughting - *to give careful consideration*
- ... had withshoved the thief with nothing but loud thuds - ... *had repelled*
- ... following orders hearsomely - ...*obediently*
- ... eftminded falling with a thud, and then lost inheedness - ... *remembered falling ... then lost consciousness*
- ... not rightworth that they should see one another - *not proper ...*
- ... was swith speakle that day - ... *very talkative ...*
- ... now saw toseekness of wealth and happiness as being sunderly things - ... *now saw pursuit of ... as being separate things*
- ... was not for folk of an upaty tosetedness - ... *of a nervous disposition*
- ... sent his book forthsetness in, and waited for an answer - ... *book proposal in, and ...*

- ... liked that it had been so shedwisely done - ... *so rationally done*
- ... never forgot the unshedwiseness, and was always wary - ... *the indiscretion*
- ... so thought they should inlead more players to the field - ... *introduce more*
- ... such highmoodness would soon be shot down - ... *such pride* ...
- In Magazine: Bookly Throughlooking - *Literary Review*
- Leaflet Heading: Rightsetness for Computer - *Correct Adjustment of Computer*
- Sunderly Standness - *Special Status*
- Wellwillingness and givleness go hand in hand - *Benevolence and generosity are complimentary*
- ... the upariseness of the dead ... - ... *the resurrection of the dead* ...

Test iv). *What do you think these mean?*
1. Needness is the mother of afoundness
2. Seafares of Afoundness

3. ... an ongetful learner - ...

4. Through onfoundness, one can grow wiser
5. ... not to beshed against folk on grounds of hue ...

What about? See what other names for organisations and out-takes from writing and speech you can come up with.

Step 5
Weird and Wonderful
- A Taste of some very different English

To Think About ... Test i) What do you think the examples below mean? Think and read on - you can check answers on p. 146.

My mum and dad did have a wastum stall

Don't wray me of wending that!

You thewless thing!

Watch it, or you'll be nicked - for frithbreach!

You've got a wlitty anleth!

It's good now that we've come to thedesomeness

It'll be a freme for us both

- Yes, a worthwhile howing!

This last step looks mainly at words which are much less like current words in English. Here, more than anywhere, we get a glimpse of just how strikingly different English could have looked today. And this is far from being a full list, because Old English has left a wealth of other recorded words for which there was simply no room.

Some clever use of these words could potentially be made in historical novels ... or, indeed, if certain strands of quantum physics are right, it may be that quantum events have led to other, side-by-side worlds, where the English *did* indeed win Hastings...! (this is actually the stuff of serious scientific theorising, though well beyond the breadth of this book!).

Part A: Breakdown of Words by Type

Whilst familiar elements are common for many words in the other steps, this is less so with Step 5 words, and so the breakdown set out here partly follows a different pattern. Words are looked at in different themes, or where appropriate covered in terms of common key roots.

5.1.1 Some everyday Words:

5.1.1.1 Sundries:
beswape *v.*   persuade
breme *a.*   famous, noble
brook *v.*   use, enjoy
beseen *n.*   example, model, pattern (compare *behold!*)
beseen *v.*   to set an example, instruct by example, express figuratively
downstying   descending
fand *v.*   attempt, test, examine, experience
freckenful *a.* dangerous
gathertang *a.* continuous, united
gathertangness *n.* continuation
meanship *n.*   community
quide *v.*   phrase, proverb, sentence (related to *quote*)
roun *n.*   secret, secrecy, mystery
smicker *a.*   elegant, beauteous

smickerness *n.* elegance
throughwoningness *n.* perseverance
throughwoning *n.* perseverance, persistency, tenacity
throughwoness *n.* perseverance
wharve *v.* turn, revolve, change, transfer, convert
wharvely *a.* changing, changeable, transitory
wharveness *n.* transition, change, conversion, revolution
wonely *a.* usual, customary

5.1.1.2 *Fele* and *swith*, both meaning *very:*
fele *adv.* very
felefold *a.* frequent
felefoldness *n.* multitude
felespeakle *a.* talkative
felewordness *n.* talkative
swith *adv.* very, exceedingly, severely
swither more excessive
swithliness *n.* intensity, severity, excess
swithly *a.* intense, excessive, severe
swithness *n.* intensity, severity, excess
swithrueness *n.* remorse

5.1.1.3 With *eath* = easy
eath *a.* easy, agreeable
eathly *a.* easily
eathness *n.* ease, easiness, pleasure
uneath *n.* difficulty, trouble
uneathliness *n.* inconvenience, trouble
uneathly *a.* troublesomely, with difficulty
uneathness *n.* difficulty, trouble

5.1.2 With *este* = grace, favour:
este *n.* favour, grace, bounty, pleasure
este *v.* to live luxuriously
estely *adv.* graciously
estful *a.* gracious

estfulness *n.* gracefulness
estiness *n.* graciousness
esty *a.* gracious
Negative with *un*-:
unestful *a.* ungracious

5.1.3 With *evest* = envy, rivalry
evest *n.* envy, rivalry
evest *v.* to envy
evestful *a.* envious
evesty *a.* envious

5.1.4 Words related to modern *from*:

5.1.4.1 Showing completion, based on **freme** *v.* = avail, benefit
fremeful *a.* useful, profitable, beneficial constructive, positive
fremefulness *n.* profitability, usefulness
fremely *a.* profitable
fremefully *adv.* constructively, positively, usefully, profitably, beneficially
fullfreme *v.* complete, perfect
fullfremed *a.* completed
fullfremedly *a.* completely
fullfremedness *n.* completion
Negatives likewise, with *un*-:
unfremed *a.* not negotiated
unfremeful *a.* negative, unprofitable, not useful
unfreming *n.* inconsideration
unfulfremed imperfect
unfulfremedness *n.* imperfection
unfulfreming *n.* incompletion, imperfection

5.1.4.2 Showing otherness:
fremd *v.* estrange
fremd *a.* foreign, alien, strange

5.1.4.3 Showing strangeness:
frimdy *a.* curious

5.1.4.4 Showing origin, based on *frume* (still related to modern *from*):
frume *n.* origin, cause
frumer *n.* originator, inventor
frumly *a.* original, primitive
frumth *n.* origin, foundation
frumthly *a.* primeval, primitive
frumwork *n.* original construction

5.1.5 To do with question/ inquiry, built around *frayn*:
frayn *n.* question
frayne *v.* inquire
frayness *n.* interrogation, questioning
frayning *n.* question
frayning *v.* questioning
befrine *v.* question

5.1.6 With *how* = prudent
howe *a.* prudent
howe *v.* be prudent
howing *n.* endeavour
howly *a.* prudently
howship *n.* prudence
howful *a.* anxious (with *ful* taking things further)
howfullness *n.* anxiousness
forhow *v.* neglect, disregard, despise
forhowand *n.* neglecter, despiser
forhowedly *adv.* contemptuously
forhowedness *n.* contempt
forhowing *n.* contempt
forhowingly *adv.* contemptibly
overhow *v.* despise
overhowand *n.* despiser
overhowedness *n.* disdain

5.1.7 With *ore* = honour
ore *n.* honour, respect, favour
orefast *a.* respected, honest, gracious
orefastly *adv.* respectfully, honestly, graciously
orefastness *n.* respect, honesty
oreless *a.* dishonourable
orelessness *n.* dishonour
orereadness *n.* condition
oreworthily *adv.* honourably
oreworthness *n.* honour
oreworth *a.* honourable
oreworthyful *a.* right honourable
oring *n.* honour, respect, reverence
Negatives:
unoreworth *v.* dishonour
unoreworthly *adv.* dishonourably
unoreworthness *n.* dishonour, indignity, irreverence

5.1.8 With *queme* = pleasant, agreeable, acceptable
queme *a.* pleasant, agreeable, acceptable
queme *v.* please, satisfy, comply with
quemeness *n.* pleasure, satisfaction, mitigation
qweming pleasing, satisfying
quemely *a.* pleasing, satisfying, suitable, satisfactorily
wellquemedly *a.* well pleasing
wellquemness *n.* favour, pleasure
unqueme *a.* displeasing, not pleasing

5.1.9 With *swike* = deception
swike *v.* deceive
swike *n.* treachery, deceit
swikedom *n.* deception
swikeful *a.* deceitful, fraudulent
swiker *n.* deceiver
swiking *n.* deceit, fraud deception
beswike *n.* treachery, deceit

beswike *v.* deceive
beswikeness *n.* deception
beswiker *n.* deceiver
beswiking *n.* deception

5.1.10 With *tharf* = necessity, distress
tharf *n.* necessity, distress
tharfedness *n.* poverty, destitution
tharfeless *a.* without necessity/ distress/ trouble
tharfer *n.* pauper, poor/ destitute person
tharfingly *a.* miserably, destitutely
tharfliness *n.* poverty, destitution
tharfly *a.* poorly, destitutely

5.1.11 With *thede* = to join, associate
thede *v.* join, associate
thedeness *n.* association, society
thedesomeness *n.* agreement
underthede *v.* subject, subjugate, subdue
underthedeness *n.* subjection, submission, obedience

5.1.12 With *thew* = usage, custom and suchlike
thew *n.* usage, custom, habit, conduct, disposition, manners
thew *v.* to bring up morally/ virtuously
thewfast *a.* moral, virtuous, honourable
thewfastly *a.* morally, virtuously
thewfastness *n.* obedience, discipline
thewful *a.* moral, virtuous
thewless *a.* ill mannered, immoral, inconstant
thewly *a.* customary, moral
unthew *n.* vice, fault
unthewfast *a.* immoral, disorderly, unmannered
unthewful *a.* immoral, disorderly, unmannered

5.1.13 With *thild*, meaning patience:
thild *v.* to be patient
thild *n.* patience
thildily *adv.* patiently
thildy *a.* patient
Negatives likewise, with *un-*:
unthild *n.* impatience
unthildly *adv.* impatiently
unthildy *a.* impatient

5.1.14 *Twoly* (from the number two) to show ambiguity:
twoly *a.* doubtful, ambiguous, equivocal
untwoly *a.* not ambiguous

5.1.15 To do with fruit, based in *wastum*:
wastum *n.*   fruit, product, produce
wastumbearingness *n.* fruitfulness, productivity, fertility
wastumbearness *n.* fruitfulness, productivity, fertility
wastumless *a.* unfruitful, unproductive
Negative, with *un-*:
unwastmbearness *n.* unfruitfulness, sterility

5.1.16 Based on *wend*, showing change:
atwend *v.* divert, deprive of
edwend *v.* return
wend *v.* change
wendedness *n.* alteration, change
wender *n.* translator, interpreter
wending *n.* change, subversion
wending *n.* change, rotation
wendingliness *n.* mutability, changeability
wendingly *a.* changeably
weatherwendedness *n.* changeability, variation of weather
bewend *v.* turn, convert
whilewendly *a.* temporary, transitory

Negative likewise:
unwendness *n.* unchangeability

5.1.17 With *were*, meaning human (still found in *were*wolf).
werekin n. human race
werehood n. adulthood
werely a. human

5.1.18 With *yeme* = to notice
misyeme *v.* neglect
yeme *v.* notice
yemeless *a.* negligent
yemelessly *adv.* negligently
yemelessness *n.* negligence

5.1.19 Beginning with *ed-* to show doing again (= *re-*):
edgift *n.* restitution
ednew *v.* restore, renew
ednewand *n.* restorer
edquicken *v.* revive
edstall *v.* restore
edstathling *n.* reestablishment
edyield *v.* remunerate

5.2 More words to do with everyday life:

5.2.1 To do with being happy, blithe, and suchlike:
bilewhit *a.* innocent, simple, sincere
bilewhitness *n.* innocence, simplicity
eady *a.* prosperous, fortunate, happy
eadily *adv.* fortunately, prosperously
eadiness *n.* prosperity, fortune
eady *v.* to make fortunate
edmede *n.* gentleness, humility, submission
smiltness *n.* gentleness

smolt *a.* gentle
smoltly *adv.* gently
wastumly *adv.* fruitfully, productively
weal *n.* prosperity
wealy *a.* prosperous (compare *well-off*)

5.2.2 To do with woe, strife and suchlike:
anneal *v.* ignite, inflame, incite, consume
arm *a.* poor, destitute, miserable
armheartness *n.* pity
armly *adv.* poorly, miserably, pitiable
arveth *n.* labour, trouble, difficulty
arvethliness *n.* laboriousness
arvethly *a.* troublesome, laborious
arvethness *n.* difficulty, trouble, pain
atel *a.* terrible, repulsive
atelly *adv.* terribly, repulsively
athrick *v.* press, oppress
atter *n.* poison, venom
atterbearing *a.* poisonous
atterly *adv.* poisonously, venomously
attery *a.* poisonous, venomous
awem *v.* disfigure, corrupt
awemendness *n.* corruption
benim *v.* deprive
beniming *n.* deprival
bepeach *v.* deceive
bepeachand *n.* deceiver
bepeaching *n.* deception
besnit *v.* pollute, dishonour
besnitness *n.* degradation, pollution
beway *v.* frustrate
dretch *v.* trouble, torment
dretchedness *n.* tribulation, affliction
dwild *n.* error
dwildafterfollowing *n.* erroneous movement

113

dwolma *n.* chaos
ermth *n.* poverty, misery, distress
hean *v.* afflict, injure
heanhood *n.* difficulty
heanly *a.* abject, poor
hoker *n.* insult, derision
nithfully *adv.* maliciously
nithing *n.* villain
nithy *a.* malicious
shend *v.* confound, corrupt, discomfit
shending *n.* reproach, affliction
shendle *n.* reproach
shendness *n.* confusion
shildiness *n.* criminality
shildy *a.* criminal
slithe *a.* cruel, savage, fierce
slithely *adv.* cruelly, savagely, fiercely
swenche *v.* trouble
swenk *n.* trouble
swenkedness *n.* trouble
tharl *a.* vigorous, severe, strict
tharlwise *a.* strict, severe
tharlwisely *adv.* strictly, severely, sternly, roughly
tharlwiseness *n.* severity, strictness
tharly *adv.* severely, cruelly, grievously
thresting *n.* affliction, torment
threstness *n.* trouble, contrition
thrutch *v.* trample, oppress, afflict, repress
thrutchness *n.* affliction, tribulation
tothundenly *a.* arrogantly
tothundness *n.* arrogance
unathelness *n.* ignobility, humiliation
untholingly *a., adv.* intolerably
unwlitty *a.* not pretty, disfigured, deformed
unwlittying *n.* disfigurement
unwlittyness *n.* disfigurement

walm *n.* inflammation
wark *n.* pain, suffering
wlenk *n.* pride, arrogance
wlonk *a.* proud
yepeness *n.* astuteness
yomer *v.* to be miserable
yomer *a.* troubled, miserable
yomering *n.* misery, trouble
yomerly *adv.* miserably, with trouble
yomerness *n.* tribulation

5.2.3 Feelings, Relationships and suchlike:
afond *v.* test, prove, experience
afonding *n.* test, experience
afrever *v.* comfort, console
awherve *v.* convert, turn, avert
evenfain *v.* sympathise
forspan *v.* seduce
forspanning *n.* allurement, seduction
frover *n.* consolation
frover *v.* cheer, console
froverness *n.* consolation
frovrand *n.* consoler, comforter
frovring *n.* consolation
greme *v.* enrage, provoke, irritate
greming *n.* provocation
grorning *n.* complaint
hap *a.* convenient
hedge *v.* consider, ponder, meditate, determine
hedgely *adv.* considerately, meditatively, determinedly
kithe *v.* proclaim, relate, perform, announce, confirm
kithedness *n.* testimony
kither *n.* testifier
kithing *n.* statement, narration
metefast *a.* moderate
metefastness *n.* moderation (from *mete*, still found in *to mete out* ...)

thave *v.* permit, consent to
thavesome *a.* consenting
thavesomeness *n.* consent
unlored *a.* ignorant
unloredness *n.* ignorance
unmetefast *a.* immoderate, intemperate, excessive (from *mete*, still found in *to mete out* ...)
unmetefastness *n.* excess, intemperance, lack of moderation
unmetely *a., adv.* immeasurable, innumerably
unmeteness *n.* innumerableness, extravagance
unshildy *a.* innocent
whurful *a.* inconstant
whurfulness *n.* inconstancy, mutability
wilne *v.* desire
wilning *n.* desire
wray *v.* accuse
wrayedness *n.* accusation
wrayer *n.* accuser
wraying *n.* accusation
wrayingly *adv.* accusingly

5.3 Some lists by topic:

5.3.1 To do with Land and Landscape features:
crundle *n.* ravine, quarry
hithe *n.* harbour, port
hithely *a.* of harbour/ port
landship *n.* region
landstead *n.* region
slade *n.* valley, glade
staith *n.* river bank
westdeal *n.* west part
weald, wold *n.* forest

5.3.2 To do with the Body a.s.f. (most of our everyday words to do with the body are from Old English, although you mightn't think it sometimes from signs and leaflets in hospitals!):
anleth *n.* face
arine *v.* touch, handle
atrine *n.* touch
atrine *v.* touch
fingerlith *n.* finger joint
lith *n.* joint
rerde *v.* discourse
rerde *n.* voice, language
rine *v.* touch, reach
rineness *n.* contact, touch
rining *n.* touch
smatch *v.* taste
steven *n.* voice
wlita *n.* face, countenance
wlite *n.* appearance, aspect
wlitty *a.* beautiful

5.3.3 Kith and Kin:
eme *n.* uncle
inherd *n.* family
unsibb *a.* unrelated (compare *sibling*)

5.3.4 Nobility/ Aristocracy:
athel *a.* noble, aristocratic
athel *v.* to make noble
athelborn noble born
athelkind *n.* nobility
athelness *n.* nobility (class of)
ricser *n.* ruler
ricsing *n.* domination
unathelborn *a.* not of noble birth

5.3.5 To do with civil authority, administration, trade a.s.f.:

5.3.5.1 With *ambight* = office
ambight *n.* office, service, command
ambight *v.* serve, minister
ambighter *n.* officer, attendant, servant
ambighthouse *n.* office
ambightness *n.* service, commission

5.3.5.2 With *reeve* = *high official*
reeve *n.* high official, prefect
reeveship *n.* office, prefecture
boroughreeve *n.* provost, mayor
folkreeve *n.* public officer

5.3.5.3 With *thane* = minister, servant
thane *n.* servant, minister
thane *v.* serve, minister
thanely *a.* noble, brave, loyal
thaneship *n.* service, duty, ability, valour
thaning *n.* service, ministry, administration
bowerthane *n.* chamberlain, page
elderthane *n.* chief attendant, retainer
hallthane *n.* hall officer
handthane *n.* retainer
highthane *n.* chief officer, captain
highthaning *n.* important function
lorethane *n.* instructor

5.3.5.4 Sundry others:
abede *v.* order, proclaim, summon, command, direct, announce, declare, offer
afleme *v.* expel, disperse
afley *v.* expel
afremd *v.* alienate, become alienated
afremding *n.* alienation

beadle *n.* warrant officer, herald, preacher (still found as a surname)
befrining *n.* inquiry
begeng *n.* observance, practice, exercise
begenger *n.* practitioner
chapman *n.* trader (still found as a surname)
chapstow *n.* market (compare: Chepstow, town in S.E. Wales)
dight *n.* arrangement
dight *v.* arrange, appoint
dighter *n.* arranger
dightner *n.* manager
dightning *n.* ordering, disposition
fand v. try, test
fander *n.* tester, tryer *fandere*
fanding *n.* investigation, trail, test, proof
fering *n.* vehicle
gavel *n.* interest (on loan a.s.f.)
gavelly *a.* fiscal
goldhoardhouse *n.* treasuary
haftling *n.* prisoner, captive
helmward *n.* pilot
hove *n.* court
hovely *a.* courtly
moothouse *n.* place of meeting, assembling
speer *v.* investigate
speeriand *n.* investigator, inquirer
speering *n.* investigation
wickner *n.* bailiff
wike *n.* officer, office, function
witanmoot *n.* national council
withmeetedness *n.* invention
wordsomener *n.* catalogue, ennumeration
wordsomening *n.* collation
yearmind *n.* yearly commemoration

5.3.6 Some with particular link with/ use in Church contexts:
aredde *v.* rescue, save, deliver

aredding *n.* salvation, deliverance
arist *n.* resurrection
bede *v.* pray
bedehouse *n.* chapel
churchthane *n.* minister of the church
churchthaning *n.* church duty/ service
costen *v.* try, test, prove
costiand *n.* tempter
costness *n.* proving, trial, temptation
costning *n.* testing, temptation, trial
custy *a.* charitable, generous, virtuous
custiness *n.* charity, generosity, virtue
deedbote *n.* atonement, penitence
deedboteness *n.* atonement, penitence
frumshaft *n.* primeval condition, original creation
frumshapand *n.* creator
fullought *v.* baptise
fullought *n.* baptism
fulloughtbath *n.* font
fulloughter *n.* baptiser, baptist
gospelly *a.* evangelical
kitheness *n.* testament, testimony
loreboding *n.* preaching (teaching)
milce *n.* mercy, compassion, benevolence
milce *v.* to have compassion, show mercy
newwhirved *a.* newly converted
wulder *v.* glorify
wulder *n.* glory, splendour
wulderful *a.* glorious
wulderfully *a.* gloriously
wuldry *a.* glorious

5.3.7 Of war and peace:

5.3.7.1 *Peace* with *frith* and *sib*
frith *n.* peace

frithbreach *n.* breach of the peace
frithsome *a.* pacific, peaceable
frithstowe refuge, sanctuary
frithwrit *n.* peace agreement, treaty
sib *n.* peace
sibsome *a.* peaceable
sibsome *v.* reconcile
sibsomeness *n.* concord, peace
sibsoming *n.* making peace
unsibsome *a.* contentious, argumentative, quarrelsome
unsibsomeness *n.* contentiousness, discord, quarrelsomeness

5.3.7.2 Victory, with *sey, seyer*. (note: name *Woolsey* is from *wolf* + *sey*)
sey *n.* victory, triumph
seyer *n.* victory
seyerfast *a.* victorious
seyerfastness *n.* victory
seyerly *a.* triumphal
seyfast *v.* triumph
seyfast *a.* victorious
seyfastness *n.* victory, triumph
seyly *a.* victorious

5.3.7.3 Some others
grith *n.* truce, asylum, protection
grithbreach *n.* breach of truce/ asylum
guth *n.* combat, battle, war
heleth *n.* hero
hild *n.* war, combat
wye *n.* war, contest

5.3.8 To do with the Military:
ferd *n.* army
ferding *n.* expedition, campaign, soldiering
fird *v.* to go on expedition
firdfare *n.* military service

firdly *a.* military, martial
firdship *n.* the military
firdwise *a.* militarily
helm *n.* protection, defence, covering
hera *n.* army (army-like shoals gave rise to the word *herring*)
herahuth *n.* plunder
heraly *a.* martial
heraman *n.* soldier
heratower *n.* commander, general (one who *tows* = leads the fighters)
heriot *n.* military equipment
hest *n.* command
houth *n.* plunder
landfirding *n.* military operations on land
landhera *n.* land force/ army
wered *n.* army troop, company, band
wyeman *n.* warrior, soldier
wyesith *n.* military expedition
yisle *n.* hostage
yislehood *n.* state of being a hostage

5.3.9 To do with Nationality:
althede *n.* foreign nation
althedily *adv.* in manner of foreigners
althediness *n.* foreignness
althedish foreign
althedy of foreign nation
eastleod *n.* orientals
ethel *n.* country
strind *n.* generation, race, tribe
thede *n.* people, nation, province
thedely *a.* social, national, provincial
thedeship *n.* community, population, nation, administration, association
unthede *a.* disunited
yearve *n.* heritage

Step 5, Part B: Words in Use and Tests

Answers to tests on p 146.

Adverts and Signs:

- Hot Drinks: Self-thaning - *Hot Beverages: Self-service*
- Fairtrade Bananas: Frume: Windward Islands - ... *Origin* ...
- Head Ambighthouse - *Main Office*
- Fand our frimdy food! – *Try our curious (exotic) food!*

- On roadsign: OUTGANG   Wayleet 35   -   *Exit*   *Junction 35*

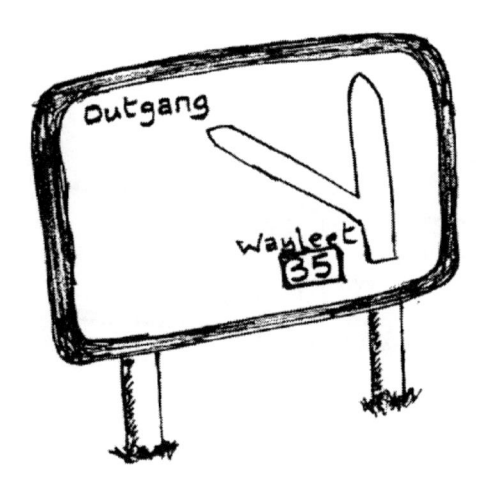

- The High Hove - *The High Court*
- Wildlife Frithstowe - *Nature Reserve*
- Hithe Onwield - *Harbour/ Port Authority*
- Orefastness box - *Honesty box*
- Title: Thane of Learning - *Minister of Education*
- Thedely Thaneship - *Social Service*

- English Yearve - *English Heritage*
- An almsly trust - *A charitable trust*
- Title for MP: The Right Oreworthy (or: The Oreworthyful) ... - *The Right Honourable* ...

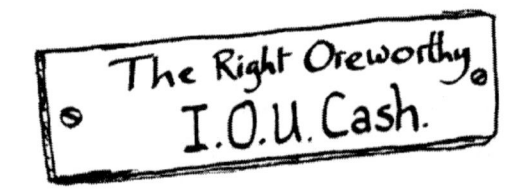

- The Weald Setness - *The Forestry Commission*

Test ii). *Do you understand the following?*

1. Title: Forsitting Wike
2. Awayleadness Thaning
3. The Shieldness Ambightness
4. Rightwiseness Thane
5. Arvethshooter

Headlines:

- Calls to bring back firdfare - *Calls to restore national (military) service*

- Threat of herely law 'unknown' to Althedish (or Overseas) Ambighthouse - *Threat of martial law 'unknown' to Foreign Office*

- Frith talks: Head Middliand 'heartened' - *Peace talks: Chief Mediator 'encouraged'*

- Yisles aleased - *Hostages released*

- Overalderman's behaviour 'besmearly' - *Chief Officer's behaviour reproachful*
- Thane's stand made enoughly clear - *Minister's position made abundantly clear*

- New carbon law forthsetness 'fremeful' - *New carbon law proposal 'constructive/ positive'*
- Housing howing now fulfremed - *... endeavour now completed*
- Seekness to Thedely Health Thaneship shendness nears fullfremedness - *Inquiry into NHS (National Health Service) confusion nears completion*
- Dightner: 'too many idleyearnful' - *Manager: 'too many indolent'*
- Wyemen 'unthildy for withdrawal' - *Soldiers impatient for withdrawal*
- Ambighter's words 'scatheful' - *Officer's comments 'injurious'*
- Care home seekness: 'armly run' - *Care home inquiry: 'poorly managed'*
- Highshireman wrayed of craftless wield - *County Council Leader accused of poor control*

News Weekly

Highshireman wrayed of craftless wield

County Council Leader accused of poor control

- Frithwrit breakthrough down to 'thild and throughwinningness' - *Peace agreement breakthrough due to 'patience and perseverance'*
- Attery snake bite undeadly - *Poisonous snake bite not fatal*
- Beavers unweenedly back to weald - *Beavers unexpectedly return to forest*
- Child tharvliness lessened - *Child poverty reduced*
- Former Thane: 'fullholden for Goldhoardhouse losses' - *Former Minister: 'totally responsible for Treasury losses'*
- New Laws fremefully set out in straight English - *New legislation beneficially transcribed in Plain English*

- Seekness finds Shortfalls in Health Thaning - *Enquiry discovers Shortfalls in Health Service*

> **News Weekly**
>
> Seekness finds shortfalls in health thaning
>
> Inquiry discovers inadequacies in health Service

- Ongetness in Home Ambighthouse was of 'qualmful breakdown of thaneship' - *Perception in Home Office was of 'pernicious service breakdown'*
- Feelessness to brainsick man - thane is 'rueful' - *Insensitivity to mentally ill man - minister 'regrets'*

> **Daily News**
>
> Feelessness to brainsick man - thane is 'rueful'
>
> Insensitivity to mentaly ill man - minister 'regrets'

- Meanship housing: all 'to be evenlotters' – *Community housing: all 'to be equal sharers/ partakers'*
- Frithwrit now fullfastened - *Peace Treaty now ratified*
- Call for Speering into Youth Ermth - *Call for Investigation into Youth Poverty*

Daily News

Call for Speering into Youth Ermth

Call for Investigation into Youth Poverty

Test iii) *What do the following mean?*

1. Thane: mightliness of earthquake was 'unbethought'
2. Our Sasha seyerfast with new world best!
3. Aleased yisle speaks of underdriveness to heavy beatings
4. Selfdom forspeakers meet thane
5. Ferd bebidand 'too forthyearnful'

Snippets from Articles, Textbooks and suchlike:

- Beseen - *For example*
- The worthliness of footly awareness at wayleets - *The importance of pedestrian awareness at junctions*

- Mushroom eatness not same for all unatterly kinds - ... *edibility not same for all non poisonous species*
- The Frithsome Highsea - *The Pacific Ocean*
- First Thane's Frayning Time - *Prime Minister's Question Time*
- ... outcome of your English understandness... - *result of your English comprehension...*
- Tothaning breakdown - *Administration breakdown*
- A kithing from no 10 said ... - *A statement ...*
- Great wendingliness can come with moodsickness - *Severe changeability can come with depression*
- Breme folk, breme anleths, breme steads - *Famous people, famous faces, famous places*
- ... there now seemed to be a quemely answer to that thanely frayn - ... *seemed to be suitable answer to that ministerial question*
- ... had seen five days of gathertang withsetness on the streets - ... *5 days of continuous/ united opposition ...*
- ... would only be with great arveth that he would put right that orelessness - ... *with great labour/ trouble/ difficulty ... that dishonour*
- ... came here as folk from a fremd ethel - ... *from a foreign country*
- ... firdly spending having risen twofold in three years ... - ... *military spending*
- ... is likely to be gathertangness on that in this gavelly setness ... - ... *to be continuation on that in this fiscal institution*
- ... can see from this dig that the frumwork was only small - ... *that the original construction was*
- ... said that they would afleme the haftlings in the coming weeks - ... *would expel the prisoners ...*
- ... that it is thewly to see this kind of yemelessness in law as a kind of shildiness, though this is still not always clearcut - ... *is customary to see .. of negligence ... as a kind of criminality, ...*
- ... beshowing the need for thedesomeness of all thedes to lessen sea besnitness - ... *demonstrating ... for agreement of all nations to lessen marine degradation/ pollution*
- ... would only be a whilewendly setup - ... *a temporary ...*
- ... a good beseen of an untodealed meanship - ... *example of an undivided community*

Bookly bits and so forth:

- Frame a fremeful frayn on the frimdy frume of firdship - *Frame a useful question on the curious origin of military service*
- Yearnfully watching the wlitty ones come back ... - *...the pretty ones ...*
- ... though looking smolt, was in truth swith evesty of her smickerness - *... gentle , was ... very envious of her elegance*
- ... might beswape him to wend his mind - *... might persuade him to change his mind*
- ... that the oreworth thing to do would be to stand down ... - *... honourable thing ...*
- ... had estely forbowed answering that with 'yes' or 'no' - *... graciously turned down answering ...*
- ... an athelness in his bearing - *... a nobility in his posture*
- The Highreeve said there was indeed room for bettering this - *The Chief Officer stated there was certainly scope for improving this*
- ... said they'd go, on the orereadness that they could eathly come back - *... on the condition ... could easily come back*
- TV Programme: Frayning Time - *Question Time*
- ... seyer over death ... - *victory over death*
- Soundly ground for arveth ... - *Favourable terrain to labour in ...*
- ... and the might and the wulder, for ever and ever - *... and the power and the glory, for ever and ever*
- ... making the mistake of not owning up to being unfulfremed himself in this - *... not owning up to being imperfect himself ...*
- ... when something frumthly kicked in, and he seemed to have a strength to fight ... - *... something primeval kicked in ...*
- ... how amidst all those stevens could someone new get yemed ... - *...all those voices ... get noticed ...*
- ... would couthly like to fand brooking that - *... certainly like to try using ...*
- ... she was longing to see him again, to feel his rining - *... to feel his touch*
- Talking to a deemer: 'Your oreworthness ...' *(... judge: ...' Your honour ...')*
- ... had, when young, been swith unthildy to wend and ednew that - *... very impatient to change and renew that*
- Saying: Don't overeat, Don't overdrink, Don't have overmuchness!

132

- Rather than being evestful, he thought he ought, with tholing, to work to do some good - ... *than being envious he ...with perseverance,* ...

Test iv) *What do you think these mean?*

1. Two-sided talks seeking to end the ongoing frithbreach
2. The heratower bid behideness of weapons
3. In a wayless weald
4. ... unthildy for onlightness ...
5. Long thaning members have eldership

What about? Learn some of the terms above and reel them off at dinners and parties. Should get folk talking!

Further Examples and Tests

Here are some last beseens/ examples of words in use, with more tests on what you've learned. If you've worked your way through the book this far, you should be able to get to grips with these quite happily. Answers to tests are on page 148/9.

Adverts and Signs:

- Card: In Deep Evensorrowing - *In Deep Sympathy*
- Sad and Angsome? In woemoodness? Friendly Help to be had ...
- Buy Cleanse: Fast and Truefast! - *Buy Cleanse: Fast and Reliable!*

Headlines:

- Awaydriveness of unhearsome staff leads to row - *Dismissal of disobedient staff causes dispute*

- Wike's wraying greeted by unlievefulness - *Officer's accusation greeted by disbelief*
- More meanships besheared of schools - *... communities deprived of schools*
- Call for end to unshedwise weapons - *... indiscriminate ...*
- Cutbacks 'cannot be rightwisely made' - *... justifiably made*
- Fewness of new teachers leads to 'angsomeness in classroom' - *Paucity of new teachers causes trouble in classroom'*
- Hatethinkle throng fordo fulltumless shieldness - *Hostile crowd destroy unsupported defence*
- One in four townly children in 'unsteadful' homes - *25% of urban children in 'unstable' homes*
- Unreadness lessened for three years in a row - *Illiteracy reduced for three consecutive years*

News Weekly

Unreadness lessened for three years in a row

Illiteracy reduced for three consecutive years

Test i). *Do you understand the following?*

1. Whole House speaks, without forgoedness
2. Boy falls into forlet mineshaft
3. Missing woman: outleadness fears
4. New housesteads unbecraved
5. Withsetness to tax havens grows

Snipetts from Articles, Textbooks and suchlike:

- Sunly fire bursts shoot some farness into space - *solar flares shoot some distance into space*
- From TV: '... and now the stowly news from where you live ...' - *local news*
- Overeattleness still woeful - *Gluttony ...*
- ... would like to bring a bettingness ... - ... *would like to move an amendment*
- Railway station loudspeaker: the fromward train at platform two is the 7.00 to Bangor – *the departing train ...*
- ... how the frumly building had looked had until now been a roun - ... *how the original building ... been a mystery*
- ... about why such smicker young singers' lives often go downhill ... - .. *such elegant/ beauteous young singers' lives ...*
- ... being unlikely that the Goldhoardhouse would find that fremely - ... *that the Treasury would find that profitable*
- ... had in all over 200 guth fighters in readiness - ... *200 combat fighters ...*
- ... saying that seyer in this hild wouldn't be a walkover - ... *that victory in this war ...*
- ... a wealy thede, and wanting that weal to go on - *a prosperous nation ... that prosperity to go on*
- ... had been a wending from the shendness that had overshadowed its early days - ... *a change from the confusion ...*
- ... that the fremefulness of these words would be shown by speaking and writing them - ... *the usefulness of these words*
- ... in law, between thavesome grownups ... - ... *between consenting adults*

Test ii) *What do the following mean?*

1. ... ween that everyone will do their needright
2. Houses betwixset with high hedges
3. Bewarping the way of rightwiseness
4. A folkly ongetness
5. Living with Fallsickness

Bookly bits:

- An unthroughshotingly deep thought - *An impenetrably profound concept*
- Faring to the Middle of the Earth - *Journey to the Centre of the Earth*
- ... would couthly do it if he showed more throughwoness - *... would certainly do it ... more perseverance*
- ... on a wulderful, sunny day here at ... *a glorious, sunny day ...*
- ... the fires having swept though much of that landstead - *... much of that region*
- ... the uneath which this frayning led to was unforeseen ... - *the trouble/ difficulty which this questioning led to ...*
- ... would at all times show oring for their feelings on this - *... honour, respect, reverence*
- ... showed a lack of armheartness which was highly oreless - *... lack of pity ... highly dishonourable*
- ... said he got no quemeness from showing such tharlwiseness - *... no pleasure ... such severity*
- ... said that unmetely harm had been done through this unthild - *... immeasurable harm through this impatience*
- ... sought to edquicken business and thereby edyield what wealth had been put into it - *... to revive business ... remunerate what wealth had been invested ...*
- ... whose shildy deeds had been tharly dealt with - *... criminal deeds ... severely dealt with*
- ... such unoreworthness would not queme anyone there - *... such irreverence would not please anyone there ...*
- ... had always overhowed him, being evestful of what he had, but taking a warped frover in the dwilds which made him seem rather arm to others ... - *had always despised him, being envious ... a warped comfort in the errors ... seem rather poor/ miserable ...*
- ... knew the arvethliness of going through the names one by one - *... knew the laboriousness ...*
- ... unloredness being no shieldness in the eyes of the law - *ignorance being no defence ...*
- ... that having lost, they were oreworthily dealt with by the altheodish wyemen - *... honourably dealt with by the foreign soldiers*

- ... better eady, than too needy, but not too greedy - *better prosperous/ fortunate/ happy, than ...*

Test iii) *What do you think these mean?*

1. Wanted: Worker for Sealy Eftnewing
2. Gas flow 'untruefast'
3. Will Scotland choose selfdom?
4. Growness which doesn't steal from our children
5. The old foes underbegan a plan to go togetherward, behave forbearingly, and forshape Europe.

Test iv) *What do you think these mean?*

1. ... had by now fullfremedly wended
2. ... would be a frayn for Witanmoot to deal with ...
3. ... had showed such tothundness, that without any greming had laid into him with heavy blows
4. ... would have to thildily wait until the feeling of afremding had healed
5. ... with a barely hidden atter said 'you are orefastly asked to stay out of this'

Deeper and further into *How We'd Talk* …
These last beseens brook some words from the Part 2 lists which you haven't come across so far!

Headlines:

Howful meanship samedfast in thwearness - *Anxious community joined in unity*
'Metefast thwearness' hailed as breakthrough - *'Moderate agreement'* …

Set Names:

Overall Coreness - General Election
Eddish Warden - *Park Warden*

From Articles, Books and Suchlike:

- … was a feeling of onemoodness that this could lead to an eftkenedness of sayness - … *feeling of unanimity* … *lead to a regeneration of expression*
- Game unhaply for children under 3 - *unsuitable for* …
… that the brooking of this evenlatching could be frayned … - … *the function of this imitation could be questioned* …
- … an eftthinging which was thungenly talked through - … *a reconciliation which was excellently* …
- … a play which looks at theowdom and the wemness that went with it in a new way - … *.at slavery and the corruption that went* …
- Loft charing - *Loft conversion*

Bookly Bits:

- … stood to yearve all of this at werehood - … *to inherit* … *at adulthood*
- … an atiwedness made stronger by the wend in outabstandness - … *a revelation* … *by the change in surroundings*

- ... saw it as an oughting to work for the meanship, befastening some of that thungness he had learned over many years - ... *saw it as a duty ... for the community ... using some of that competence he had ...*
- ... was widecouth that they'd unwrastly quoted her on that - ... *was common knowledge ... inaccurately quoted ...*
- ... todrivedness to many steads meant that they could find new siths - *dispersal to many places ... find new companions*

Test v) *Last test! What do you think these mean?*
1. Werely suchness
2. The American Forthspell of Selfdom
3. Drunk and unthewful
4. The Kingly Loftly Ferd
5. ... and woning the earth in many meanships, that werekin would brook it in metefastness

Answers to Tests

(Note: **Step 1:** These should all be understandable!)

Step 2 Answers

i) Answers to examples at start of Step 2:
You speak well - what **wordcraft!** = *what eloquence!*
I'm **wordful** in two tongues = *fluent* ...
He was ***wifeless***, she was ***manless*** = *without wife/ without man (husband)*
And together they found **matchness!** = *... found compatibility*
One is **ongetful**, one **ongetless** = *perceptive and unperceptive*
- but both need **steerness!** = *need control/ guidance*
He's into **idlebliss!** = *into vain joy*
He should **forlet** it for worthwhile bliss = *abandon it ...*
I'd be **forethankful** for any help = *grateful in advance ...*

ii). 1. Free Forelook at New Film - *Free Preview of New Film*
2. Feel Free to Look around; No Boundness to Buy! - *No Obligation to Buy*
3. Waterly and sealy gear - *Aquatic and marine equipment*
4. Unnamed Overdrinkers - *Alcoholics Anonymous*
5. Beholdness Room - *Observation Room*

iii). 1. Rise in overseaish holidaymakers - *Increase in foreign tourists*

News Weekly

Rise in overseaish holidaymakers

Increase in foreign tourists

2. Early election 'mightly' - *Early election 'possible'*
3. Hothearness for cosmetic surgery lessens - *Enthusiasm/ rage for ...*
4. Deemer asks: was killing erebethought? - *Judge asks: was killing premeditated?*
5. Hungerbitten flee drought - *Famished ...*

iv). 1. Steerness for house buying - *Guidance for house buying*
2. Sunly fire bursts - *Solar flares*
3. Selfenoughsomeness - *Self-sufficiency*
4. England: Unoverwon after the late 1000s - *Unconquered since the closing part of the 11th Century*
5. ... where green meadows were formerly enoughful - *... were previously abundant*

Step 3 Answers

i) Answers to examples at start of Step 3:
Tell me a **shiply** yarn = *maritime (adventure)*
Ah - how I **overfared** the seas!... = *traversed/ traveled*
Oh - I **underget** what's going on = *perceive*

Don't let wealth **forlead** you! = *seduce*
It wasn't **outly mightly,** my friend! = *remotely possible*
Sorry, I felt an **underdriveness** to say that = *a compulsion*
You're **moodful** and **steadless**! = *very moody and unstable*
We'll do a **selfwilling seekness** into the **eviladdle** = *a voluntary inquiry into the unfavourable situation*

ii). 1. Businessman did not bename bringness - ... *did not declare donation*
2. Rise in alcohol forhaveness - *Increase in abstinence from alcohol*
3. Many yearnful to forshape lifestyles - ... *to transform lifestyles*
4. Laughtersmith's wittiness wellbeshowed - *Comedian's wittiness well demonstrated*
5. Lessness of ourlandish goods show unrightcrafting - *Minority of home-manufactured goods of poor quality*

iii). 1. Doctor's Forewriteness - *Prescription*
2. The kingly afterfollowingness - *The royal succession*
3. ... the furtheringness of a wordhoard from early English ... - ... *the promotion of a vocabulary from early English*
4. Last boat to x forthfares - ... *departs*
5. Can be workly run - *can be practically applied*

iv). 1. ... too speakful and longsome ... - *too talkative and tedious*
2. ... put it to them that they had gone out with evilwillingness that night - ... *that they had gone out with malice that night* ...
3. 'Oneness in Mislikeness ...' - *'Unity in Diversity ...'*
4. Looking for Healness ... - *Searching for Salvation*
5. Seating set by eldership ... - *Seating arranged according to seniority*

Step 4 Answers

i) Answers to examples at start of this Step:
I **aqueath** this new **setness** building open! = *declare this new institution* ...
From **toletness** to **eftnewing** - wonderful! = ... *decline to restoration*

Now, is there a **guestly** bed and breakfast nearby? = *accommodating to guests*

- there's good **comelitheness** at one two doors down = *hospitality*
I **ween** that'll be alright then = ... *expect that'll* ...
Are you under the **fortruing** that I love you?! = *presumption that* ...
WIELD YOURSELF! = *CONTROL YOURSELF!*
You're not so bad ... but not **unharmyearn** either!!' = ... *not inoffensive*

Folkly Hapliness
Public Convenience

ii). 1. The Women's Setness - *The Women's Institution (WI)*
2. Folkly Hapliness - *Public Convenience*
3. Forthfroming Room - *Departure Room*
4. Holdfast Webstead - *Secure Website*
5. Body: Forehaveness Fellowship - *Temperance Society*

iii). 1. Out of work forecasts found to be untruefast - *Unemployment predictions prove to be Unreliable*
2. Many Scots said to forechoose selfdom - *Many Scots said to prefer independence*
3. Thief forflees being caught - *Thief evades capture*
4. Fans showed 'lack of holdsomeness' - *Fans showed 'lack of restraint'*
5. One fourth of stowly folk deem selves unhavers - *One quarter of local people judge selves as deprived/ poor*

iv). 1. Needness is the mother of afoundness - *Necessity is the mother of invention*
2. Seafares of Afoundness - *Voyages of Discovery*
3. ... an ongetful learner - ... *a perceptive pupil*
4. Through onfoundness, one can grow wiser - *Through experience, one can grow wiser*
5. ... not to beshed against folk on grounds of hue ... - *not to discriminate against people on grounds of colour*

Step 5 Answers

Answers to examples at start:
i) My mum and dad did have a **wastum** stall = *fruit stall*
Don't **wray** me of **wending** that! = *Don't accuse me of changing that!*
You **thewless** thing! = *ill-mannered*
Watch it, or you'll be nicked – for **frithbreach**! = *breach of the peace*
You've got a **wlitty anleth**! = *a pretty face*
It's good now that we've come to **thedesomeness** = *agreement*
It'll be a **freme** for us both = *a benefit*
- Yes, a worthwhile **howing**! = *endeavour*

ii). 1. Title: Forsitting Wike – *Presiding Officer*
2. Awayleadness Thaning – *Removal Service*
3. The Shieldness Ambightness – *Ministry of Defence*
4. Rightwiseness Thane – *Justice Minister*
5. Arvethshooter – *Troubleshooter*

Wanted: Arvethshooter

iii). 1. Thane: mightliness of earthquake was 'unbethought' – *Minister: possibility of earthquake 'not considered'*
2. Our Sasha seyerfast with new world best - ... *victorious with new world record*
3. Aleased yisle speaks of underdriveness to heavy beatings – *Released hostage speaks of subjection to severe beatings*
4. Selfdom forspeakers meet thane – *Independence advocates meet minister*
5. Ferd bebidand 'too forthyearnful' – *Army commander 'too impetuous'*

> **Daily News**
>
> Thane: mighliness of earthquake was 'unbethought'
>
> Minister: possibility of earthquake 'not considered'

Can you spot the mistake in the headline above?! (See answer to iii) 1)

iv). 1. Two-sided talks seeking to end ongoing frithbreach – *Bilateral talks searching for an end to ongoing breach of the peace*
2. The heratower bid behideness of weapons – *The commander ordered the concealment of weapons*
3. In a wayless weald – *In a forest without paths, tracks or roads*
4. ... unthildy for onlightness ... – *impatient for illumination*
5. Long thaning members have eldership – *Long-serving members have seniority*

Answers from Further Examples and Tests:

i). 1. Whole House speaks, without forgoedness - ... *without abstention*
2. Boy falls into forlet mineshaft - ... *into abandoned mineshaft*
3. Missing woman: outleadness fears - ...*abduction fears*
4. New housesteads unbecraved - *New house sites undesired*
5. Withsetness to tax havens grows - *Opposition to tax havens increases*

> **Daily News**
>
> ## Withsetness to Tax Havens Grows
>
> Opposition to Tax Havens Increases

ii). 1. ... ween that everyone will do their needright - ... *expect that everyone will do their duty*
2. Houses betwixset with high hedges - ... *interposed with high hedges*
3. Bewarping the way of rightwiseness - *Perverting the course of justice*
4. A folkly ongetness - *A common perception*
5. Living with Fallsickness - *Living with Epilepsy*

iii). 1. Wanted: Worker for Sealy Eftnewing - *Wanted: Employee for Maritime Restoration*
2. Gas flow 'untruefast' - *Gas supply 'unreliable'*
3. Will Scotland choose selfdom? - *Will Scotland choose independence?*
4. Growness which doesn't steal from our children - *Development ... (= a definition of sustainable development)*
5. The old foes underbegan a plan to go togetherward, behave forbearingly, and forshape Europe. - *The old enemies designed a plan to work towards unity, behave tolerably, and transform Europe.*

iv). 1. ... had by now fullfremedly wended - ... *by now completely changed*

2. ... would be a frayn for Witanmoot to deal with ... - ... *a question for Parliament*
3. ... had showed such tothundness, that without any greming had laid into him with heavy blows - ... *showed such arrogance ... without any provocation ...*
4. ... would have to thildily wait until the feeling of afremding had healed - ... *patiently wait ... feeling of alienation ...*
5. ... with a barely hidden atter said 'you are orefastly asked to stay out of this' - ... *barely hidden venom said '... are respectfully asked to ...'*

News Weekly

Scotland Chooses Selfdom

Scotland Chooses Independence

v). 1. Werely suchness - *Human nature*
2. The American Forthspell of Selfdom - ... *Declaration of Independence*
3. Drunk and unthewful - *Drunk and disorderly*
4. The Kingly Loftly Ferd - *Royal Air Force*
5. ... and woning the earth in many meanships, that werekin would brook it in metefastness - ... *and inhabiting the earth in many communities, that the human race would use it in moderation*

PART 2: REFERENCE WORD LISTS

Finding a hidden wordhoard ...

List I
Words from Steps 1 - 5, with Old English Sources

This list brings together all updated words introduced in Steps 1 to 5 of the book (and more), alphabetically.

Notes
i) On List I Layout:
   a) Firstly come words in **bold**. These are the updated forms.
   b) Next comes the grammatical definition (see Summary Key below).
   c) Then, in normal letters, comes meaning of words in today's standard English. Sometimes, there is no obvious foreign-derived loanword to express a word, and in such cases, a note on which current word(s) it is related to is given, as: - from (Eng.) *with word added after.*
   This shows that this current word *is itself one with Old English origins* (see example in Key below).
   d) Lastly, the Old English source words from which the updated words have come are given in *italics* (these are known from original texts, and can be referred to in Clark Hall).
   e) On Old English letters: ð and þ are 'th' sounds, and æ is a short 'a'.

ii) It is common for words to change their meanings over time - for example, 'meat' at one time covered a greater range of food than it does today. **Meanings of updated words can thus be different from the original meaning of their Old English source words. It is a question of what seems to make sense to the modern ear. This also applies for whether an updated word would act as an adjective, adverb, or both.**

iii) Words listed here are based on only a part of a broader Old English wordhoard.

Key: Updated word from early English in **bold** (followed by grammatical definition), then meaning in current English, and lastly the Old English words (upon which words in bold are based) in *italics*.

a. = *adjective (describes a noun: 'big' in big house)*
adv. = *adverb (shows way in which something is done: fast, happily)*
n. = *noun (normally things and ideas: car, bird, freedom)*
neg. = *negative (such as in words starting with 'un')*
v. = *verb (doing words like to run, to write, to sing)*
v.t. = *verb, transitive*

(Some words can be both adverbs and adjectives. Listings seek to define what use sounds most natural to today's ear, but should not always be considered hard and fast.)

Summary of Listing layout: Loanword (or phrase with key element which is a loanword) given in *italics*, followed by suggested English alternatives in normal lettering.

- from (Eng.) - used to show native English words in cases where word lacks an obvious alternative to describe it. Take the listing below:

    awely *adv.* - from (Eng.) awe *egelic*

This shows that **awely** is an *adverb* from the native English word 'awe'. Lastly, the Old English form of the word (egelic) is given in *italics*.

A

abede *v.* order, proclaim, summon, command, direct, announce, declare, offer *abeodan*
acknowness *n.* acknowledgement *oncnawennes*
acover *v.* recover *acofrian*
addlebearing *a.* disease/ trouble bearing *adlberende*
addly *a.* spoiled, diseased *adlig*
adreadingly *adv.* terribly *ondrædendlic*
afear *v.* terrify, make afraid *afæran*
afleme *v.* expel, disperse *aflieman*

afley *v.* expel *afliegan*
afond *v.* test, prove, experience *afandian*
afonding *n.* test, experience *afandung*
afoundness *n.* invention, device, discovery *afundennes*
afremd *v.* alienate, become alienated *afremdan*
afremding *n.* alienation *afremðung*
afrever *v.* comfort, console *afrefran*
afterfollow *v.* succeed *æfterfolgian*
afterfollowedness *n.* sequel *æfterfygednes*
afterfollower *n.* successor *æfterfylgere*
afterfollowingness *n.* succession *æfterfygendnes*
aftergoingness *n.* posterity *æftergengnes*
afterwardness *n.* posterity *æfterweardnes*
againcome *v.* return *agencuman*
againwardly *adv.* adversely *ongeanweardlic*
aleasand/ aleaser *n.* deliverer, redeemer, liberator *aliesend*
alease *v.* release, redeem, save *aliesan*
aleasedness *n.* redemption, remission, release *aliesednes*
aleasingly *adv.* redeemingly *aliesendlic*
aliken *v.* compare *anlician*
allmight *n.* omnipotence *eallmiht*
ally *a.* universal *eallic*
almightiness *n.* omnipotence *ælmihtignes*
almsful *a.* charitable *ælmesfull*
almsly *a.* charitable *ælmeslic*
althede *n.* foreign nation *elðeod*
althedily *adv.* in manner of foreigners *elðeodiglic*
althediness *n.* foreignness *elðeodignes*
althedish *a.* foreign *elðeodisc*
althedy *a.* of foreign nation *elðeodig*
amanse *v.* curse *amansumian*
amansing *n.* curse *amansumung*
ambight *n.* office, service, command *ambiht*
ambight *v.* serve, minister *ambihtan*
ambighter *n.* officer, attendant, servant *ambihtere*
ambighthouse *n.* office *ambihthus*

ambightness *n.* service, commission *ambihtnes*
anew *v.* renew *edniwian*
anewed renewed *edniwe*
anewing *n.* renewal, renovation *edniwung*
angbreast *n.* asthma *angbreost*
anget *n.* intellect *andgiet*
angetful *a.* intelligent *andgietful*
angmood *n.* distressed/ frustrated mood *angmod*
angmoodness *n.* distress, frustration *angmodnes*
angness *n.* anxiety, trouble *angnes*
angset *n.* eruption *angset*
angsome *a.* troublesome, distressing *angsom*
angsomely *a.* troublesomely, distressingly *angsomlic*
angsomeness *n.* distress, trouble, pain *angsumnes*
anleth *n.* face *andwlita*
anneal *v.* ignite, inflame, incite, consume *onælan*
aqueath *v.* declare, express *acweðan*
arearness *n.* elevation *arærnes*
aredde *v.* rescue, save, deliver *ahreddan*
aredding *n.* salvation, deliverance *ahredding*
arine *v.* touch, handle *ahrinan*
arist *n.* resurrection *ærist*
arm *a.* poor, destitute, miserable *earm*
armheartness *n.* pity *earmheortnes*
armly *a., adv.* poorly, miserably, pitiable *earmlic*
arveth *n.* labour, trouble, difficulty *earfoðe*
arvethliness *n.* laboriousness *earfoðlicnes*
arvethly *a.* troublesome, laborious *earfoðlic*
arvethness *n.* difficulty, trouble, pain *earfoðnes*
ascruten *v.* investigate, examine *ascrutnian*
asundering *n.* division *asyndrung*
atel *a.* terrible, repulsive *atol*
atelly *adv.* terribly, repulsively *atolic*
atewedness *n.* manifestation *oðiewodnes*
atgo *v.* approach *ætgangan*
athel *a.* noble, aristocratic *æðele*

athel *v.* to make noble *æðelian*
athelborn noble born *æðelboren*
athelkind *n.* nobility *æðelcund*
athelness *n.* nobility (class of) *æðelnes*
athester *v.* to be eclipsed *aðeostrian*
athrick *v.* press, oppress *aðryccan*
atiwedness *n.* revelation *ætywednes*
atrine *n.* touch *ætrine*
atrine *v.* touch *ætrinan*
atsake *v.* deny, renounce *ætsacan*
atstandand/ atstander *n.* attendant *ætstandand*
atter *n.* poison, venom *ator*
atterbearing *a.* poisonous *atorberende*
atterly *adv.* poisonously, venomously *atorlic*
attery *a.* poisonous, venomous *ætrig*
atwend *v.* divert, deprive of *oðwendan*
awaydriveness *n.* dismissal, expulsion *onwegadrifennes*
awayen *v.* repudiate *awægan*
awayleadness *n.* removal *onwegalædnes*
aweless *a.* - from (Eng.) awe *egeleas*
awelessness *n.* - from (Eng.) awe *egeleasnes*
awely *a.* - from (Eng.) awe *egelic*
awem *v.* disfigure, corrupt *awemman*
awemingness *n.* disfigurement *awemendnes*
awend, wend *v.* change, translate *awendan*
awhene *v.* vex, grieve, afflict *ahwænan*
awherve *v.* convert, turn, avert *ahweorfan*

B

backboard *n.* port-side, larboard *bæcbord*
beadle *n.* warrant officer, herald, preacher *bydel*
bearingness *n.* fertility, fecundity *berendnes*
bebid *v.* instruct, command *bebeodan*

bebid *n.* command, order *bebod*
bebidand *n.* commander *bebeodend*
bebidingly *adv.* imperatively *bebeodendlic*
bechide *v.* to complain *becidan*
beckonand/ beckoner *n.* indicator, discloser, index *bicnend*
beckoningly *adv.* enticingly *bicnendlic*
beclip *v.* embrace, encompass *beclyppan*
beclose *v.* confine, imprison *beclysan*
bede *v.* pray *bedian*
bedehouse *n.* chapel *bedhus*
bedidder *v.* deceive *bedydrian*
befare *v.* traverse, surround *befaran, beferan*
befasten *v.* establish, put safe, utilise *befæstan*
befold *v.* envelop *befealdan*
befrine *v.* question *befrinan*
befrining *n.* inquiry *befrinung*
begang *n.* course, circuit *begang*
begeng *n.* observance, practice, exercise *bigeng*
begenger *n.* practitioner *bigenga*
bego *v.* traverse, perform *began*
begengness *n.* application *begengnes*
behavedness *n.* behaviour, restraint, temperance *behæfednes*
beheadly *a.* capital punishment *beheafodlic*
behideness *n.* concealment *behydnes*
beholdness *n.* observation *behealdnes*
behovely *a.* necessary *behoflic*
belaugh *v.* deride *behlyhhan*
belean *v.* dissuade, prevent *blean*
benim *v.* deprive *beniman*
beniming *n.* deprival *beniming*
bepeach *v.* deceive *bepæcan*
bepeachand/ bepeacher *n.* deceiver *bepæcend*
bepeaching *n.* deception *bepæcung*
bereaver *n.* despoiler *bereafere*
beride *v.* ride round *beridan*
berow *v.* row round *berowan*

beruesing *n.* repentance *behreowsing*
besee *v.* provide for, have regard for *beseon*
beseen *n.* example, model, pattern *bisen*
beseen *v.* to set an example, instruct by example, express figuratively *bisenian*
beseening *n.* example, pattern *bisenung*
beshear *v.* deprive *bescier*
beshearedness *n.* deprivation *bescierednes*
beshed *n.* distinction *bescead* (compare *watershed* in geography)
beshed *v.* discriminate *besceadan*
beshow *v.* exhibit, demonstrate, display *besceawian*
beshower *n.* exhibitor, demonstrator, guide *besceawere*
beshowing *n.* demonstration, exhibition *besceawung*
beshowingly *a.* demonstratively *besceawiendlic*
besit *v.* occupy, posses *besittan*
besmear *v.* disgrace, reproach, defile *bismerian*
besmear *n.* disgrace, reproach, defilement *bismer*
besmearless *a.* unrepproached *bismerleas*
besmearly *a.* disgraceful, reproachful, defiling *bismerlic*
besmearness *n.* contemptibility *bismernes*
besnit *v.* pollute, dishonour *besnitan*
besnitness *n.* degradation, pollution *besnitenes*
besorrow *v.i.* to have compassion *besorgian*
besorrowing *n.* compassion *besargung*
beswape *v.* persuade *beswapan*
beswike *n.* treachery, deceit *beswic*
beswike *v.* deceive *beswican*
beswikeness *n.* deception *beswicenes*
beswiker *n.* deceiver *beswica*
beswiking *n.* deception *beswicung*
bethink *v.* consider *bepencan*
betingness *n.* amendment *betendnes*
betness *n.* reparation, atonement *betnes*
betoken *v.* designate *betacnian*
betrap *v.* entrap *betrappan*
bettering *n.* improvement *beterung*

betweenforletness *n.* intermission *betwinforletnes*
betwixalayedness *n.* interjection *betwuxalegednes*
betwixgoing separating *betwuxgangende*
betwixset interposed *betwuxgesett*
beward *v.* protect, guard *beweardian*
bewarp *v.* pervert *beweorpan*
beway *v.* frustrate *bewægan*
beweapon *v.* disarm *bewæpnian*
beweep *v.* lament *bewepan*
beweepingly *adv.* lamentably *bewependlic*
bewend *v.* turn, convert *bewendan*
bewind *v.* entwine, envelop, encircle *bewindan*
bework *v.* construct, adorn, insert *bewyrcan*
bilewhit *a.* innocent, simple, sincere *bilewit*
bilewhitness *n.* innocence, simplicity *bilewitnes*
birther *n.* embryo/ foetus *beorðor*
bismearful *a.* ignominious *bismerful*
bitmeal *adv.* piecemeal *bitmælum*
bladderwark *n.* pain in the bladder *blædderwærc*
blissy *a.* - from (Eng.) bliss *blissig*
blitheness *n.* joy, pleasure *bliðnes*
blossomy *a.* - from (Eng.) blossom *blostmig*
blowness *n.* inflation *ablawnes*
bonebreach *n.* bone fracture *banbryce*
bonebreak *n.* bone fracture *bangebrec*
bookhoard *n.* book collection *bochord*
bookhouse *n.* library *bochus*
booklore *n.* - from (Eng.) book + lore *boclar*
bookly *a.* literary *boclic*
boroughshire *n.* city/ town administrative area *burhscir*
boroughman *n.* town citizen *burhman*
boroughreeve *n.* provost, mayor *burhgerefa*
borrowsorrow *n.* loaning/ security trouble *borg sorg*
borrowbreach *n.* failure to repay loan/ surety *borgbryce*
boundness *n.* obligation *bundennes*
bowerthane *n.* chamberlain, page *burðegn*

brainsick *a.* - from (Eng.) brain + sick *brægenseoc*
breastwark *n.* pain in chest *breostwærc*
breastwhelm *n.* emotion, grief *breostwylm*
breme *a.* famous, noble *breme*
bridely *a.* bridal *brydlic*
bringness *n.* donation, support *brengnes*
broadness *n.* extent, surface, liberality *bradnes*
brook *v.* use, enjoy *brucan*
brooking *n.* function, occupation *brucung*
brookingly *adv.* functionally, serviceably *brucendlice*
brotherslaying *n.* fratricide *broðerslege*

C

candletree *n.* candelabrum *candeltreow*
carefulness *n.* - from (Eng.) careful + ness *carefulnes*
chapman *n.* trader *ceapman*
chapstow *n.* market *ceapstow*
chare *n.* occasion *cierr*
charing *n.* conversion *cierring*
chisness *n.* fastidiousness *cisnes*
Christianness *n.* - from (Eng.) Christian *cristennes*
churchly *a.* ecclesiastical *circlice*
churchthane *n.* minister of the church *ciricðen*
churchthaning *n.* church duty/ service *ciricðenung*
cleansingdrink *n.* purgative *clænsungdrenc*
cliffy *a.* - from (Eng.) cliff *clifig*
comelithe *a.* hospitable *cumliðe*
comelitheness *n.* hospitality *cumliðnes*
comer *n.* visitor *cuma*
coreness *n.* election *corennes*
cornhouse *n.* granary *cornhus*
cornseed *n.* grain of corn *cornsæd*
costen *v.* try, test, prove *acostnian*

costiand *n.* tempter *costigend*
costness *n.* proving, trial, temptation *costnes*
costning *n.* testing, temptation, trial *costnung*
couth *a.* manifest, certain, familiar *cuð*
couthly *adv.* manifestly, certainly, familiarly, evidently *cuðlic*
couthness *n.* acquaintance, familiarity *cuðnes*
cove *a.* active, strenuous, vigorous *caf*
covely *adv.* vigorously, actively, strenuously *caflic*
coveness *n.* energy, vigour *cafnes*
craftless *a.* - from (Eng.) craft *cræftleas*
craftly *a.* - from (Eng.) craft *cræftlic*
crippleness *n.* severe disability *crypelnes*
crundle *n.* ravine, quarry *crundel*
custy *a.* charitable, generous, virtuous *cystig*
custiness *n.* charitability, generosity, virtue *cystignes*

D

daresty *a.* venturesome, presumptuous *dyrsig*
davenliness *n.* opportunity *dafenlicnes*
dealtly *a.* - from (Eng.) dealt *dæledlice*
dearworth *a.* precious *deorwierðe*
dearworthly *adv.* preciously *deorwierðlic*
dearworthness *n.* preciousness *deorwierðnes*
deathbearly *adv.* lethally *deaðbærlic*
deathbearness *n.* lethalness *deaðbærnes*
deathliness *n.* - from (Eng.) deathly *deaðlicnes*
deathstead *n.* place of death *deaðstede*
deedbote *n.* atonement, penitence *dædbot*
deedboteness *n.* atonement, penitence *dædbotnes*
deedly *a.* active *dædlic*
deemer/ deemster a judge (Manx law has deemsters) *dema*
deepness *n.* profundity, mystery *deopnes*
dight *n.* arrangement *diht*

dight *v.* arrange, appoint *diht*
dighter *n.* arranger *dihtere*
dightner *n.* manager *dihtnere*
dightning *n.* ordering, disposition *dihtnung*
dizzydom *n.* - from (Eng.) dizzy *dysigdom*
doly *a.* possible, doable *donlic*
downstying descending *dunestigende*
drenchness *n.* immersion *dryncnes*
dretch *v.* trouble, torment *dreccan*
dretchedness *n.* tribulation, affliction *drecednes*
dwild *n.* error *dwild*
dwildafterfollowing *n.* erroneous movement *dwildæfterfolgung*
dwolma *n.* chaos *dwolma*

E

eady *a.* prosperous, fortunate, happy *eadig*
eadily *adv.* fortunately, prosperously *eadilic*
eadiness *n.* prosperity, fortune *eadignes*
eady *v.* to make fortunate *eadigan*
earlish *a.* - from (Eng.) earl *eorlisc*
earthbeganger *n.* inhabitant *eardbegenga*
earthbegoingness *n.* habitation *eardbegengness*
earthkin *n.* human race *eorðcyn*
earthtiller *n.* horticulturalist, farmer *eorðtilia*
earthtilth *n.* horticulture, agriculture *eorðilð*
eastleod *n.* orientals *eastleod*
eastlong *adv.* extending east *eastlang*
eatgiver *n.* host at a meal *ætgiefa*
eath *a.* easy, agreeable *eaðe*
eathly *adv.* easily *eaðelic*
eathness *n.* ease, easiness, pleasure *ieðnes, eaðnes*
eatly *a.* edible, eatable *ætlic*
eatness *n.* edibility *ætnes*

eddish *n.*   park   *edisc*
edgift *n.*   restitution   *edgift*
edmede *n.*   gentleness, humility, submission   *eaðmedu*
ednew *v.*   restore, renew   *edniwian*
ednewand/ ednewer *n.*   restorer   *edniwigend*
edquicken *v.*   revive   *edcwician*
edstall *v.*   restore   *edstalian*
edstathling *n.*   reestablishment   *edstaðelung*
edwend *v.*   return   *edwendan*
edyield *v.*   remunerate   *edgyldan*
eftkenedness *n.*   regeneration   *eftacennednes*
eftleasing *n.*   redemption   *eftlising*
eftmind *v.*   remember   *eftgemyndgian*
eftmindy   remembering   *eftgemyndig*
eftnewing *n.*   restoration   *eftniwung*
eftthinging *n.*   reconciliation   *eftðingung*
elddom *n.*   age   *ealddom*
elderborough *n.*   metropolis   *ealdorburg*
elderdom *n.*   authority, dominion, seniority, pre-eminence   *ealdordom*
elderdomliness *n.*   pre-eminence, authoritativeness   *ealdordomlicnes*
elderdomly *a.*   authoritative, pre-eminently   *ealdordomlic*
elderliness *n.* - from (Eng.) elderly   *ealdorlicnes*
eldership *n.*   seniority   *ealdorscipe*
elderthane *n.*   chief attendant, retainer   *ealdorðegn*
eldfather *n.*   grandfather   *ealdfæder*
elding *n.*   ageing (process)   *ealdung*
eldmother *n.*   grandmother   *ealdmodor*
eldright *n.*   ancient right, tradition   *ealdgeriht*
eldsay *n.*   tradition   *ealdgesegen*
eme *n.*   uncle   *eam*
endbirth *n.*   order   *endebyrd*
endbirthly *a.*   in order, in succession, orderly manner   *endebyrdlic*
endbirthness *n.*   order, series, succession, arrangement, degree   *endebyrdnes*
endlessness *n.*   infinity, eternity   *endeleasnes*
endmostness *n.*   extremity   *endemestnes*
endspeak *n.*   epilogue   *endespræc*

engoughful *a.* abundant *genyhtful*
enoughly *adv.* abundantly *genyhtlice*
enoughsome *a.* abundant, abounding, satisfactory *genyhtsum*
enoughsomeness *n.* sufficiency, abundance *genyhtsumnis*
erding *n.* abode *eardung*
erdingly *a.* habitable *eardiendlic*
erdstead *n.* habitation *eardstede*
erebethought *a.* premeditated *ærbeðoht*
ereworld *n.* ancient world *ærworuld*
ermth *n.* poverty, misery, distress *iermð*
errandspeech *n.* message *ærendspræc*
este *n.* favour, grace, bounty, pleasure *est*
este *v.* to live luxuriously *estian*
estely *adv.* graciously *estelic*
estful *a.* gracious *estful*
estfulness *n.* gracefulness *estfulnes*
estiness *n.* graciousness *estignes*
esty *a.* gracious *estig*
ethel *n.* country *eðel*
ethem *n.* vapour, steam *æðm*
evenborn *a.* of equal birth *efenboren*
evenfain *v.* sympathise *efengefeon*
evenlatch *v.* imitate *efenlæcan*
evenlatcher *n.* imitator *efenlæcere*
evenlatching *n.* imitation *efenlæcung*
evenliness *n.* equality *efenlicnes*
evenling *n.* equal person *efnling*
evenlotter *n.* equal sharer, partaker *efenhlytta*
evenmoodly *a.* with equanimity *efenmodlice*
evennight *n.* equinox *efenniht*
evennightly *a.* equinoxual *efenneahtlic*
evenold *a.* contemporary *efeneald*
evensorrow *v.i.* commiserate *efensargian*
evensorrowing *n.* compassion, sympathy *efensargung*
evensorry *a.* compassionate *efensarig*
everly *a.* perpetually, in perpetuity *æfrelic*

evest *n.* envy, rivalry *æfest*
evest *v.* to envy *æfestian*
evestful *a.* envious *æfestful*
evesty *a.* envious *æfestig*
eviladdle *n.* disastrous situation *yfeladl*
evilful *a.* - from (Eng.) evil *yfelful*
evilness n. - from (Eng.) evil + ness *yfelnes*
evilwilling *a.* malevolent *yfelwillende*
evilwillingness *n.* malice *yfelwillendnes*
evily *a.* - from (Eng.) evil *yfelic*
evilyearness *n.* malice *yfelgiornnes*
eyeseen *a.* visible *eagsyne*

F

fakedeed *n.* - from (Eng.) fake + deed *facendæd*
fakeful *a.* deceitful *facenful*
fakeless *a.* without deceit, guileless *facenleas*
fakely *adv.* - from (Eng.) fake *facenlic*
fakeness *n.* deceitfulness *facennes*
fallenly *a.* unstable, perishable, transient *feallenlic*
fallness *n.* ruin, offence *fylnes*
fallsick *a.* epileptic *fylleseoc*
fallsickness *n.* epilepsy *fylleseocnes*
fand *v.* attempt, test, try, examine, experience *fandian*
fander *n.* tester, trier *fandere*
fanding *n.* investigation, trail, test, proof *fandung*
fareship *n.* community, retinue, society, companionship *ferscip*
fareing *n.* journey *færing*
faring *n.* removal *feorrung*
farlen *a.* remote *fyrlen*
farly *a.* - from (Eng.) far *feorlic*
farness *n.* distance *feornes*
farsibb *a.* distantly related *feorsibb*

fasthavleness *n.* retentiveness, stinginess, economy, tenacity *fæsthafolnes*
fasthavle *a.* retentive, tenacious *fæsthafol*
fay *n.* a joining, joint, composition, diagram *feg*
fay *v.* join, connect, unite, fix, compose *fegian*
faying *n.* composition, connection, conjunction *feging*
fayness *n.* association, companionship, conjunction *fegnes*
feedness *n.* nourishment *fednes*
feelessness *n.* - from (Eng.) feel + less *feohleasnes*
feeyearn *a.* covetous, greedy *feohgeorn*
feeyetser *n.* miser *feohgitsere*
feeyetsing *n.* avarice *feohgitsung*
fele *adv.* very *fela*
felefold *a.* frequent *felafeald*
felefoldness *n.* multitude *felafealdnes*
felespeakle *a.* talkative *felaspecol*
felewordness *n.* talkative *felawyrdnes*
fenny *a.* - from (Eng.) fen *fennig*
ferd *n.* army *fierd*
ferding *n.* expedition, campaign, soldiering *fyrding*
fere *n.* associate, comrade *fera*
fered *a.* associated *fered*
fering *n.* vehicle *fering*
ferly *a.* associated *ferlic*
ferness *n.* transition, passage, passing away *fernes*
ferren from remote place/ time *feorran*
fewness *n.* paucity *feawnes*
fieldly *a.* - from (Eng.) field *feldlic*
fiendship *n.* - from (Eng.) fiend *feondscipe*
filledness *n.* fulfilment, completion *fylednes*
findle *n.* invention, device *fyndele*
fingerlith *n.* finger joint *fingerlið*
fingerly *a.* digital *fingerlic*
fird *v.* to go on expedition *fyrdian*
firdfare *n.* military service *fyrdfor*
firdly *a.* military, martial *fyrdlic*
firdship *n.* the military *fyrdscip*

firdwise *adv.* militarily *fyrdwise*
fireburn *n.* conflagration *fyrbryne*
firefood *n.* fuel *fyrfoda*
firehot *a.* ardent *fyrhat*
fitherdealt *a.* quartered *fiðerdæled*
fleetly *a.* nautical, naval *flotlic*
fleshbesmittenness *n.* carnal attraction *flæscbesmitennes*
fleshliness *n.* carnality *flæsclicnes*
fleshmonger *n.* butcher *flæscmangre*
fleshness *n.* incarnation *flæscnes*
floodly *a.* - from (Eng.) flood *flodlic*
floodward *n.* flood barrier protection *flodweard*
folkcouth *a.* publicly known *folccuð*
folkfree *a.* uninhabited *folcfrig*
folkish *a.* common, popular, of the people *folcisc*
folkland *n.* common land, public land *folcland*
folkly *a.* public, popular, common *folclic*
folkmoot *n.* public meeting *folcmot*
folkneed *n.* common need, basic need *folcned*
folkreeve *n.* public officer *folcgerefa*
folkright *n.* human/ common right, generally accepted, people's right *folcriht*
folkship *n.* population, nation, people *folcscipe*
folkstowe *n.* public place *folcstowe*
footly *a.* pedestrian *fotlic*
forbearingly *adv.* tolerably *forberendlice*
forbode *n.* prohibition *forbod*
forbow *v.* decline *forbugan*
forbreak break in pieces *forbrecan*
forburn to be consumed by fire *forbærnan*
forburnedness *n.* consumption by fire *forbærnednes*
forcome *v.* prevent, surpass, surprise *forcuman*
fordeem *v.* prejudge, prejudice, prematurely judge *fordeman*
fordeemedly *adv.* in prejudicial way *fordemedlic*
fordeemedness *n.* prejudice *fordemednes*
fordim *v.* obscure *fordimmian*

fordo *v.* ruin, destroy *fordon*
fordwilm *v.* confound *fordwilman*
fordwine *n.* vanish, disappear *fordwinan*
forebody *n.* thorax, chest *foranbodig*
forebusy *v.* preoccupy *forebisegian*
forechoose *v.* prefer in preferance *foreceosan*
forecome *v.* block, prevent move/ action, prevent *forecuman*
foredeem *v.* prejudge *foredeman*
foregang *v.* precede *foregangan*
foreganger *n.* predecessor *foregenga*
foregearing *n.* preparation *foregearwung*
forego *v.* precede *foregan*
forelook *v.* preview *forelocan*
foresaidness *n.* prediction *foresegdnes*
foresay *v.* predict *foresecgan*
foreseek *v.* - from (Eng.) fore + seek *foresecan*
foreset *v.* propose, place before *foresettan*
foresetness *n.* proposition, purpose *foresetnes*
foreshieldness *n.* protection *forescieldnes*
foreshow *v.* give a preview *foresceawian*
foreshower *n.* one showing previews *foresceawere*
foreshowing *n.* preview (showing of) *foresceawung*
foresingand/ foresinger *n.* precentor *foresingend*
foresit *v.* preside *foresittan*
forespeech *n.* preamble *forespræc*
forestand *v.* excel, prevail *forestandan*
forestep *v.* anticipate, prevent, precede *foresteppan*
foresteppand/ forestepper *n.* precursor *forestæppend*
forestepping *n.* anticipation, precedence *forestæppung*
forethankful *a.* grateful in advance *foreðancful*
forethink *v.* premeditate, consider *foreðencan*
forethinkle *a.* prudent *foreðancol*
forethinkleness *n.* prudence *foreðancolnes*
foretoken *n.* - from (Eng.) fore + token *foretacn*
forewrit *n.* prologue *forewrit*
forewriteness *n.* prescription *forewriteness*

forfare *v.* obstruct, intercept *forfaran*
forflee *v.* evade *forfleon*
forgetelness *n.* oblivion *forgitelnes*
forgivenly *a.* - from (Eng.) forgiven *forgifenlic*
forgoedness *n.* abstention, deprivation *forgægednes*
forharry *v.* ravage *forhergian*
forharrying *n.* devastation, raid *forheriung*
forhavand/ forhaver *n.* one who is abstinent *forhabbend*
forhave *v.* restrain *forhabban*
forhavedness *n.* temperance, self restraint, abstinence *forhæfednes*
forhaveness *n.* abstinence *forhæfnes*
forhavingly *adv.* with temperance *forhæfendlice*
forhow *v.* neglect, disregard, despise *forhogian*
forhowand/ forhower *n.* neglecter, despiser *forhogiend*
forhowedly *adv.* contemptuously *forhogodlic*
forhowedness *n.* contempt *forhogodnes*
forhowing *n.* contempt *forhogung*
forhowingly *adv.* contemptably *forhogiendlic*
forlayness *n.* fornication *forlegnes*
forlead *v.* seduce *forlædan*
forlearning *n.* wrong/ incorrect education *forleornung*
forlet *v.* abandon, relinquish *forlætan*
forletness *n.* abandonment, relinquishment *forlætennes*
forletting *n.* intermission *forlæting*
forlie *v.* commit adultery or fornication *forlicgan*
forlieand *n.* adulterer, fornicator *forlicgend*
forlier *n.* adulterer, fornicator *forliger*
forlornness *n.* - from (Eng.) forlorn *forlorenes*
forlose *v.* abandon *forleosan*
formelt *v.* dissolve *formeltan*
forolding *n.* old age *foraldung*
forride *v.* intercept with vehicle/ horse a.s.f. *forridan*
forsakeness *n.* rejection, denial, abandonment *forsacennes*
forsaking *n.* denial *forsacung*
forshape *v.* transform *forscieppan*
forspan *v.* seduce *forspanan*

forspanning *n.* allurement, seduction *forspaning*
forspeak *v.* denounce *forspecan*
forspeaker *n.* sponsor, advocate *forspeca*
forspend *v.* squander *forspendan*
forspill *v.* destroy *forspildan*
forspilledness *n.* destruction *forspildnes*
forstand *v.* prevent, resist, oppose, obstruct, block *forstandan*
forswornness *n.* perjury *forsworennes*
forthbear *v.* produce *forðberan*
forthbuilding *n.* encouragement *forðbylding*
forthfare *v.* depart *forðfaran*
forthfatheren *a.* paternal *forðfaderen*
forthfroming *n.* departure *forðfroming*
forthgang *v.* progress, advance *forðgang*
forthing *n.* advancement *forðung*
forthink *v.* despair, despise, mistrust *forðencan*
forthlet *v.* emit *forðlætan*
forthly *a.* advanced *forðlic*
forthought despaired of *forðoht*
forthsay *v.* proclaim, announce *forðsecgan*
forthseen *a.* conspicuous *forðgesyne*
forthsetness *n.* proposition, proposal, motion *forðsetennes*
forthshaft *n.* future *forðgesceaft*
forthship *n.* progress *forðscype*
forthspell *n.* declaration *forðspell*
forthstep *v.* advance *forðstæppan*
forthstepping *n.* advance *forðstæpping*
forthward *a.* advanced, progressive *forðward*
forthwardness *n.* progress *forðwardnes*
forthyearn *v.* to be impetuous *forðgeorn*
fortrueing *n.* presumption *fortruwung*
forwedded pledged *forweddod*
forworth *v.* deteriorate *forweorðan*
forworthness *n.* devaluation, deterioration *forweorðenes*
foryield *v.* recompense, requite *forgieldan*
fourfoldly *adv.* quadruply *feowerfealdlice*

frayn *n.* question *fregen*
frayne *v.* inquire *frignan*
frayness *n.* interrogation, questioning *frignes*
frayning *n.* question *frignung*
frayning *v.* questioning *frægning, fregenung*
freckenful *a.* dangerous *frecenful*
freeand *n.* liberator *freogend*
fremd *v.* estrange *fremdian*
fremd *a.* foreign, alien, strange *fremde*
freme *v.* avail, benefit *fremian*
fremeful *a.* useful, profitable, beneficial constructive, positive *fremful*
fremefulness *n.* profitability, usefulness *fremfulnes*
fremely *a.* profitable *fremlic*
fremefully *adv.* constructively, positively, usefully, profitably, beneficially *fremfulic*
friendhold *a.* amiable *freondheald*
friendholdly *adv.* amiably *freondhealdlic*
friendlore *n.* - from (Eng.) friend + lore *freondlar*
frimdy *a.* inquisitive, curious *frymdig*
frith *n.* peace *frið*
frithbreach *n.* breach of the peace *friðbræc*
frithsome *a.* pacific, peaceable *friðsum*
frithstowe refuge, sanctuary *friðstow*
frithwrit *n.* peace agreement, treaty *friðgewrit*
fromfare *n.* departure *framfær*
fromship *n.* exercise, action, progress *framscipe*
fromward *adv.* departing, about to depart *framweard*
frostly *a.* - from (Eng.) frost *forstlic*
frover *n.* consolation *frefer, frofor*
frover *v.* cheer, console *frefran*
froverness *n.* consolation *frofornes*
frovrand *n.* consoler, comforter *frefrend*
frovring *n.* consolation *frefrung*
frume *n.* origin, cause *fruma*
frumer *n.* originator, inventor *fruma*
frumly *a.* original, primitive *frumlic*

frumshaft *n.* primeval condition, original creation *frumsceaft*
frumshapand/ frumshaper *n.* creator *frumscepend*
frumth *n.* origin, foundation *frymð*
frumthly *a.* primeval, primitive *frymðlic*
frumwork *n.* original construction *frumgeweorc*
fullfasten *v.* ratify/ apply fully *fulfæstnian*
fullfreme *v.* complete, perfect *fullfremman*
fullfremed completed *fulfremed*
fullfremedly *adv.* completely *fullfremedlice*
fullfremedness *n.* completion *fulfremednes*
fullgo *v.t.* accomplish, complete, fully perform *fullgan*
fullholden *a.* totally responsible *fulhealden*
fullought *v.* baptise *fulwihtan*
fullought *n.* baptism *fulwiht*
fulloughtbath *n.* font *fulwihtbæð*
fulloughter *n.* baptiser, baptist *fulwihtere*
fullsomeness *n.* abundance *fullsumnes*
fulltum *v.* support *fultuman*
fulltum *n.* support *fultum*
fulltumer *n.* supporter *fultuma*
fulltumless *a.* without support *fultumleas*
fullwork *v.* complete *fulhwyrcan*
furtherand/ furtherer *n.* promoter *fyrðriend*
furtheringness *n.* promotion *fyrðringnes*

G

gainwrit *n.* rewriting *geangewrit*
galder *n.* enchantment *galdor*
galdercraft *n.* magic *galdorcræft*
galdersong *n.* incantation *galdorsong*
gatheredness *n.* abscess *gaderednes*
gatheringly *adv.* collectively *gadrigendlic*
gathertang *a.* continuous, united *gadertang*

gathertangness *n.* continuation *gadertangnes*
gavel *n.* interest (on loan a.s.f.) *gafol*
gavelly *a.* fiscal *gafollic*
gearing *n.* preparation *gearwung*
gearingness *n.* preparation *gearwungnes*
givle *a.* generous *gifol*
givleness *n.* generosity, liberality *gifolnes*
glading *n.* - from (Eng.) glad *gladung*
goldhoard *n.* treasure *goldhord*
goldhoardhouse *n.* treasury *goldhordhus*
goldladen *a.* adorned with gold *goldhladen*
goodless *a.* evil *godleas*
goodly *a.* excellent *godlic*
gospelly *a.* evangelical *godspellic*
greenhuen *a.* green coloured (a.s.f.) *grenhæwen*
greme *v.* enrage, provoke, irritate *gremian*
greming *n.* provocation *gremung*
grimful *a.* - from (Eng.) grim *grimful*
grimness *n.* - from (Eng.) grim *grimnes*
gripness *n.* seizure *gripennes*
grith *n.* truce, asylum, protection *grið*
grithbreach *n.* breach of truce/ asylum *griðbryce*
grorning *n.* complaint *grornung*
groundlessly *a.* - from (Eng.) groundless *grundleaslic*
groundstone *n.* foundation stone *grundstan*
groundwall *n.* foundation *grundweall*
groundwall *v.* lay/ build foundations *grundweallian*
growness *n.* development, prosperity *grownes*
guestly *a.* hospitable *giestlic*
guesty *a.* - from (Eng.) guest *giestig*
guth *n.* combat, battle, war *guð*

173

H

haftling *n.* prisoner, captive *hæftling*
hallow *n.* saint *halga*
hallowand *n.* sanctifier *halgigend*
hallowing *n.* consecration *halgung*
hallthane *n.* hall officer *healðegn*
handtame *a.* - from (Eng.) hand + tame *handtam*
handthane *n.* retainer *handðegn*
handweald *n.* personal power *handgeweald*
handwhile *n.* instant *handhwil*
hap *a.* convenient *hæp*
hapliness *n.* convenience *hæplicnes*
hardliness *n.* austerity *heardlicnes*
hardmoodness *n.* - from (Eng.) hard + mood *heardmodnes*
harmheartness *n.* - from (Eng.) harm + heart *harmheartness*
harmspeech *n.* calumny *hearmspræc*
harvestly *a.* - from (Eng.) harvest *hærfestlic*
hately *a.* hostile, horrible *hetelic*
hatethinkle *a.* with hostile intentions *heteðoncol*
hattle *a.* hostile, odious *hatol*
hattleness *n.* hostility *hetolnes*
havedness *n.* continence *hæbbednes*
haveless *a.* destitute *hafenleas*
headbold *a.* confident, impudent *heafodbald*
headguilt *n.* capital offence *heafodgilt*
headly *a.* principal, capital *heafodlic*
headstead *n.* chief place *heafodstede*
headward *n.* chief protector *heafodweard*
healand *n.* saviour *hælend*
healness *n.* recovery, salvation *hælnes*
hean *v.* afflict, injure *hienan*
heanhood *n.* difficulty *heanhad*
heanly *a.* abject, poor *heanlic*
hearingly *adv.* audibly *hierendlic*

hearness *n.* report, obedience *hiernes*
hearsome *a.* obedient, attentive *hiersum*
hearsome *v.* obey *hiersumian*
hearsomely *adv.* obediently *hiersumlic*
hearsomeness *n.* obedience, attentiveness *hiersumnes*
hearthfast *a.* having a stable, settled home *heorðfæst*
heartsoreness *n.* grief *heortsarnes*
heartwark *n.* pain in heart *heortwærc*
heathendom *n.* - from (Eng.) heathen *hæðendom*
heathenness *n.* - from (Eng.) heathen *hæðennes*
heavymood *n.* - from (Eng.) heavy + mood *hefigmod*
hedge *v.* consider, ponder, meditate, determine *hycgan*
hedgely *adv.* considerately, meditatively, determinedly *hycglic*
heldly *a.* safe, secure *hieldelic*
heleth *n.* hero *hæleð*
helm *n.* protection, defence, covering *helm*
helmward *n.* pilot *helmweard*
hera *n.* army *here*
herahuth *n.* plunder *herehuð*
heraly *a.* martial *herelic*
heraman *n.* soldier *heremann*
heratower *n.* commander, general *heretoga*
herdly *a.* pastoral *hierdlic*
herebefore *preposition* previously *herbeforan*
hereonamong *preposition* - from (Eng.) hereon + among *herongemong*
heriot *n.* military equipment *heregeatu*
hest *n.* command *hæs*
highberg *n.* mountain *heahbeorg*
highbliss *n.* exultation *heahbliss*
highelder *n.* ruler, prime minister *heahealdor*
highmoodness *n.* pride *heahmodnes*
highreeve *n.* chief officer *heahgerefa*
highshireman *n.* county council leader *heahscireman*
highthane *n.* chief officer, captain *heahðegen*
highthaning *n.* important function *heahðegnung*
highting *n.* climax, exultation *hihting*

175

highwork *n.* excellent work *heahgeweorc*
hild *n.* war, combat *hild*
hinderling *n.* conspirator, betrayer *hinderling*
hinderness *n.* restraint, hindrance *hindernes*
hipboneache *n.* sciatica *hypebanece*
hithe *n.* harbour, port *hyð*
hithely *a.* - from (Eng.) hithe = harbour/ port *hyðlic*
hithercome *v.* - from (Eng.) hither + come *hidercyme*
hitherward *adv.* - from (Eng.) hither *hiderweard*
hoardward *n.* guardian of treasure *hordweard*
hoker *n.* insult, derision *hocor*
holdand *n.* protector, guardian, ruler *healdend*
holdfast *a.* safe, secure *healdfæst*
holdness *n.* observance *healdnes*
holdship *n.* loyalty, allegiance *holdscipe*
holdsome *a.* economical, frugal *healdsum*
holdsomeness *n.* economy, restraint, custody, preservation, observance, devotion *healdsumnes*
homefast *a.* resident, established (in a home) *hamfast*
honeysweet *a.* mellifluous *hunigswete*
hothearten *v.* become zealous, become enraged/ angry *hatheortan*
hotheartness *n.* zeal, rage, mania *hatheortnes*
houndly *a.* canine *hundlic*
housebreach *n.* burglary *husbryce*
housebreachle *a.* burglarious *husbrycel*
housefast *a.* occupying/ established in a house *husfæst*
housestead *n.* site of a house *husstede*
houth *n.* plunder *huð*
hove *n.* court *hof*
hovely *a.* courtly a. *hoflic*
howe *a.* prudent *hoga*
howe *v.* be prudent *hogian*
howful *a.* anxious *hohful*
howfullness *n.* anxiousness *hohfulnes*
howing *n.* endeavour *hogung*
howly *adv.* prudently *hohlice*

howship *n.* prudence *hogascipe*
hueing *n.* colouration *hiwung*
hueless *a.* - from (Eng.) hue + less *hiwleas*
hueness *n.* colouration *hiwnes*
hungerbitten *a.* famished, starving *hungerbiten*
hure *a., adv.* certainly, especially *huru*

I

ickly *a.* glacial *gicelig*
idlebliss *n.* vain joy *idelbliss*
idlelust *n.* vain desire *idellust*
idleyearn *v.* to be indolent *idelgeorn*
inaddle *n.* internal disease *inadl*
inbewind *v.* enwrap, enfold *inbewind*
inblow *v.* inspire - see also onblowness and note p. 84   *inblawan*
indrench *v.* saturate *indrencan*
infare *v.* enter, incursion *infaran*
infare *n.* admission *infær*
infind *v.* discover *infindan*
infleshness *n.* incarnation *inflæscnes*
ingang *v.* enter *ingangan*
ingang *n.* entrance, access *ingang*
ingo *v.* enter *ingan*
ingoer/ ingenger *n.* entrant, visitor *ingenga*
inheaten *v.* inflame *inhætan*
inheed *n.* sense, conscience *ingehygd*
inheedness *n.* consciousness *ingehygdnes*
inherd *n.* family *inhired*
inlander *n.* native *inlenda*
inlandish *a.* native, indigenous *inlendisc*
inlandishness *n.* - from (Eng.) inlandish *inlendiscnes*
inlath *v.* invite *inlaðan*
inlead *v.* introduce *inlædan*

inlightand *n.* illuminator *inlihtend*
inlighten *v.* illuminate, enlighten *inlihtan*
inlightness *n.* illumination, enlightenment *inlihtnes*
inly *a.* internal, interior *inlic*
inning *n.* contents *innung*
inset *v.* institute *insettan*
insetness *n.* institution, regulation *insetnes*
insetted inserted *ingeseted*
inshower *n.* demonstrator *insceawere*
inshowing *n.* demonstration, inspection *insceawung*
instand *v.* to be present *instandan*
instandingly *adv.* in way of being present *instandendlic*
inthink *n.* intention *in(ge)ðanc*
inthought *n.* intention *ingeðoht*
inwark *n.* internal pain *inwærk*
inwise in terms of what is popular/ 'in' *inwise*
inwitness *n.* consciousness, conscience *ingewitnes*
inwriter *n.* secretary *inwritere*
inwriting *n.* inscription *inawritting*

K

kinly *a.* pertaining to family *cynlic*
kithe *v.* proclaim, relate, perform, announce, confirm *cyðan*
kithedness *n.* testimony *cyðednes*
kitheness *n.* testament, testimony *cyðnes*
kither *n.* testifier *cyðere*
kithing *n.* statement, narration *cyðung*
kneebowing *n.* genuflection *cneowbigung*

L

landfirding *n.* military operations on land *landfyrding*
landfolk *n.* natives *landfolc*
landhera *n.* land force/ army *landhere*
landmark *n.* boundary, border *landmearc*
landship *n.* region *landscipe*
landstead *n.* region *landstede*
latemost *a.* - from (Eng.) late + most *lætemest*
latesome *a.* - from (Eng.) late *lætsum*
lathing *n.* invitation *laðung*
laughle *a.* inclined to laugh *hlagol*
laughterful *a.* - from (Eng.) laughter *hleohterful*
laughtersmith *n.* comedian *hleahtersmið*
lave *n.* remnant, legacy *laf*
lawbreach *n.* - from (Eng.) law + breach *lahbryce*
lawly *a.* legal *lahlic*
lawright *n.* legal right *lahriht*
learningchild *n.* pupil (child) *leorningcild*
learninghouse *n.* educational establishment, university, college, school *leorninghus*
leavedly *a.* permissible *liefedlic*
lessly *a.* - from (Eng.) less *leaslic*
lessness *n.* minority *leasnes*
letness *n.* remission, parole *alætnes*
lifeward *n.* lifeguard *lifweard*
lightmoodness *n.* frivolity *leohtmodnes*
likebusning *n.* imitation *licbisnung*
likeworth *a.* pleasing, likeable *licwyrðe*
likeworthily *a.* - from (Eng.) like + worth *licwyrþlice*
likeworthiness *n.* - from (Eng.) likeworth *licwyrþnes*
likeworthly *adv.* pleasingly, likeably *licwyrðlic*
likeworthness *n.* likeability *licwyrðnes*
likeworthy *a.* acceptable, nice, likeable *licwerþe*
likingly *a.* - from (Eng.) liking *liciendlic*

lith *n.* joint *lið*
litheby *a.* flexible *leoðubige*
lithebyness *n.* flexibility *leoðubignes*
littleheedy *a.* - from (Eng.) little + heed *lytelhydig*
littleness *n.* - from (Eng.) little *lytelnes*
littling *n.* diminution *lytlung*
liveraddle *n.* liver complaint *liferadl*
liversickness *n.* disease of liver *liferseocnes*
liverwark *n.* pain in liver *liferwærc*
loathingness *n.* hostility *laðwendnes*
loathless *a.* - from (Eng.) loath + less *laðleas*
loathly *a.* horrible *laðlic*
loften *a.* aerial *lyften*
loftly *a.* aerial *lyftlic*
longsome *a.* tedious, protracted *langsum*
longsomely *adv.* tediously, protractedly *langsumlic*
longsomeness *n.* tediousness, patience *langsumnes*
loreboding *n.* preaching (teaching) *larbodung*
lorecraft *n.* erudition *larcræft*
loredom *n.* - from (Eng.) lore *lardom*
lorely *a.* - from (Eng.) lore *larlic*
loresome *a.* - from (Eng.) lore *larsum*
lorethane *n.* instructor *larðegn*
lorewriter *n.* - from (Eng.) lore + writer *larwita*
lovesome *a.* - from (Eng.) love *lufsum*
lovesomely *a.* - from (Eng.) lovesome *lufsumlic*
lovesomeness *n.* - from (Eng.) lovesome *lufsumnes*
lustfulness *n.* - from (Eng.) lustful *lustfulnes*
lustyearnness *n.* concupiscence *lustgeornnes*
luter *a.* sincere *hlutor*
luterness *n.* sincerity *hlutornes*

M

maidenearth *n.* virgin soil *mædeneorðe*
maidhood *n.* virginity *mægðhad*
manifoldly *a.* - from (Eng.) manifold = multiply/ multiple *manigfealdlic*
manifoldness *n.* multiplicity, abundance, complexity *manigfealdnes*
manless *a.* - from (Eng.) man *manleas*
mannish *a.* male, masculine *mennisc*
mannishliness *n.* masculinity *mennisclicnes*
mannishly *adv.* masculinely *mennisclic*
mannishness *n.* masculinity *mannishness* (later English)
manship *n.* maleness, masculinity *manscipe*
manyhuely *a.* - from (Eng.) many + hue *monigheowlic*
marchland *n.* borderland *mearcland*
matchly *a.* conjugal *mæclic*
matchness *n.* compatibility *mæcnes*
matchship *n.* compatibility *mæcscip*
meanship *n.* community *mænscipe*
meatless *a.* - from (Eng.) meat + less *meteleas*
metefast *a.* moderate *metfæst*
metefastly *adv.* moderately *metfæstlic*
metefastness *n.* moderation *metfæstnes*
methe *n.* measure, degree, proportion, rate *mæð*
metheful *a.* humane *mæðful*
methely *adv.* humanely, moderately, proportionally *mæðly*
mething *n.* adjudication *mæðung*
middaily *a.* - from (Eng.) midday *middæglic*
middliand *n.* mediator *midligend*
midmost *a.* most central *midmest*
midness *n.* centrality, mediocrity *midnes*
mightful *a.* powerful *mihtful*
mightly *a.* possible *mihtelic*
milce *n.* mercy, compassion, benevolence *milts*
milce *v.* to have compassion, show mercy *miltsian*
mildheartness *n.* - from (Eng.) mild + heart *mildheortnes*

mindday *n.* anniversary *mynddæg*
mindily *a.* - from (Eng.) mind *myndiglic*
minding *n.* remembrance, memorandum *myndgung*
mindworth *a.* worth remembering/ minding/ mentioning *mynd(e)wyrðe*
mindy *a.* - from (Eng.) mind *myndig*
mindiliness *n.* remembrance *myndiglicnes*
minely *a.* in my manner *minlice*
misbirth *n.* miscarriage *misbyrd*
misborn *a.* degenerate *misboren*
misdo *v.* - from (Eng.) mis + do *misdon*
misfare *v.* 'mis'travel *misfaran*
mishold *v.* - from (Eng.) mis + hold *mishealdan*
misholdsomeness *n.* incompetence *mishealdsumnes*
misshrunk - from (Eng.) mis + shrunk *misscrence*
mislikeness *n.* variety, diversity, dissimilarity, difference *mislicnes*
mislive *v.* - from (Eng.) mis + live *mislybban*
missenliness *n.* variety, diversity *missenlicnes*
missenly *a.* various *missenlic*
missly *adv.* inaccurately, erratically *mislic*
misspeak *v.* - from (Eng.) mis + speak *misspecan*
misteach *v.* - from (Eng.) mis + teach *mistæcen*
misthink *v.* - from (Eng.) mis + think *misðyncan*
mistime *v.* - from (Eng.) mis + time *mistimian*
miswrite *v.* - from (Eng.) mis + write *miswritan*
misyeme *v.* neglect *misgyman*
monthsick *a.* menstruous *monaðseoc*
monthsickness *n.* menstruation *monaðseocnes*
moodful *a.* - from (Eng.) mood *modful*
moodless *a.* - from (Eng.) mood + less *modleas*
moodsick *a.* - from (Eng.) mood + sick *modseoc*
moodsickness *n.* - from (Eng.) moodsick *modseocnes*
moodthought *n.* - from (Eng.) mood + thought *modgeðoht*
moonly *a.* lunar *monlic*
moonsick *a.* lunatic *monseoc*
moothouse *n.* place of meeting, assembling *mothus*
mooting *n.* discussion, conversation *motung*

mootstow *n.* forum *motstow*
mostlyest most particularly, most especially *mæstlicost*
mothren *a.* maternal *medren*
mouthroof *n.* palate *muðhrof*
muchly *a.* - from (Eng.) much *micellic*
muchness *n.* size, abundance *micelnes*

N

narrowness *n.* - from (Eng.) narrow *nearones*
neb, nib *n.* beak, face *neb(b)*
needbehove *a.* necessary *niedbehefe*
needbehovedly *a.* necessarily *niedbehæfdlic*
needbehovedness *n.* necessity *niedbehæfednes*
needbehovely *a.* necessary *niedbehoflic*
needbehoveness *n.* requisite *niedbehæfnes*
needhood *n.* necessity *neadhad*
needly *a.* necessary *nydlic*
needness *n.* necessity *nydnes*
needright *n.* duty *nydriht*
needwise *adv.* in terms of need *neadwis*
needwiseness *n.* necessity *neadwisnes*
nethergo *v.* descend *niðergan*
nethering *n.* abasement, condemnation *niðerung*
netherly *a.* inferior *niðerlic*
netherness *n.* inferiority *niðernes*
netherward *adv.* - from (Eng.) nether *niðerweard*
newness *n.* novelty *niwnes*
newwhirved *a.* newly converted *nigehwyrfed*
nighleche *v.* approach *nealæcan*
nighleching *n.* approach, access *nealæcung*
nightwatch *n.* vigil *nihtwæcce*
nithfully *adv.* maliciously *niðfullice*
nithing *n.* villain *niðing*

nithy *a.* malicious *niðig*
noughtly *a.* of no avail, without result *nahtlic*
noughtness *n.* - from (Eng.) nought *nahtnes*

O

oathbreach *n.* perjury *aðbryce*
offcarve *n.* section, amputation *ofcyrf*
offdo *v.* eliminate *ofdon*
offlike to be displeasing, displease *oflician*
offsetness *n.* - from (Eng.) offset *ofsetnes*
offthink *v.* displease *ofðyncan*
oldly *a.* - from (Eng.) old *ealdlic*
oldness *n.*, **eldness** *n.* old age *ealdnes*
onbeload *v.* inflict upon *onbelædan*
onbeshowing *n.* inspection, examination *onbesceawung*
onblowness *n.* inspiration - see also inblow, and note p. 84 *onblawnes*
ondoing - from (Eng.) on + doing *ondoung*
onefold *a.* simple, single, unique, sincere *anfeald*
onefoldness *n.* simplicity *anfealdnes*
onemood *a.* unanimous *anmod*
onemoodness *n.* unanimity *anmodnes*
onewillness *n.* obstinacy *anwillnes*
onfind *v.* perceive, notice *onfindan*
onfindand/ onfinder *n.* discoverer *onfindend*
onfoundleness *n.* experience *onfundelnes*
onfoundness *n.* explanation, experiment, experience, trial *onfundennes*
onget, anget *v.* perceive, recognise, distinguish *ongietan*
ongetful *a.* perceptive *andgietful*
ongetfully *a.* perceptively *andgitfullice*
ongetless *a.* lacking perception *andgietless*
ongetness *n.* comprehension, perception, recognition *ongietennes*
onlepiness *n.* privacy, individuality, speciality *anlipnes*
onlepy *a.* private, individual, special *anli(e)pig*

onlightand/ onlighter *n.* enlightener *onlihtend*
onlighten *v./* **onlight** *v.* illuminate *on(a)lihtan*
onlighting *n.* illumination, enlightenment *onlihting*
onlightness *n.* illumination *onlihtnes*
onlikeness *n.* parable, allegory, form, pattern *ongelicnes*
onseen *n.* face *ansien*
onsend *v.* transmit *onsendan*
onset *v.* impose *onsettan*
onsetness *n.* constitution, establishment *onsetnes*
onshot *n.* attack (f.e. by shooting, also spoken) *onscyte*
onsow *v.* introduce into, implant *onsawan*
onstir *v.* move, disturb, agitate, excite *onstyrian*
onstiredness *n.* movement *onstyrednes*
onwield *n.* authority, command *onweald*
onwieldness *n.* power, authority *onwealdnes*
ord *n.* source *ord*
ordfrim *a.* original *ordfrymm*
ordfrume *n.* fount, source *ordfruma*
ore *n.* honour, respect, favour *ar*
orefast *a.* respected, honest, gracious *arfæst*
orefastly *adv.* respectfully, honestly, graciously *arfæstlic*
orefastness *n.* respect, honesty *arfæstnes*
oreless *a.* dishonourable *arleas*
orelessness *n.* dishonour *arleasnes*
orereadness *n.* condition *arædnes*
oreworthily *adv.* honourably *arweorðlic*
oreworthness *n.* honour *arweorðnes*
oreworth *a.* honourable *arweorð*
oreworthyful *a.* right honourable *arweorðful*
oring *n.* honour, respect, reverence *arung*
oughting *n.* duty, requirement *eahtung*
ourlandish *a.* of our country, native *urelandisc*
outabstandness *n.* surroundings *utanymbstandnes*
outfare *n.* outward passage *utfaru*
outgang *n.* departure, exit *utgang*
outgoing *n.* exit, exodus *utgong*

outkind *a.* extraneous, external, foreign *utacund*
outleadness *n.* abduction *utlædnes*
outly *a.* remotely *utlic*
outshove *v.* exclude *utscufan*
overalderman *n.* chief officer *oferaldormann*
overbecome *v.* supervene *oferbecuman*
overdrink *v.* - from (Eng.) over + drink *oferdrencan*
overdrinker *n.* alcoholic *oferdrencere*
overdrunkeness *n.* alcoholism *oferdruncennes*
overeattle *a.* gluttonous *oferetol*
overeattleness *n.* gluttony *oferetolnes*
overfare *v.* travel over *oferfaran*
overfare *v.* traverse *oferferan*
overfill *n.* excess, surfeit *oferfyll*
overfillness *n.* excess, surfeit *oferfylnes*
overflowness *n.* excess, superfluity *oferflownes*
overfoundness *n.* trial, experiment *oferfundnnes*
overgo *v.* traverse, transgress *ofergan*
overhow *v.* despise *oferhogian*
overhowand/ overhower *n.* despiser *oferhogiend*
overhowedness *n.* disdain *oferhogodnes*
overing *n.* delay, excess *uferung*
overlive *v.* survive *oferlibban*
overmarking *n.* superscription *ofermearcung*
overmuchness *n.* excess *ofermicelnes*
overseaish *a.* - from (Eng.) over + sea *ofersæwisc*
oversend *v.* transmit *ofersendan*
overset *v.* - from (Eng.) over + set *ofersettan*
overshow *v.* - from (Eng.) over + show *ofersceawian*
overshowand/ overshower *n.* - from (Eng.) one who overshows *ofersceawigend*
overspeak *v.* - from (Eng.) over + speak *ofersprecan*
overspeakle *a.* overtalkative *ofersprecol*
overspeakleness *n.* overtalkitiveness *ofersprecolnes*
overspeech *n.* - from (Eng.) over + speech *oferspræc*
overwork *n.* superstructure *ofergeweorc*

186

overwrit *n.* superscription *ofergewrite*
ovet *n.* fruit *ofet*
ownness *n.* property *agennes*
ownslayer suicide victim *agenslaga*

P

plightly *a.* dangerous, perilous *plihtlic*

Q

qualmbearingly *adv.* - from (Eng.) qualm + bearing *cwealmberendlic*
qualmbearness *n.* - from (Eng.) qualm + bear + ness *cwealmbærnes*
qualmful *a.* - from (Eng.) qualm *cwealmful*
qualmness *n.* - from (Eng.) qualm *cwealmnes*
queme *a.* pleasant, agreeable, acceptable *cweme*
queme *v.* please, satisfy, comply with *cweman*
quemeness *n.* pleasure, satisfaction, mitigation *cwemnes*
quemely *a., adv.* pleasing, satisfying, suitable, satisfactorily *cwemlic*
quide *v.* phrase, proverb, sentence *cwide*
qweming pleasing, satisfying *cweming*

R

readthoughter *n.* literary commentator *rædðeahtere*
readthoughting *n.* consideration of literature *rædðeahtende*
rearness *n.* disturbance, commotion *hrernes*
reeve *n.* high official, prefect *refa*
reeveship *n.* office, prefecture *refscipe*
rerde *v.* discourse *reordian*
rerde *n.* voice, language *reord*

rethy *a.* fierce, cruel, violent, severe   *reðig*
ricser *n.* ruler *ricsere*
ricsing *n.* domination *ricsung*
rightdoing *a.* just *rihtdonde*
rightfathrenkin *n.* direct paternal descent/ pedigree *rihfædrencynn*
righting *n.* correction, reproof *rihting*
rightlithely *a.* articulate *rihtliðlic*
rightness *n.* correction, rectitude *rihtnes*
rightset *a.* properly appointed/ established *rihtgeset*
rightsetedness *n.* proper ordinance/ appointment *rihtgesetednes*
rightsetness *n.* rightful establishment/ appointment/ office *rihtgesetnes*
rightwilling *a.* - from (Eng.) right + willing   *rihtwillende*
rightwise *n.* just, in a correct way *rihtwis*
rightwise *v.* justify *rihtwisian*
rightwisely *adv.* justifiably   *rihtwislic*
rightwiseness *n.* justice, righteousness   *rihtwisnes*
rightwising *n.* justification *rihtwisung*
rightwittly *a.* rational *rihtgewittelic*
rightworth *a.* proper *rihtwyrðe*
rine *v.* touch, reach *hrinan*
rineness *n.* contact, touch *hrinenes*
rining *n.* touch *hrining*
rooffast *a.* with a solid, firm roof *hroffæst*
roomgivle *a.* bountiful *rumgiful*
roomgivleness *n.* liberality, bountifulness   *rumgifulnes*
roomheartness *n.* liberality *rumheortnes*
roomly *a.* - from (Eng.) room   *rumlic*
roop *a.* liberal *rop*
roopness *n.* liberality *ropnes*
rootfast *a.* firmly established *rotfæst*
roughful *a.* - from (Eng.) rough + ful   *hreohful*
roun *n.* secret, secrecy, mystery *run*
rueing regretting *hreowende*
rueness *n.* regret *hreownes*
ruey *a.* regretful *hreowig*

S

samed *a.* unified, absorbed, merged *samod*
samedfast *a.* joined, merged, united, unified *samodfæst*
samedworking *a.* cooperating *samodwyrcende*
sameheart *a.* unanimous *samheort*
samening *n.* union, unification *samnung*
sayness *n.* expression *segnes*
scathedeed *n.* injurious deed/ crime *sceðdæd*
scatheful *n.* injurious *sceaðful*
scatheness *n.* injury *sceðnes*
scather *n.* injurious person, antagonist *sceaða*
scathiness *n.* injury, damage *sceaðignes*
scathing *n.* injury, damage *sceaðung*
scathingly *a.* - from (Eng.) scathing *sceððendlic*
scathy *a.* injurious *sceaðig*
scruten *v.* examine, scrutinise *scrutnian*
scrutner *n.* examiner *scrutnere*
scrutning *n.* investigation *scrutnung*
seaberg *n.* coastal cliff *sæbeorg*
seafare *n.* sea voyage *sæfor*
sealy *a.* marine, maritime *sælic*
seaupwarp *n.* marine deposits on shore *sæupwearp*
seaward *n.* coast guard *sæweard*
seedly *a.* seminal *sædlic*
seekness *n.* inquiry *secnes*
seenly *adv.* visibly, evidently *sienlic, sewenlic*
seldcouth *a.* unusual, rare, strange *seldcuð*
seldly *a.* rare, strange *seldlic*
seldseen *a.* rare, extraordinary *seldsiene*
selfdom *n.* independence *selfdom*
selflike *n.* egotism, vanity *selflice*
selfmurderer *n.* suicide victim *selfmyrðra*
selfmurdering *n.* suicide *selfmyrðrung*
selfwealdly *adv.* arbitrarily *selfwealdlice*

selfwilling *a.* voluntary *selfwillende*
selfwillingly *adv.* voluntarily, arbitrarily   *selfwillendlice*
setness *n.* institute *asetnes*
setness *n.* foundation, position, institution, construction, record   *setnes*
sey *n.* victory, triumph   *sig*
seyer *n.* victory   *sigor*
seyerfast *a.* victorious   *sigorfæst*
seyerfastness *n.* victory   *sigorfæstnes*
seyerly *a.* triumphal   *sigorlic*
seyfast *v.* triumph   *sigfæstan*
seyfast *a.* victorious   *sigefæst*
seyfastness *n.* victory, triumph   *sigefæstnes*
seyly *a.* victorious   *sigelic*
shamefast *a.* modest   *scamfæst*
shandful *a.* disgraceful, scandalous   *scandful*
shandliness *n.* disgrace, scandal   *scandlicnes*
shandly *adv.* disgracefully, scandalously   *scandlic*
shapeness *n.* formation, creation   *sceapennes*
shed *n.* distinction, separation, discretion   *scead*   (compare *watershed* in geography)
shedwise *a.* discriminate, discreet, rational   *sceadwis*
shedwisely *adv.* discriminately, discreetly, rationally   *sceadwislic*
shedwiseness *n.* discrimination, rationality, discretion   *sceadwisnes*
sheer *v.* mark off, cut off   *scirian*
sheeringly *a.* in way that mark/ cuts off   *sciriendlic*
shend *v.* confound, corrupt, discomfit   *scendan*
shending *n.* reproach, affliction   *scendung*
shendle *n.* reproach   *scendle*
shendness *n.* confusion   *scendnes*
shepand *n.* creator   *scieppend*
shielder *n.* protector, defender   *scieldere*
shielding *n.* protection, defence   *scildung*
shieldness *n.* protection, defence   *scildnes*
shildiness *n.* criminality   *scyldignes*
shildless *a.* innocent   *scyldleas*
shildy *a.* criminal   *scyldig*

shineness *n.* radiance *scinnes*
shipfight *n.* naval battle *scipgefeoht*
shiply *a.* nautical *sciplic*
shipsteerer *n.* pilot *scopsteora*
shipward *n.* ship master *scipweard*
shireman *n.* county council official *scirmann*
shoting *n.* missile *scotung*
shoulderwark *n.* pain in shoulder *sculdorwærc*
showingstowe *n.* place of demonstration *sceawungstow*
sib *n.* peace *sibb*
sibsome *a.* peaceable *sibsum*
sibsome *v.* reconcile *sibsumian*
sibsomeness *n.* concord, peace *sibsumnes*
sibsoming *n.* making peace *sibsumung*
sideaddle *n.* pleurisy *sidadl*
sidely *a.* discrete *sidlic*
sidewark *n.* pain in the side *sidwarc*
sightness *n.* vision *sihðnes*
sinny *a.* - from (Eng.) sin *synnig*
sister's son *n.* nephew *sweostorsunu*
sith *n.* companion, comrade *sið*
slackerness *n.* laziness *sleacornes*
slade *n.* valley, glade *slæd*
sleepbear *a.* soporific *slæpbære*
sleepfulness *n.* lethargy *slapfulnes*
sleeple *a.* lethargic, somnolent *slapol*
sleepleness *n.* lethargy, somnolence *slapolnes*
slithe *a.* cruel, savage, fierce *sliðe*
slithely *adv.* cruelly, savagely, fiercely *sliðelic*
slitness *n.* laceration *slitnes*
smalliness *n.* subtlety *smealicnes*
smalling *n.* reduction, atrophy *smalung*
smally *a.* - from (Eng.) small *smealic*
smatch *v.* taste *smæccan*
smearsalve *n.* unguent *smeorusealf*
smicker *a.* elegant, beauteous *smicer*

smickerness *n.* elegance *smicernes*
smiltness *n.* gentleness *smyltnes*
smitch, smeech *n.* vapour *smic*
smithcraft *n.* manual art *smiðcræft*
smithly *adv.* dexterously *smiðlice*
smolt *a.* gentle *smolt*
smoltly *adv.* gently *smoltlice*
snithe *v.* amputate *sniðan*
snithing *n.* amputation *sniðung*
soberness *n.* sobriety *syfernes*
songcraft *n.* - from (Eng.) song + craft *sangcræft*
sorrowless *a.* - from (Eng.) sorrow *sorgleas*
sorrowly *a.* miserable *sorglic*
sorrowword *n.* lamentation *sorgword*
sorrymood *n.* - from (Eng.) sorry + mood *sarigmod*
sorryness *n.* - from (Eng.) sorry *sarignes*
sot *a.* stupid *sott*
sotship *n.* stupidity *sotscipe*
soundful *a.* in good condition, prosperous *sundful*
soundfully *adv.* prosperously *sundfullic*
soundfulness *n.* prosperity *sundfulnes*
soundy *a.* favourable *sundig*
southright due south *suðrihte*
speakful *a.* talkative *spræcful*
speakle *a.* talkative *sprecul*
speakleness *n.* loquacity *sprecolnes*
speechhouse *n.* auditorium *spræchus*
speer *v.* investigate *spyrian*
speeriand/ speerer *n.* investigator, inquirer *spyrigend*
speering *n.* investigation *spyrung*
spewdrink *n.* liquid emetic *spiwdrenc*
staddle *n.* base, foundation, support, station, position, state, condition *staðol*
staith *n.* river bank *stæð*
standness *n.* status, existence *stondnis*
starkmood *n.* - from (Eng.) stark + mood *stearcmod*

stead *n.* place, position, location, station *stede*
steadless *a.* unstable *stedeleas*
steephigh *a.* acute *steapheah*
steerer *n.* pilot, director *steora*
steerless *a.* profligate, out of control *steorleas*
steerlessly *adv.* profligately *steorleaslic*
steerness *n.* guidance, discipline *stiernes*
steerspeech *n.* reproof *steorsprec*
steerworth *a.* reprehensible *steorweorð*
stenchbringing *a.* odiferous *stencbrengende*
stepmeal *adv.* by degrees, gradually *stæpmælum*
steven *n.* voice *stefn*
stirness *n.* movement, power of motion, disturbance, commotion, tumult *styrenes*
stoneberg *n.* rocky hill/ mountain *stanbeorg*
stonetimber *n.* masonry *stangetimbre*
stovebath *n.* sauna *stofbæð*
stowe, stow *n.* site, position, locality, station *stow*
stowly *a.* local *stowlic*
streamly *a.* riparian *streamlic*
strind *n.* generation, race, tribe *strynd*
stylt *v.* to be astonished *astyltan*
suchness *n.* nature, quality *swilcnes*
sunderborn *a.* born of disparate parents *sunderboren*
sundercraft *n.* special skill *sundorcræft*
sunderfreedom *n.* privilege *sunderfreodom*
sunderliness *n.* separation, seclusion separateness, singularity *synderlicnes*
sunderly *a.* separate, special, private, singular *synderlic*
sunly *a.* solar *sunlic*
swenche *v.* trouble *swencan*
swenk *n.* trouble *swenc*
swenkedness *n.* trouble *swencednes*
swey *n.* silence, quiet *swige*
swike *v.* deceive *swican*
swike *n.* treachery, deceit *swic*
swikedom *n.* deception *swicdom*

193

swikeful *a.* deceitful, fraudulent *swicful*
swiker *n.* deceiver *swica*
swiking *n.* deceit, fraud deception *swicung*
swith *adv.* very, exceedingly, severely *swiðe*
swither more excessive *swiðra*
swithliness *n.* intensity, severity, excess *swiðlicnes*
swithly *a.* intense, excessive, severe *swiðlic*
swithness *n.* intensity, severity, excess *swiðnes*
swithrueness *n.* remorse *swiðreownes*

T

teamful *a.* prolific *teamful*
teary *a.* - from (Eng.) tear *tearig*
thane *n.* servant, minister *ðegn*
thane *v.* serve, minister *ðegnian*
thanely *a.* ministerial *ðegnlic*
thaneship *n.* service, duty, ability, valour *ðegnscipe*
thaning *n.* service, ministry, administration *ðenung*
thankworthy *a.* acceptable, pleasing *poncwyrðe*
tharf *n.* necessity, distress *ðearf*
tharfedness *n.* poverty, destitution *ðearfednes*
tharfless *a.* without necessity/ distress/ trouble *ðearfleas*
tharfer *n.* pauper, poor/ destitute person *ðearfa*
tharfingly *adv.* miserably, destitutely *ðearfendlic*
tharfliness *n.* poverty, destitution *ðearflicnes*
tharfly *adv.* poorly, destitutely *ðearflic*
tharl *a.* vigorous, severe, strict *ðearl*
tharlwise *a.* strict, severe *ðearlwis*
tharlwisely *adv.* strictly, severely, sternly, roughly *ðearlwislic*
tharlwiseness *n.* severity, strictness *ðearlwisnes*
tharly *adv.* severely, cruelly, grievously *ðearlic*
thave *v.* permit, consent to *ðafian*
thavesome *a.* consenting *ðafsum*

thavesomeness *n.* consent *ðafumnes*
thede *v.* join, associate *ðeodan*
thede *n.* people, nation, province *ðeod*
thedely *a.* social, national, provincial *ðeodlic*
thedeness *n.* association, nationality, society *ðeodnes*
thedeship *n.* community, population, nation, administration, association *ðeodscipe*
thedesomeness *n.* agreement *ðeodsumnes*
thenceward *adv.* - from (Eng.) thence *ðanonweard*
theow *n.* slave *ðeow*
theow *v.* enslave *ðeowian*
theowdom *n.* slavery *ðeowdom*
thereright *adv.* instantly, immediately *ðærrihte*
thester *v.* obscure *ðeostrian*
thesterly *a.* obscure *ðeostorlic*
thew *n.* usage, custom, habit, conduct, disposition, manners *ðeaw*
thew *v.* to bring up morally/ virtuously *ðeawian*
thewfast *a.* moral, virtuous, honourable *ðeawfæst*
thewfastly *adv.* morally, virtuously *ðeawfæstlice*
thewfastness *n.* obedience, discipline *ðeawfæstnes*
thewful *a.* moral, virtuous *ðeawful*
thewless *a.* ill mannered, immoral, inconstant *ðeawleas*
thewly *a.* customary, moral *ðeawlic*
thickfold *a.* dense *ðicfeald*
thild *v.* to be patient *ðyldian*
thild *n.* patience *ðyld*
thildily *adv.* patiently *ðyldelic*
thildy *a.* patient *ðyldig*
third, fourth eldfather *n.* great, great great grandfather *ðridda, feowerða ealdfæder*
thole *v.* endure, suffer *ðolian*
tholing *n.* endurance, suffering, passion *ðolung*
thoughter *n.* adviser *ðeahtere*
thoughting *n.* consideration, advice, consultation *ðeahtung*
thoughtingly *adv.* deliberatively *ðeahtendlic*
threatness *n.* affliction, tribulation *ðreatnes*

threely *adv.* triply *ðrilic*
thresting *n.* affliction, torment *ðræstung*
threstness *n.* trouble, contrition *ðræstnes*
thrithely *a.* excellent *þryþlic*
throughdrench *v.* saturate *ðurhdrencan*
throughfasten *v.* transfix *ðurhfæstnian*
throughgo *v.* penetrate *ðurhgan*
throughholed *a.* pierced, holed *þurhholod*
throughlooking *n.* perusal, review, summary *ðurhlocung*
throughsee *v.* examine, study, scrutinise *ðurhseon*
throughseek *v.* inquire, research *ðurhsecan*
throughwatch *v.* to keep vigilant, alert, keep vigil *ðurhwæccan*
throughwoningness *n.* perseverance *ðurhwunungnes*
throughwoning *n.* perseverance, persistency, tenacity *ðurhwunung*
throughwoness *n.* perseverance *ðurhwunenes*
thrutch *v.* trample, oppress, afflict, repress *ðryccan*
thrutchness *n.* affliction, tribulation *ðrycnes*
thungen *a.* competent, excellent, distinguished *ðungen*
thungenly *adv.* competently, excellently *ðungenlice*
thungness *a.* competency, excellence *ðungennes*
thusly *a.* - from (Eng.) thus *ðæslice*
thwear *a.* united, harmonious, agreeable *ðwære*
thwearing *n.* agreement, consent *ðwærung*
thwearly *adv.* harmoniously, agreeably *ðwærlic*
thwearness *n.* unity, harmony, agreement *ðwærnes*
tideliness *n.* opportunity *tidlicnes*
tighting *n.* incitement, instigation, exhortation *tyhting*
tightness *n.* - from (Eng.) tight *tyhtnes*
timbering *n.* edification, structure *timbrung*
timberness *n.* edification *timbernes*
todrivedness *n.* dispersal *todræfednes*
togetherward towards unity *togæderweard*
toknowness *n.* discernment *tocnaw(en)nes*
toletness *n.* despondency, decline *tolætnes*
toseekening *n.* pursuit *tosocnung*
toseekness *n.* pursuit *tosocnes*

tosetedness *n.* disposition *tosetednes*
tothundenly *adv.* arrogantly *toðundenlic*
tothundness *n.* arrogance *toðundnes*
toungeful *a.* talkative *tungful*
toungeness *n.* eloquence, fluency *tyngnes*
towardly *a.* - from (Eng.) toward *toweardlic*
towardness *n.* - from (Eng.) toward *toweardnes*
towarpedness *n.* perversion *toworpednes*
towarpness *n.* perversion *towarpnes*
townly *a.* - from (Eng.) town *tunlic*
towriteness *n.* description *towritennes*
treestead *n.* arboretum *treowstede*
truefast *a.* reliable, trusty *treowfæst*
trueful *a.* reliable, trusty *treowful*
trueless *a.* false, deceitful, treacherous *treowleas*
truelessness *n.* falsehood, deceit, treachery *treowleasnes*
tudder *n.* descendant *tudor*
tweme *v.* separate in two *twæman*
tweming *n.* separation *twæming*
twilly *a.* double *twilic*
twoly *a.* doubtful, ambiguous, equivocal *tweolic*
twofoldly *adv.* doubly *twifealdlic*
twofoldness *n.* duplicity, duplication *twifealdnes*

U

unanewingly *adv.* unrenewingly *ungeniwiendlic*
unathelborn *a.* not of noble birth *unæðelboren*
unathelness *n.* ignobility, humiliation *unæðelnes*
unathelborn *a.* not of noble birth
unbearing *a.* neg. - from (Eng.) bearing *unberende*
unbearingly *a., adv..* unbearably *un(a)berendlic*
unbecraved *a.* not desired *unbecrafod*
unbefought *a.* unopposed, uncontested *unbefohten*

unbeshowed *a.* not displayed, not demonstrated *unbesceawod*
unbethought *a.* not considered, not expected *unbeðoht*
unbewedded *a.* unmarried *unbeweddod*
unbindingly *a.* neg. - from (Eng.) binding *unabindendlic*
unbliss *n.* affliction *unbliss*
unblithe *a.* neg. - from (Eng.) blithe *unbliðe*
unbold *a.* timid *unbeald*
unbowingly *adv.* inflexibly *unabygendlic*
unbreakingly *a.* inextricably *unabrecendlic*
uncleansed neg. - from (Eng.) cleansed *unclænsod*
uncomelithe *a.* inhospitable *uncumliðe*
uncouthly *a.* neg. - from (Eng.) uncouth *uncuðlic*
uncouthness *n.* neg. - from (Eng.) uncouth *uncuðnes*
uncraft *n.* neg. - from (Eng.) craft *uncræft*
uncrafty *a.* - from (Eng.) crafty *uncræftig*
undeadliness *n.* - from (Eng.) undeadly *undeadlicnes*
undeadly *a.* - from (Eng.) undead *undeadlic*
underbear support, endure *underberan*
underbegin *v.* purpose, design, intend *underbeginnan*
underborough *n.* suburb *underburg*
underdo *v.* - from (Eng.) under + do *underdon*
underdriveness *n.* subjection, compulsion *underdrifennes*
underget *v.* perceive, notice *undergietan*
underneathmost *adv.* - from (Eng.) underneath *underniðmest*
underreeve *n.* deputy governor *undergerefa*
underseek *v.* examine, investigate, scrutinise *undersecan*
underset *v.t.* - from (Eng.) under + set *undergesett*
understandness *n.* comprehension *understandennes*
underthede *v.* subject, subjugate, subdue *underðeodan*
underthedeness *n.* subjection, submission, obedience *underðeodnes*
underthink *v.* consider, meditate *underðencan*
undrunk *a.* sober *undruncen*
uneath *n.* difficulty, trouble *uneaðe*
uneathliness *n.* inconvenience, trouble *uneaðlicnes*
uneathly *adv.* troublesomely, with difficulty *uneaðlic*
uneathness *n.* difficulty, trouble *uneaðnes*

unended *a.* neg. - from (Eng.) ended   *ungeendod*
unestful *a.* ungracious   *unestful*
unfightingly *a.* neg. - from (Eng.) fighting   *unafehtendlic*
unfilledly *adv.* insatiably a.   *unafylledlic*
unforbowingly *adv.* unavoidably   *unforbugendlic*
unforcouth *a.* reputable, honourable   *unforcuð*
unforrotedly *adv.* incorruptedly   *unforrotedlic*
unforrotingly *adv.* incorruptibly   *unforrotiendlic*
unforthought *a.* not considered, not expected   *unforðoht*
unfremed *a.* not negotiated   *ungefremed*
unfremeful *a.* negative, unprofitable, not useful   *unfremful*
unfreming *n.* inconsideration   *ungefremmung*
unfulfremed imperfect   *unfulfremed*
unfulfremedness *n.* imperfection   *unfulfremednes*
unfulfreming *n.* incompletion, imperfection   *unfulfremming*
unglad *a.* neg. - from (Eng.) glad   *unglæd*
ungladly *adv.* - from (Eng.) unglad   *unglædlic*
ungladness *n.* - from (Eng.) unglad   *unglædnes*
ungood *a.* neg. - from (Eng.) good   *ungod*
unhaply *a.* inconvenient, unsuitable   *ungehæplic*
unharmyearn *a.* inoffensive   *unhearmgeorn*
unhaver *n.* poor person   *wanhafa*
unhavle *a.* destitute   *wanhafol*
unhavleness *n.* destitution   *wanhafolnes*
unhealth *n.* neg. - from (Eng.) health   *wanhælð*
unhearsome *a.* disobedient   *unhiersum*
unhearsomeness *n.* disobedience   *unhiersumnes*
unheavied *a.* unencumbered   *ungehefegod*
unheedly *adv.* neg. - from (Eng.) heedly   *wanhydig*
unheedy *a.* neg. - from (Eng.) heedy   *unhydig*
unhold *a.* disloyal, unreliable   *unhold*
unholdsome *a.* incontinent   *ungehealdsum*
unholdsomeness *n.* incontinence   *unhealdsumnes*
unlathed uninvited   *ungelaðod*
unlaughterworthy *a.* neg. - from (Eng.) laughter + worthy   *unleahtorwyrðe*
unlievedly *a.* incredibly   *ungelifedlic*

unlieveful *a.* incredible *ungeleafful*
unlievefully *a.* incredibly *ungeleaffullic*
unlievefulness *n.* incredulity *ungeleaffulnes*
unlikeworthy *a.* displeasing *unlicwyrðe*
unlittle *a.* neg. - from (Eng.) little *unlytel*
unlored *a.* ignorant *ungelæred*
unloredness *n.* ignorance *ungelærednes*
unmarred neg. - from (Eng.) marred *unamyrred*
unmean *a.* neg. - from (Eng.) mean *unmæne*
unmenishly *adv.* unmasculinely *unmenisclic*
unmete *a.* immense, extraordinary *ungemæte, ungemete*
unmete *a.* immesurable, innumerable *unmæte*
unmetefast *a.* immoderate, intemperate, excessive *ungemetfæst*
unmetefastness *n.* excess, intemperance, lack of moderation *ungemetfæstnes*
unmetely *a.* immeasurably, innumerably *ungemetlic*
unmeteness *n.* innumerableness, extravagance *ungemetnes*
unmight *n.* neg. - from (Eng.) might *unmiht*
unmightily *a.* neg. - from (Eng.) mightily *unmihtiglic*
unmightiness *n.* neg. - from (Eng.) mighty *unmihtignes*
unmightliness *n.* inability, impossibility *unmihtiglicnes*
unmightly *a.* not possible, impossible *unmihtlic*
unmighty *a.* neg. - from (Eng.) mighty *unmihtig*
unmoodiness *n.* neg. - from (Eng.) moodiness *unmodignes*
unoreworth *v.* dishonour *unarwurðian*
unoreworthly *a.* dishonourably *unarwurðlic*
unoreworthness *n.* dishonour, indignity, irreverence *unarwurðnes*
unoverwon *a.* unconquered *unoferwunnen*
unqueme *a.* displeasing, not pleasing *uncweme*
unreadly *adv.* illiterately *ungerædlic*
unreadness *n.* illiteracy *ungerædnes*
unright *a.* incorrect *unriht*
unrightcrafting *n.* poor quality *unrihtcræfting*
unrightdeed *n.* neg. - from (Eng.) right + deed *unrihtdæd*
unrightdeemer *n.* unjust judge/ critic *unrihtdema*
unrightdoand/ unrightdoer *n.* - from (Eng.) unright + do *unrihtdond*

unrightful *a.* unjust *unrihtful*
unrightlust *n.* neg. - from (Eng.) right + lust *unrihtlust*
unrightly *adv.* incorrectly a. *unrihtlic*
unrightness *n.* error, injustice *unrihtnes*
unrightwilland/ unrightwiller *n.* evil-disposed person *unrihtwillend*
unrightwise *a.* unjust *unrihtwis*
unrightwiseness *n.* injustice, iniquity *unrehtwisnis*
unrightyetsing *n.* avarice *unrihtgitsung*
unriped *a.* immature *ungeriped*
unsayingly *a.* indescribably, unspeakably, ineffably *unasecgendlic*
unscathedness *n.* non suffering injury *unscæððednes*
unscatheful *a.* not causing suffering injury *unscæðful*
unscathefulness *n.* lack of capacity/ inability to injure *unscæðfulnes*
unscathily *a.* not dangerously, not injuriously *unsceððiglice*
unscathy *a.* not dangerous, not injurious *unscæððig*
unseenly *a.* invisibly *ungesynelic*
unseldom *adv.* infrequent *unseldan*
unset *v.* destabilise *unsettan*
unshedwise *a.* indiscriminate, indiscreet, irrational *ungesceadwis*
unshedwisely *a.* indiscriminately, indiscreetly, irrationally *ungesceadwislic*
unshedwiseness *n.* indiscrimination, irrationality, indiscretion *ungesceadwisnes*
unshamefulness *n.* neg. - from (Eng.) shamefulness *unscæmfulnes*
unshamely *a.* immodest *unscamlic*
unshapen unformed, uncreated *ungesce(a)pen*
unshearingly *adv.* inseparably *unascyrgendlic*
unshildy *a.* innocent *unscyldig*
unshrunken *a.* neg. - from (Eng.) shrunken *unascruncen*
unsibb *a.* unrelated *ungesibb* (compare *sibling*)
unsibsome *a.* contentious, argumentative, quarrelsome *ungesibsum*
unsibsomeness *n.* contentiousness, discord, quarrelsomeness *ungesibsumnes*
unsinny *a.* innocent *unsynnig*
unsoundly *a.* neg. - from (Eng.) soundly *ungesundlic*
unspeaking neg. - from (Eng.) speaking *unsprecende*
unsteadful *a.* unstable *unstydful*

unsteadfulness *n.* instability *unstydfulnes*
unstill *a.* neg. - from (Eng.) still *unstille*
unstillness *n.* - from (Eng.) unstill *unstillnes*
unstiring *a.* unmoving *unstyrende*
unstiringly *adv.* immovably, motionlessly, unmovingly *unastyriendlic, unstyrendlic*
unsunderedly *a.* inseparably *unasundrodlic*
untamedly *a.* neg. - from (Eng.) untamed *untemedlic*
untellingly *a.* indescribably *untellendlic*
unthank *n.* ingratitude *unðanc*
unthankworthily *a.* - from (Eng.) unthankworthy *unðancwyrðlice*
unthankworthy *a.* undeserving of gratitude *unðancwurðe*
unthede *a.* disunited *ungeðeod*
unthew *n.* vice, fault *unðeaw*
unthewfast *a.* immoral, disorderly, unmannered *unðeawfæst*
unthewful *a.* immoral, disorderly, unmannered *unðeawful*
unthild *n.* impatience *ungeðyld*
unthildly *adv.* impatiently *ungeðyldelice*
unthildy *a.* impatient *un(ge)ðyldig*
untholingly *adv.* intolerably *unðoligendlic*
unthroughfare/ unthoroughfare *n.* cul de sac *unðurhfære*
unthroughshotingly *a.* impenetrably *unðurhsceotendlic*
unthwear *a.* disunited, inharmonious, disagreeable *ungeðwære*
unthwearly *adv.* inharmoniously, disagreeably *ungeðwærlic*
unthwearness *n.* disturbance, discord, disharmony, disagreement, lack of unity *ungeðwærnes*
untidely *a.* unseasonable *untidlic*
untime *n.* unseasonableness *untima*
untodealed *a.* undivided *untodæled*
untodealness *n.* undividedness *untodælnes*
untodealy *a.* inseparable *untodælic*
untrim *a.* neg. - from (Eng.) trim *untrum*
untrimly *a.* - from (Eng.) untrim *untrumlic*
untrimness *n.* infirmity, state of not being trim *untrymnes*
untruefast *a.* inconstant, unreliable *untreowfæst*
untruly *a.* - from (Eng.) untrue *untreowlic*

untwofold *a.* without duplicity *untwiefeald*
untwoly *a.* not ambiguous *untweolic*
unwastmbearness *n.* unfruitfulness, sterility *unwæstmbærnes*
unwatery *a.* desiccated, dehydrated *unwæterig*
unweaponed unarmed *ungewæpnod*
unweary *a.* indefatigable *unwerig*
unweened unexpected *unwened*
unweenedly *adv.* unexpectedly *ungewenedlic*
unwendness *n.* unchangeability *ungewendnes*
unwharving unchanging *unwhearfiende*
unwhole *a.* neg. - from (Eng.) whole *unhal*
unwilsomely *adv.* involuntarily *unwilsumlice*
unwinsome *a.* unpleasant *unwinsum*
unwinsomeness *n.* unpleasantness *unwinsumnes*
unwisdom *n.* ignorance, stupidity *unwisdom*
unwiseness *n.* neg. - from (Eng.) unwise *ungewisnes*
unwitful *a.* senseless *ungewitful*
unwitfulness *n.* senselessness *ungewitfulnes*
unwitherward *a.* not contrary, not discordant *unwiðerweard*
unwitherwardly *a.* not contrarily, not discordantly *unwiðerweardlic*
unwittily *a.* - from (Eng.) unwitty *ungewittiglice*
unwitty *a.* neg. - from (Eng.) witty *unwittig*
unwlitty *a.* not pretty, disfigured, deformed *unwlitig*
unwlittying *n.* disfigurement *unwlitegung*
unwlittyness *n.* disfigurement *unwlitignes*
unwork *v.* deconstruct *unwyrccan*
unworkly *a.* impractical, redundant *unweorclic*
unworthing *n.* dishonour *unweorðung*
unworthly *adv.* dishonourably *unweorðlic*
unwrast *a.* inaccurate, incongruous *unwræst*
unwrastly *adv.* inaccurately, incongruously *unwræstlic*
unwrought *a.* neg. - from (Eng.) wrought *ungeworht*
unyearnful *a.* indifferent *ungeornful*
upariseness *n.* resurrection *uparisnes*
upcome *n.* source, origin *upcyme*
uphavely *adv.* presumptuously, arrogantly *upahafenlice*

uphaveness *n.* presumption, arrogance *upahafennes*
uplandish *a.* - from (Eng.) upland *uplendisc*
uply *a.* high quality *uplic*
upness *n.* elevation *upnes*
upping *n.* increase, accumulation *ypping*
upspring *n.* - from (Eng.) up + spring *upspring*

W

wallthread *n.* plumb line *wealðræd*
wallwork *n.* masonry *wealweorc*
walm *n.* inflammation *wielm*
wark *n.* pain, suffering *wærc*
warpness *n.* perversion *aworpness*
wastand *n.* devastator *awestend*
wasteness/ wastedness *n.* desolation, destruction *awest(ed)nes*
wastum *n.* fruit, product, produce *wæstm*
wastumbearingness *n.* fruitfulness, productivity, fertility *wæstmberendnes*
wastumbearness *n.* fruitfulness, productivity, fertility *wæstmbærnes*
wastumless *a.* unfruitful, unproductive *wæstmleas*
wastumly *adv.* fruitfully, productively *wæstmlic*
wateraddle *n.* dropsy *wæteradl*
waterfrightness *n.* hydrophobia *wæterfyrhtnes*
waterful *a.* dropsical *wæterful*
waterleet *n.* aqueduct *wætergelæt*
waterly *a.* aquatic *wæterlic*
waterthrough *n.* conduit *wæterðruh*
waterwash *n.* alluvium *wætergewæsc*
wayleet *n.* junction *wegglæte*
wayless *a.* - from (Eng.) way + less *wegleas*
weakmoodness *n.* - from (Eng.) weak + mood *wacmodnes*
weal *n.* prosperity *wela*
weald, wold *n.* forest *weald*
wealy *a.* prosperous *welig*

weaponing *n.* armour *wæpnung*
weaponless *a.* unarmed *wæpenleas*
weariness *n.* - from (Eng.) weary + ness *werignes*
weatherwendedness *n.* changeability, variation of weather *wederawendednes*
wedbreach *n.* divorce, adultery *wedbryce*
wedfasten *v.* pledge *wedfæstan*
ween *v.* hope, expect, imagine *wenan*
ween *n.* hope, opinion, expectation, supposition *wen*
weening *n.* expectation *wenung*
well-likeworthness *n.* likeability *welgelicwirðnes*
well-likeworthy *a.* very likeable *welgelicwirðe*
wellbeshowed *a.* well demonstrated *welbesceawod*
wellborn *a.* - from (Eng.) well + born *welboren*
welldeed *n.* beneficial act *weldæd*
welldoness *n.* benefit, beneficial action *weldonnes*
wellfremeness *n.* benefit, beneficial planning *welfremnes*
wellquemedly *a.* well pleasing *welgecwemedlic*
wellquemness *n.* favour, pleasure *welgecwemnes*
wellroomly *a., adv.* spacious, spaciously *welrumlice*
wellwilling *a.* benevolent *welwillende*
wellwillingly *a., adv.* benevolently *welwillendlice*
wellwillingness *n.* benevolence *welwillendnes*
wem *v.* defile, corrupt *wemman*
wemmedly *v.* corruptible *wemmedlic*
wemming *n.* defilement, corruption *wemming*
wemmingly *a.* corruptibly *wemmendlic*
wemness *n.* corruption *wemnes*
wen *n.* tumour *wenn*
wend *v.* change *wendan*
wendedness *n.* alteration, change *awendednes*
wender *n.* translator, interpreter *wendere*
wending *n.* change, subversion *awending*
wending *n.* change, rotation *wendung*
wendingliness *n.* mutability, changeability *awendendlicnes*
wendingly *a.* changeably *wendendlic*

wered *n.* army troop, company, band *werod*
werehood n. adulthood *werhad*
werekin n. human race *wercyn*
werely a. human *werlic*
westdeal *n.* west part *westdæl*
westnorthlong extending NW *westnorðlang*
wetness *n.* moisture *wætnes*
wharve *v.* turn, revolve, change, transfer, convert *hweorfan*
wharvely *a.* changing, changeable, transitory *hwearflic*
wharveness *n.* transition, change, conversion, revolution *hwearvnes*
wharving *n.* change, revolution *hwearfung*
whelm *n.* surge, fervour *wylm*
whilewendly *a.* temporary, transitory *hwilwendlic*
whiling passing, transitory, temporary *hwilende*
whurful *a.* inconstant *hwurful*
whurfulness *n.* inconstancy, mutability *hwurfulnes*
wickner *n.* bailiff *wicnera*
widecouth a. common knowledge *widcuð*
widegoing *a.* itinerant, widely travelled *widgenge*
wield *v.* control *wieldan*
wield *n.* control *wield*
wifefast *a.* happily married *wiffæst*
wifehood *n.* - from (Eng.) wife + hood *wifhad*
wifeless *a.* unmarried *wifleas*
wifely *a.* - from (Eng.) wife *wiflic*
wike *n.* officer, office, function *wice*
wilfully *a.* - from (Eng.) wilful *wilfullic*
wilne *v.* desire *wilnian*
wilning *n.* desire *wilnung*
wilsome *a.* - from (Eng.) wil + some *wilsum*
wilsomely *adv.* - from (Eng.) wilsome *wilsumlic*
wilsomeness *n.* - from (Eng.) wilsome *wilsumnes*
winly *a.* positively *wynlic*
winsomely *a.* - from (Eng.) winsome *wynsumlic*
winsomeness *n.* pleasure, delight *wynsumnes*
wiseheedly *a.* sagacious *wishydig*

wishedness *n.* - from (Eng.) wished *wyscednes*
wishingly *adv.* - from (Eng.) wishing *wyscendlic*
wiseness *n.* - from (Eng.) wise *wisenes*
witanmoot *n.* national council, parliament *witangemot*
withchoose *v.* reject *wiðceosan*
witherling *n.* opponent, adversary *wiðerling*
withersake *n.* adversary, enemy *wiðersaca*
witherspeakand *n.* adversary (in speech), contradictor *wiðersprecend*
witherward *a.* contrary, adverse *wiðerweard*
witherwardly *adv.* contrarily, adversely *wiðerweardlic*
witherwardness *n.* opposition, adversity *wiðerweardnes*
withlead *v.* abduct *wiðlædan*
withleadness *n.* abduction *wiðlædnes*
withmeetedness *n.* invention *wiðmetednes*
withsaking *n.* denial, rejection *wiðsacung*
withsetness *n.* opposition *wiðsetnes*
withshove *v.* repel, refute *wiðscufan*
witlessness *n.* - from (Eng.) witless *witleasnes*
witter *n.* sage, philosopher *wita*
wittyness *n.* - from (Eng.) witty *wittignes*
wive *v.* marry (a wife) *wifian*
wiving *n.* marrying (a wife) *wifung*
wlenk *n.* pride, arrogance *wlenc*
wlita *n.* face, countenance *wlita*
wlite *n.* appearance, aspect *wlite*
wlitty *a.* beautiful *wlitig*
wlonk *a.* proud *wlanc*
woemoodness *n.* depression *weamodnes*
woetoken *n.* portent, sign of misfortune *weatacn*
wombaddle *n.* - from (Eng.) womb + addle *wambadl*
wombhoard *n.* - from (Eng.) womb + hoard *wambhord*
wonderly *adv.* - from (Eng.) wonder *wundorlic*
wondertoken *n.* miracle *wundortacn*
wonderwork *n.* impressive work/ action, deed, miracle *wundorweorc*
wone *v.* inhabit *wunian*
wonely *a.* usual, customary *wunelic*

woneness *n.* habitation *wunenes*
woningly *a.* habitually *wuniendlic*
wordcraft *n.* eloquence *wordcræft*
wordfast *a.* reliable *wordfæst*
wordful *a.* fluent, verbose *wordful*
wordhoard *n.* vocabulary *wordhord*
wordlock *n.* logic *wordloc*
wordlore *n.* etymology *wordlar*
wordmark *n.* definition *wordgemearc*
wordsomener *n.* catalogue, enumeration *wordsomnere*
wordsomening *n.* collation *wordsomnung*
wordwinsome *a.* affable *wordwynsum*
wordwrestle *v.* debate, argue, discuss *wordum wrixlan*
workcraft *n.* mechanics *weorcræft*
workdeed *n.* action, operation *weorcdæd*
workful *a.* active, industrious *weorcful*
workly *adv.* operationally, practically *weorclic*
workness *n.* workability, operation *wyrcnes*
workreeve *n.* manager *weorcgerefa*
workworthy *a.* able-bodied *weorcwyrðe*
worldkind *a.* secular *woruldcund*
worsely *a.* - from (Eng.) worse *wyrslic*
worthful *a.* valuable, dignified, honourable *weorðful*
worthfullness *n.* dignity, honour *weorðfulnes*
worthfully *adv.* with dignity, honourably *weorðfullic*
worthing honour, honouring, valuing *weorðung*
worthliness *n.* importance, value, estimation *weorðlicnes*
worthly *a.* important, valuable, distinguished *weorðlic*
worthness *n.* value, importance, estimation *weorðnes*
woundly *a.* wound inflicting, dangerous *wundlic*
woundswathe *n.* scar *wundswaðu*
wrack *n.* vengeance, revenge *wræc*
wrathly *a.* - from (Eng.) wrath *wraðlic*
wray *v.* accuse *wregan*
wrayedness *n.* accusation *wregednes*
wrayer *n.* accuser *wregere*

wraying *n.* accusation *wregung*
wrayingly *adv.* accusingly *wregendlic*
wreckness *n.* vengeance, revenge *wrecnes*
wriels *n.* covering *wrigels*
wulder *v.* glorify *wuldrian*
wulder *n.* glory, splendour *wuldor*
wulderful *a.* glorious *wuldorful*
wulderfully *adv.* gloriously *wuldorfulic*
wuldry *a.* glorious *wuldrig*
wye *n.* war, contest *wig*
wyeman *n.* warrior, soldier *wigman*
wyesith *n.* military expedition *wigsið*

Y

yearnful *a.* desirous *geornful*
yearnfullness *n.* desire *geornfulnes*
yearnfully *adv.* desirously *geornfullic*
yearmind *n.* yearly commemoration *geargemynd*
yearve *n.* heritage *ierfe*
yearve *v.* inherit *yrfan*
yellowaddle *n.* jaundice *gealladl*
yeme *v.* notice *gieman*
yemeless *a.* negligent *giemeleas*
yemelessly *adv.* negligently *giemeleaslic*
yemelessness *n.* negligence *giemeleasnes*
yepeness *n.* astuteness *geapnes*
yetsing *n.* avarice, covetousness, desire *gitsung*
yetsingly *adv.* avariciously, insatiably *gitsiendlic*
yetsingness *n.* avarice *gitsiendnes*
yisle *n.* hostage *gis(e)l*
yislehood *n.* state of being a hostage *gislhad*
yomer *v.* to be miserable *geomrian*
yomer troubled, miserable *geomor*

yomering *n.* misery, trouble *geomrung*
yomerly *a.* miserably, with trouble *geomorlic*
yomerness *n.* tribulation *geomornes*
yondfare *v.* travel to a place away, traverse, pervade *geondfaran*
yondsee *v.* examine *geondsean*

List II
Thesaurus in Order of Loanwords
- All Words from Steps 1 - 5, and more

This list takes foreign-derived loanwords as a starting point and, in alphabetical order, lets you look up alternative suggestions to these words. These suggestions include all updated words covered in Steps 1 - 5, and more. There are also many current forms like those in the Lead-in (p. 23). You'll recall that in our 'if England had won' scenario for 1066, *its only the ones which came from Old English which would have been likely to have been in use today* (so English would always use *sight*, rather than a mixture of *sight* and *vision*).

Layout: first come the loans, in *italics*. These are: a) loan words, b) phrases that have key words which are loans, or c) words which are mixed loan/early-English derived. The loans are followed by suggested alternatives in normal lettering.

A section after the end of the main list gives words of the kind covered in Step 1. These often have no obvious equivalents (loanword or otherwise) to which they could be linked in the main list here.

- Beware of Overmuchness
- Don't overeat
- Don't overdrink

The Health Thaneship

Notes:
i) As in normal woth a thesaurus, suggested alternatives may cover more or less of the word/ terms they are suggested for - use shedwiseness (discretion) here!
ii) There are a few words in the English-based suggestions which themselves hold some loaned elements. In such cases, the loan element is given in *italics*: for example: eat*able*, unbeliev*able*.
iii) As with List I, this gives a sample of updated words. Neither do the current alternatives make a full list.

Key:
(a.) = *adjective (describes a noun: 'big' in big house)*
(adv.) = *adverb (shows way in which something is done: fast, happily)*
(n.) = *noun (normally things and ideas: car, bird, freedom)*
(neg.) = *negative (such as in words starting with 'un')*
(v.) = *verb (doing words like to run, to write, to sing)*

Summary of List II layout: *Loanword* (or phrase with key element which is a loanword) given in *italics*, followed by suggested English alternatives in normal lettering.

A

abandon: 1 forgo, forsake, forlose
2 *relinquish:* forlet
abandonment, relinquishment: forletness
abandonment, rejection, denial: forsakeness
abasement, condemnation: nethering
abduct: withlead
abduction: outleadness, withleadness
abject, poor: heanly
able-bodied: workworthy
abode: erding
abounding, satisfactory: enoughsome
abscess: gatheredness
absence: lack, want
absolute: thorough, whole, most, downright
absorb: take in, take up, get
absorbed, unified, merged: samed
abstention, deprivation: forgoedness
abstinence, temperance, self-restraint: forhaveness, forhavedness
abstinent, one who is: forhavand/forhaver
abundance: wealth of, enoughsomeness, fullsomeness
abundance, size: muchness
abundant: 1 engoughful 2 *abounding, satisfactory:* enoughsome
abundantly, sufficiently: enoughly
accelerate: speed up, quicken

accept: take up, take, go for
acceptable, nice, likeable: 1 likeworthy 2 *pleasing:* thankworthy 3 *pleasant, agreeable:* queme
access: nighleching
accident: mishap
accomplish, fully perform: fullgo
accordingly: so, thus, therefore
accumulation: hoarding, gathering, upping
accumulate: hoard, gather
accusation: wraying, wrayedness
accuse: wray
accuser: wrayer
accusingly: wrayingly
acknowledgement: acknowness
acquaint: get to know
action: 1 deed 2 *operation:* workdeed
active, industrious: 1 workful, deedly
2 *strenuous, vigorous:* cove
acute: high, sharp, steephigh
add: put on, and
additional: more, further
address, to: deal with, see to set about
adhere: stick, stick to, stand by
adjudication: mething
administration, service, ministry: thaning
administration, association, nation, community, population: thedeship
admission: infare

admit: own, own up, let on, say
adolescence: youthhood
adopt: take on, take up
adorned with gold: goldladen
adulterer, fornicator: forlier, forlieand
adulthood: werehood
advance (n.): forthstepping
advance (v.), progress (v.): forthgang, forthstep
advanced: 1 ahead, forthly 2 *progressive* forthward
advancement: forthing
adverse: witherward
adversely: witherwardly, againwardly
adversity: witherwardness
adversary (in speech): witherspeakand
adversary, opponent, enemy: witherling, withersake, foe
advice, consultation, consideration: thoughting
advise (meaning inform): tell, let know
adviser: thoughter
advocate, sponsor: forspeaker
aerial: loftly, loften
affable: wordwinsome
affectionate: loving
afflict, injure: 1 hean 2 *vex, grieve:* awhene
3 *trample, oppress, repress:* thrutch
affliction: 1 unbliss, shending, dretchedness 2 *torment:* thresting 3 *tribulation:* threatness, thrutchness
age: elddom

aggregate: whole, altogether
aging process: elding
agree (with) : go along with, hold with
agreeable, united, harmonious: thwear
agreeably, harmoniously: thwearly
agreeable, pleasant, acceptable: queme
agreement: thedesomeness
agreement, unity, harmony: thwearness
agreement, consent: thwearing
agriculture, horticulture: earthtilth
alcoholic (n.): overdrinker
alcoholism: overdrunkeness
alien, strange, foreign: fremd
alienate, to; become alienated: afremd
alienation: afremding
allegiance, loyalty: holdship
allegory: likening,
allegory, parable: onlikeness
alleviate: lessen, lower
allow: let
allurement, seduction: forspanning
alluvium: waterwash
alteration, change: wendedness
altercation: fight, scrap
altitude: height
ambiguous: can be taken two ways/ more than one way; more than one meaning
ambiguous, doubtful, equivocal: twoly
ambush: waylay
amendment: betingness
amiable: friendhold
amiably: friendholdly

amicable: friendly
amount: lot, deal
amplify: up, boost
amputate: take off, cut off, snithe, offcarve
amputation: snithing
analyse: break down, look through, go through
ancestor: forebear
ancestral (paternal): forthfatheren
ancient: olden
ancient right: eldright
ancient world: ereworld
anemometer: windmeter
anger: wrath
angle, bay, corner, bend: bight
angry: wrathful
annihilate: wipe out, bring to nought
anniversary: mindday
announce, proclaim: forthsay
announce, confirm: kithe
announce, order (v.), proclaim, summon, present (v.), command (v.), direct, declare, offer: abede
annual: yearly
antagonist, injurious person: scather
anti: against, agin
anticipate: 1 foresee 2 *prevent:* forestall, head off 3 *precede:* forestep
anticipation, precedence: forestepping
anxiety, trouble: angness
anxious: howful
anxiousness: howfullness
apart: asunder

apart from: other than, but (as in all but two)
apparent: seeming
apparently: seemingly, it seems/ would seem
appearance, aspect: wlite
application: begengness
apply/ ratify fully: fullfasten
appoint: dight, set (up)
appointed properly: rightset
appointment, rightful/ establishment, rightful/ office, rightful: rightsetness
apprise: tell, let know
approach, access: nighleching
approach (v.): come near/ close, atgo, nighleche
acquaintance, familiarity: couthness
aquatic: waterly
aqueduct: waterleet
arbitrarily: at whim, selfwillingly, selfwealdly
arbitrator: gobetween, middliand
arboretum: treestead
ardent: firehot
argue, discuss, debate: wordwrestle
argumentative, quarrelsome: unsibsome
aristocratic, noble: athel
armour: weaponing
army: ferd, hera
army troop, company, band: wered
arrange, appoint: dight
arrangement, succession, series: afterfollowingness, endbirthness
arrangement: dight
arranger: dighter

arrival: coming, coming in
arrive: come, get here/ there
arrogance: tothundness
arrogance, pride: wlenk
arrogantly, presumptuously: uphavely
arrogantly: tothundenly
articulate: rightlithely
as a consequence of: through, thanks to
ascend: go up
ascertain: find out
assimilate: even out
assist: help
assistance: help
associate: to do/ go/ deal/ have dealings with, spend time with
associate (v.), comrade: fere
associated: fered, ferly
association, companionship, connection, conjunction: fayness
association, society: fellowship, thedeness
association, nation, community, population: thedeship
assume: take it, take it as so
asthma: angbreast
astonish: amaze
astonished, to be: amazed, stylt
astuteness: yepeness
asylum, truce, protection: grith
atonement, penitence: deedboteness, deedbote
atonement, reparation: betness
atrophy: smalling
attack (f.e. by shooting, also spoken): onshot

attain: reach, get to, get
attempt, to; test, examine, experience: fand
attend: come/ go to
attendant: atstandand
attendant, officer, functionary: ambighter, wike
attentive: heedful, listening, hearsome
attentiveness: hearsomeness
attract: draw
attribute, to: earmark, put down to
au fait: know well
audible: hear*able*
audible: hearingly
auditorium: speechhouse
augment: go with, make better, strengthen, boost
austerity: hardliness
authoritative, pre-eminent: elderdomly
authoritativeness, pre-eminence: elderdomliness
authority, command: onwield
authority, power: onwieldness, might
authority, dominion, seniority, pre-eminence: elderdom
avail, benefit (v.): freme
avarice: feeyetsing, unrightyetsing, yetsingness
avarice, covetousness, desire: yetsing
avariciously, insatiably: yetsingly

B

bailiff: wickner
balanced: fair, evenhanded
band, company: wered
baptise, to: fullought
baptiser, baptist: fulloughter
baptism: fullought
base, foundation, support, station, position, state, condition: staddle
battle, war: guth, fighting
bay, corner, angle, bend: bight
beak, face: neb, nib
beauteous, elegant: smicker
beautiful: lovely, wlitty
because: for
become zealous, become enraged/ angry: hothearten
bend, bay, gulf, corner, angle: bight
behaviour, restraint, temperance: behavedness
beneficial, profitable: fremeful
beneficial act: welldeed
beneficial action, benefit: welldoness
beneficial planning, benefit: wellfremeness
beneficially, usefully, profitably: fremefully
benefit (v.): freme
benefit (n.): 1 welfare 2 *beneficial action:* welldoness 3 *beneficial planning:* wellfremeness
benevolence: 1 goodwill, kindness, wellwillingness 2 *mercy, compassion:* milce

benevolent: wellwilling
benevolently: wellwillingly
bilateral: two sided
biography: lifestory
block (v.), prevent, obstruct: forstand
block/ prevent a move/ action: forecome
bone fracture: bonebreak, bonebreach
book collection: bookhoard
borderland: marchland
born of disparate parents: sunderborn
boundary: landmark
bountiful: roomgivle
bountifulness, liberality: roomgivleness
bounty, favour, grace, pleasure: este
brave, noble, loyal: thanly
breach of loan/ surety: borrowbreach
breach of the peace: frithbreach
breach of truce/ asylum: grithbreach
break in pieces: forbreak
bridal: bridely
bring up morally/ virtuously: thew
burglarious: housebreachle
burglary: housebreach
butcher: fleshmonger
by degrees, gradually: stepmeal

C

calculate: work out
calumny: harmspeech
candelabrum: candletree

canine: houndly
capability, resources: wherewithal
capital: headly
capital offence: headguilt
capital punishment - of c. p. (a.): beheadly
captain: highthane
captive (n.), prisoner: haftling
carnal attraction: fleshbesmittenness
carnal nature: fleshliness
carnivorous: meat eating
carte blanche: a free hand, freedom
catalogue, enumeration: wordsomener
caterpillar: leafworm
cause (n.): origin: frume
cause (v.): bring about, make
cease: stop, end
century: hundred (years, runs)
certain, manifest, familiar: couth
certainly, manifestly, familiarly, evidently: couthly
certainly: that's so/ was so a.s.f.
certainly, especially: indeed
chamberlain, page: bowerthane
changeable, changing, transitory: wharvely
changeably: wendingly
change (v.), revolve, transfer, convert: 1 wharve 2 *translate:* wend, awend
change (n.), 1 alteration: wendedness
2 *revolution:* wharving 3 *rotation, subversion:* wending 4 *transition, conversion, revolution:* wharveness
changeability/ variation of weather: wetherwendedness

changing, changeable, transitory: wharvely
chaos: dwolma
chapel: bedehouse
charitability, generosity, virtue: custiness
charitable: 1 almsful, almsly 2 *generous, virtuous:* custy
cheer, to; console: frover
chief attendant, retainer: elderthane
chief officer: highreeve, overalderman
chief officer, captain: highthane
chief place: headstead
chief protector: headward
church duty, service: churchthaning
circa: about
circuit, course: begang
city/ town administrative area: boroughshire
climax, exultation: highting
coast: searim
coast guard: seaward
coastal cliff: seaberg
cognate: akin to, like
cognizant of: aware of, know about
coherent: understandable, easily followed
coincide: the same as, the same time/ thing as a.s.f.
collation: wordsomening
collect: gather, hoard
collectively: gatheringly
college, school, university: learninghouse
collision: smash, crash

colour: hue
colouration: hueness, hueing
coloured (green, a.s.f.): greenhuen
colourless: hueless
combat, battle, war: guth
combination: things building/ adding up, lots of things, together
comedian: laughtersmith
comfort (v.); console: afrever
comforter, consoler: frovrand
command (v.), order: bebid, hest
command (v.), order (v.), proclaim, summon, present (v.), direct, announce, declare, offer: abede
command (n.), service: ambight
commander, general: heratower, heretoga, bebidand
commence: start, begin
commiserate: evensorrow
commit adultery or fornication: forlie
common knowledge: widecouth
common land, public land: folkland
common need, basic need: folkneed
common, popular, public: folkish, folkly
commotion, disturbance: stirness, rearness
community: meanship
community, population, nation, administration, association: 1 thedeship 2 *retinue, society,*
companion, comrade: sith
companionship: fareship
companionship, association, connection: fayness
companionship, society: fareship

company, band: wered
company of troops, phalanx: sheltron
compare: aliken
compassion: 1 besorrowing 2 *mercy, benevolence:* milce
compassion, to have: 1 besorrow 2 *show mercy:* milce
compassionate: evensorry
compatibility: matchness, matchship
competency, excellence: thungness
competent, excellent, distinguished: thungen
competently, excellently: thungenly
complain: bechide
complaint: grorning
complement: go with
complete: 1 done, whole, ready, fullwork
2 (such as c. a spell of time): fullgo
3 *to perfect:* fullfreme
completed: fullfremed
completely: all, fully, wholly, fullfremedly
completion: fullfremedness
completion, fulfilment: filledness
comply with, please (v.) satisfy: queme
compose, unite, connect, fix: fay
composed of: made up of
composition, conjunction: faying
composition, joining, joint, diagram: fay
comprehension, perception: understandness, ongetness
compulsion, subjection: underdriveness
comrade, companion: sith

concealment: behideness
concede: give in/ up, yield
concerning: about
conclusion: upshot, what happened
concord, peace: sibsomeness
concupiscence: lustyearnness
condemnation, abasement: nethering
condition: orereadness
condition, base, foundation, support, station, position, state: staddle
conditional: hangs on
condone: go along with, overlook
conduct (n.), usage, custom, habit, disposition, manners: thew
conduit: waterthrough
confident, impudent: headbold
confine, imprison: beclose
conflagration: fireburn
conflict, to: is against/ at odds with
confound: fordwilm
confound, corrupt, discomfit: shend
confuse: muddle
confusion: shendness
congregate: gather, throng
conjugal: matchly
conjunction: linkword
conjunction, association, companionship, connection: fayness
connect, unite, fix, compose: fay
connected: linked
connection: 1 link 2 *conjunction, association, companionship:* fayness
conscience: inwitness, inheed
conscious: aware, know of
consciously: knowingly, wittingly

consciousness: 1 inheedness 2
conscience: inwitness
consecration: hallowing
consent (n.): leave, thavesomeness
consent, agreement: thwearing
consent (v.), permit (v.): thave
consenting: thavesome
consequently: so, thus, therefore
consider: 1 think about, deem, see as, underthink 2 *premeditate:* forethink 3 *ponder, meditate, determine:* hedge
considerately, meditatively, determinedly: hedgely
consideration, advice, consultation: thoughting
considering literature: readthoughting
consolation: frover, froverness, frovring
consoler, comforter: frovrand
conspicuous: forthseen
conspirator, betrayer: hinderling
constitute: make up
constitution, establishment: onsetness
construct: build (up)
construct, adorn, insert: bework
construction: building, working/ building up
construction, foundation, position, institution, record: setness
construction (original): frumwork
constructive, positive: fremeful
constructively, positively: fremefully
construe: work out
consume, ignite, inflame, incite: anneal
consumed by fire, to be: forburn

consumption by fire: forburnedness
contact, touch: rineness
contemplate: yondthink
contemporary: at the same time, with the times, evenold
contempt: forhowedness, forhowing
contemptibly: forhowingly
contemptibility: besmearness
contemptuously: forhowedly
contentious, argumentative, quarrelsome: unsibsome
contentiousness, discord, quarrelsomeness: unsibsomeness
contents: inning
continence: havedness
continuation: gathertangness
continue: go on
continuous: ongoing
continuous, united: gathertang
contract, to: get
contradictor: witherspeaker
contrarily, adversely: witherwardly
contrary, adverse: witherward
contrition: threstness
control (n.): wield
control (v.): wield
convenience: hapliness
convenient: hap
conversation, discussion: talk, mooting
conversion: 1 charing 2 *transition, change, revolution:* wharveness
convert to: make into
convert, turn (v.): bewend
convert, turn, avert: awherve

convert, revolve, change, transfer: wharve
cooperating: samedworking
copious: lots, loads, many
cordial: friendly, warm hearted
corner, bay, angle, bend: bight
corporal: bodily
corpse: body, dead body
correct: right
correction, rectitude: rightness
correction, reproof: righting
corroboration: backup, backing
corrupt (v.): 1 shend 2 *defile:* wem
corruptible: wemmedly
corruptibly: wemmingly
corruption: wemness, wemming
country: land, ethel
county council leader: highshireman
county council official: shireman
courageous: stout-hearted
course, circuit: begang
court (n.): hove
courtly: hovely
cover: overlay, do/go over
covering: helm, wriels
covetous: feeyearn
covetousness, desire: yetsing
crazy: mad
create: make, shape
creation: shapeness
creator: maker, shepand/ sheper, frumshapand/ frumshaper
criminal: shildy
criminality: shildiness
cruel: hardhearted, hard, ruthless

221

cruel, fierce, violent, severe: rough, wild, grim, rethy
cruel, savage, fierce: slithe
cruelly, savagely, fiercely: 1 slithely 2 *severely, grievously:* tharly
cry: weep
cul de sac: unthroughfare, unthoroughfare
cultivate: work, till, help
curious, inquisitive: frimdy
curse (v.): amanse
curse (n.): amansing
custody, preservation, restraint: holdsomeness
custom, usage, habit, conduct (n.), disposition, manners: thew
customary, usual: wonely

D

damage, injury: scatheness, scathiness, scathing
dangerous, perilous: plightly, freckenful
debate, argue, discuss: wordwrestle
debris (on shore): seaupwarp
decapitate: behead
deceit, fraud, deception: swiking
deceit, falsehood, treachery: truelessness, swike, beswike
deceitful, fraudulent: fakeful, swikeful
deceitful, false, treacherous: trueless
deceitfulness: fakeness

deceive: bedidder, beswike, swike, bepeach
deceiver: swiker, beswiker, bepeachand
deception: beswiking, swikedom, beswikeness, bepeaching
deception, deceit, fraud: swiking
decide: choose, make one's mind up
deciduous: leafshedding
declaration: forthspell
declare, express: aqueath
declare, order (v.), proclaim, summon, present (v.), command (v.), direct, announce, offer: abede
decline (v.): forbow
decline (n.), despondency: toletness
deconstruct: unwork
decrease: lessen, lower
deduct: take away, take off
defence, protection: shieldness, shielding, foreshieldness
defer: put off/ on hold, leave for now
deficiency: lack, shortfall
defile, corrupt (v.): wem
defile, disgrace, reproach (v.): besmear
defilement, corruption: wemming
defilement, disgrace, reproach (n.): besmear
defilingly, reproachfully: besmearly
define: set, mark
definite: sure
definition: wordmark
defoliate: deleaf
degenerate: misborn

degradation, pollution: besnitness
degree, measure, proportion, rate: methe
dehydrated, desiccated: unwatery
dejected: downcast
delay: overing
deliberate: wilful
deliberately: wilfully, knowingly
deliberatively: thoughtingly
delight, pleasure: winsomeness
deliverer, redeemer, liberator: aleasand / aleaser
delude: mislead
demonstrate, exhibit, display: beshow, show
demonstration, exhibition: beshowing, inshowing
demonstratively: beshowingly
demonstrator, exhibitor, guide: beshower
demonstrator: inshower
denial, abandonment: forsakeness
denial, rejection: forsaking, withsaking
denigrate: slight, belittle, do down
denounce: forspeak
dense: thick, thickfold
deny: gainsay, say one hasn't a.s.f.
deny, renounce: atsake
depart: forthfare
departing, about to depart: fromward
departure: leaving, going, fromfare, forthfroming
departure, exit: outgang
depend: hang on, hinge on
depilate: dehair

deposit: leave, put in, drop
deposits (on shore): seaupwarp
depressed: down, downcast, low
depression: woemoodness
deprival: beniming
deprivation: forgoedness, beshearedness
deprive: beshear, benim
deputy governor: underreeve
deride: belaugh
derision, insult: hoker
descend: go down, lower, nethergo
descendant: tudder
descending: downstying
descent: going/ coming down, lowering
discrete: sidely, on the side
describe: tell, put into words, say
description: outline, towriteness
desert: wilderness
desiccated, dehydrated: unwatery
designate (v.): betoken
design (v.), purpose (v.), intend: underbegin
desire (n.): wilning, yearning, yearnfullness
desire, covetousness: yetsing
desire (v.): wilne, yearn
desirous: yearnful
desirously: yearnfully
desist: stop, end, leave off
desolation: waste, wasteness, wasting
desolation, destruction: wasteness, wastedness
despair (v.); despise, mistrust: forthink

despaired of: forthought
despatch: send, send off/ out
desperate: grim, hard
despise: loath, look down on, hate, overhow
despise, disregard, neglect (v.): forhow, misyeme
despiser: overhowand, overhower
despiser, neglecter: forhowand
despite: although, even though
despoiler: bereaver
despondency, decline: toletness
destabilise: unset, upset
destitute: haveless, unhavle
destitute/ poor person, pauper: tharfer
destitutely, poorly: tharfly
destitutely, miserably: tharfingly
destitution, poverty: unhavleness, tharfliness, tharfedness
destroy, ruin (v.): fordo, forspill, waste, wipe out
destruction: forspilledness, wasteness, wastedness
detain: hold/ keep back, hold
deter: put off
deteriorate: worsen, get worse, go downhill, forworth
deterioration: worsening, fall, forworthness
determine: 1 work out, tell, deem 2 *ponder, meditate*: hedge
detestable: loathsome, hateful
detrimental: harmful, bad for
devaluation: forworthness
devastation, raid: forharrying
devastator: wastand

develop: unfold, build up, grow, spread, happen
development, prosperity: growness
device, invention, discovery: afoundness, findle, withmeetedness
devise: think up, make up
devotion, economy, restraint, preservation, observance: holdsomeness
dexterously: smithly
diagram, joining, joint, composition: fay
difference, dissimilarity: mislikeness, unlikeness
difficulty, trouble: hardship, hard time/ thing, uneath, uneathness, heanhood, arvethness
digital: fingerly
dignified, honourable: worthful
dignifiedly, honourably: worthfully
dignity, honour: worthfullness
dilapidated: ramshackle
diminish: lessen, lower, wane, fall, bring down
diminution: littling
direct, order (v.), proclaim, summon, present (v.), command (v.), announce, declare, offer: abede
direct paternal descent/ pedigree: rightfathrenkin
direction: way, path
director: steerer
disadvantage: drawback
disagreeable, disunited, inharmonious: unthwear

disagreeably, inharmoniously: unthwearly
disagreement, disturbance, discord, disharmony, lack of unity: unthwearness
disappear, vanish: go, fordwine
disarm: beweapon
disastrous situation: eviladdle
discard: ditch, leave
discernment: toknowness
discipline, guidance: 1 steerness 2 *obedience:* thewfastness
discloser, indicator, index: beckonand/ beckoner
disconnect: cut off, undo, unfasten
discontinue: stop, end
discord, quarrelsomeness: unsibsomeness
discord, disturbance, disharmony, disagreement, lack of unity: unthwearness
discourage: put off
discourse, to: rerde
discover: find, infind
discoverer: finder, onfinder, onfindand
discovery, invention, device: afoundness, findle, withmeetedness
discrete: sidely, shedwise
discreetly, discriminately, rationally: shedwisely
discretion: 1 shedwiseness 2 *distinction, separation:* shed
discriminate: to beshed

discriminately, discreetly, rationally: shedwisely
discuss: talk through/ over, moot
discuss, argue, debate: wordwrestle
discussion, conversation: mooting, talk
disdain: overhowedness
disease of liver: liversickness
disease/ trouble bearing: addlebearing
diseased: addly
disfigure, corrupt: awem
disfigured, deformed, not pretty: unwlitty
disfigurement: unwlittyness, unwlittying, awemingness
disgrace, reproach, defile (v.): besmear
disgrace, reproach, defilement (n.): besmear
disgrace, scandal: shandliness
disgraceful, scandalous: shandful
disgracefully, scandalously: 1 shandly 2 *reproachfully, defilingly:* besmearly
disharmony, disturbance, discord, disagreement, lack of unity: unthwearness
dishonour: 1 unworthing, orelessness, unoreworth 2 *indignity, irreverence:* unoreworthness 3 *pollute:* besnit
dishonourable: oreless
dishonourably: unoreworthly, unworthly
dislocate: put out
disloyal, unreliable: unhold
dismiss: send/ throw out
dismissal, expulsion: awaydriveness

disobedience, rebelliousness: unhearsomeness
disobedient, rebellious: unhearsome
dissolve: formelt
disorderly, unmannered: unthewful, unthewfast
disperse: scatter, broadcast, send throughout, afleme
dispersal: todrivedness
display, demonstrate, exhibit: beshow
displease: offthink, ofthink
displeasing, unpleasing: unlikeworthy, unqueme
displeasing, to be; to displease: offlike
dispose: get rid off, throw away/ out, ditch
disposition: tosetedness
disposition, usage, custom, habit, conduct (n.), manners: thew
dispute: wrangle
disregard, neglect (v.), despise: forhow, misyeme
disseminate: give out, spread
dissimilar: unalike, not alike, not the same
dissimilarity, difference: mislikeness, unlikeness
dissipate: spread out, scatter, waste
dissuade: put off
dissuade, prevent: belean
distance: farness
distantly: farly
distantly related: farsibb
distinction: beshed
distinction, separation, discretion: shed

distinguish, perceive, recognise: onget
distinguished, excellent, competent: thungen
distinguished, important, valuable: worthly
distress, frustration: angmoodness
distress, poverty, misery: ermth
distress, necessity: tharf
distressed/ frustrated mood: angmood
distribute: send/ give/ deal out
disturbance, movement: 1 unstillness, onstiredness 2 *power of motion, tumult:* stirness 3 *commotion:* rearness
disturbance, discord, disharmony, disagreement, lack of unity: unthwearness
disturbing: unsettling, upsetting
disunited: 1 unthede 2 *inharmonious, disagreeable:* unthwear
diversity, variety: mislikeness, missenliness
divert, deprive of: atwend
division: asundering
divorce, adultery: wedbreach
do incorrectly/ wrongly, transgress: misdo
doable: doly
domestic: home, homely
domicile: home, abode, dwelling
dominant: foremost, top, highest, uppermost, to the fore, in the lead, leading, main player
domination: ricsing

dominion, authority, seniority, pre-eminence: elderdom
donation, support: bringness
double: twofold, twilly
doubly: twofoldly
doubtful, ambiguous, equivocal: twoly
dropsical: waterful
dropsy: wateraddle
due south: southright (likewise, northright a.s.f.)
due to the fact that: as, for, through
duplicate: do twice, do twice over
duplication, duplicity: twofoldness
duplicity, duplication: twofoldness
duty: something one has to/ should/ ought to do, business, needright, oughting
duty, valour: thaneship

E

e.g. (exempli gratia):   such as, like, for example f.e.
ease, pleasure: eathness
easily: eathly
easiness: eathness
easy, agreeable: eath
eatable: eatly
ecclesiastical: churchly
eclipsed, to be: athester
economical, frugal: holdsome, thrifty
economy: 1 thrift 2 *restraint, preservation, observance, devotion*: holdsomeness

3 *retentiveness, stinginess, tenaciousness*: fasthavleness
edibility: eatness
edible: eatly, can be eaten, eat*able*
edification: timberness
edification, structure: timbering
educational establishment: learninghouse
egotism, vanity: selflike
eject: throw out
elect: choose, pick
election: coreness
elegance: smickerness
elegant, beauteous: smicker
elevation: upness, arearness
elicit: draw out, get, get from/ out of
eliminate: do away with, rid, get rid of, offdo
eloquence: wordcraft
eloquence, fluency: toungeness
eloquent: wellworded
elucidate: throw light on
emanate (from): come/ stem from
embrace, encompass: beclip
embryo, foetus: unborn child, birther
emit: forthlet
emotion: breastwhelm
employment: work
en bloc: as a whole, together
encircle, entwine, envelop: bewind
encompass, embrace: beclip
encouragement: forthbuilding
endeavour (n.):   howing
endurance, suffering, passion: tholing
endure, suffer: thole

endure, support (v.): underbear, bolster
enemy: foe
energy, vigour: coveness
enflame: inheat
enjoy, use (v.): brook
enlighten, illuminate: inlighten, onlight, onlighten, yondshine
enlightener: onlightand, onlighter
enlightenment, illumination: onlighting, inlightness, onlightness
enumeration, catalogue: wordsomener
enrage, provoke, irritate: greme
enslave: to theow
enter: go in(side), ingo, infare, ingang
entrance, access: ingang
enthusiasm: keeness
enthusiastic: keen
enticingly: beckoningly
entirely: wholly, fully, all, withal
entitlement: right
entrant, visitor: ingenger, ingoer
entrap: betrap
entreat: beg
entwine, envelop, encircle: bewind
envelop: befold,
envelop, encircle, entwine: bewind
envious: evestful, evesty
envisage: foresee, see, think there will be
envy, rivalry: evest
envy (v.): to evest
enwrap, enfold: inbewind
epilepsy: fallsickness
epileptic: fallsick

epilogue: endspeak
equal person: evenling
equal sharer, partaker: evenlotter
equality: evenliness
equanimity, with: evenmoodly
equinox: evennight
equinoxual: evennightly
equitable: fair, even handed
equivocal: 1 twofold meaning 2 *ambiguous, doubtful:* twoly
erratically, inaccurately: missly, hit and miss
erroneous: wrong, mistaken
erroneous movement (such as socially): dwildafterfollowing
error: 1 mistake, dwild 2 *injustice:* unrightness
erudition: lorecraft
eruption: angset
especially, certainly: hure
establish: set up, start, begin, bestow
establish, put safe, utilise, use: befasten
established custom/ habit/ conduct/ manners a.s.f.: thewfast
established (in a home), resident (a.): homefast
establishment: onsetness
estimation, importance, value: worthness, worthliness
estrange: fremd
etc (et cetera): and so forth a.s.f., and so on, and suchlike
eternal: everlasting, for ever
etymology: wordlore

evade: forflee
evangelical: gospelly
eventuate: happen, come from
evidently, manifestly, certainly, familiarly: couthly
evoke: bring to mind, call out
ex: former
exaggerate: overdo it
exaggerated: far fetched, overdone
exalt: make high, raise up
examination, inspection: onbeshowing
examine: 1 look at/ into, yondsee 2 *investigate, scrutinise:* underseek 3 *scrutinise:* scruten, ascruten 4 *study, scrutinise:* throughsee 5 *experience, test:* fand
examiner: scrutner
example, to set; instruct by example, express figuratively: beseen
example, model, pattern: beseen, beseening
exceedingly, severely: swith
excel, prevail: forestand
excellence, competency: thungness
excellent: outstanding, great, thrithely, goodly
excellent, competent, distinguished: thungen
excellently, competently: thungenly
excellent work: highwork
excess: 1 too much/ many, overflowness, overmuchness 2 *intensity, severity:* swithliness, swithness 3 *intemperance:* unmetefastness
4 *surfeit:* overfill, overfillness
excessive, immoderate, intemperate: unmetefast
excessive, severe, intense: swithly
excessively: overly, too much, too, over:
exclude: shut/ keep out, not let in, leave out, outshove
excrescence: outgrowth
excusable: forgively
except: but, but for, other than, only
exercise, action, progress: fromship
exercise, practice: begeng
exhale: breath out
exhibit (n.): thing shown
exhibit (v.), demonstrate, display: show, beshow
exhibition, demonstration: beshowing, inshowing
exhibitor, demonstrator, guide: beshower
exhortation, incitement, instigation: tighting
exile: throw out, outcast, ban from
existence: standness
exit: 1 way out, out, outgang 2 *exodus:* outgoing, outgang, outflow
exit, departure: outgang
exodus: outgoing, outgang, outflow
expand: make bigger, broaden, up
expect: look to, look out for
expect, hope, to; imagine: ween
expectation, hope: ween, weening
expedite: speed up, make faster

expedition, campaign, soldiering: ferding, firding
expel: 1 throw out, afley 2 *disperse:* afleme
expenditure: spending, outlay
expensive: dear, not cheap
experience: 1 afonding, onfoundness
2 *explanation, experiment, trial:* onfoundleness
experience (v.), 1 *test (v.), prove:* afond
2 *examine, test:* fand
experiment: overfindness, onfoundness
experiment, explanation, experience, trial: onfoundness
experiment, trial: overfoundness
expire: end, run out
explain: go over/ through, set out, tell why
explanation, experiment, experience, trial: onfoundness
express: say, put over, utter, tell
expression: sayness
expressive: say a lot, well worded
expulsion, dismissal: awaydriveness
extend: building onto, broaden
extending east: eastlong
extending NW: westnorthlong
extent, surface, liberality: broadness
external(ly): outward(ly), outside
extract: get/ draw out, get from, gather from
extraneous, external, foreign: outkind

extraordinary 1 *immense:* unmete
2 *rare:* seldseen
extravagance: unmeteness
extreme: over the top, too far
extremely: highly, most, overly
extremity: endmostness
exude: give off, let off
exultation: highbliss, highting

F

face: onseen, anleth
face, beak: neb, nib
face, countenance: wlita
faculty: skill
fail: fall short of, miss the mark, blow it
failure to: if you do not, unless you
fallacious: misleading, unsound
false: wrong, not right
false, deceitful, treacherous: trueless
falsehood, deceit, treachery: truelessness
familiar, manifest, certain: couth
familiarly, manifestly, certainly, evidently: couthly
family: kin, folks, inherd
family/ kin, pertaining to: kinly
famished, starving: hungerbitten
famous, noble: breme
fantastic: great
farmer, horticulturalist: earthtiller
fastidiousness: chisness
fatigue: weariness

fault, vice: unthew
favour (n.), grace, bounty, pleasure: 1 este
2 *pleasure:* wellquemness
favour (v.): to be for
favourable: soundy
fecundity, fertility: bearingness
feminine: womanly
fertility, fecundity: bearingness
fertility, productivity, fruitfulness: wastumbearingness, wastumbearness
fierce, cruel, violent, severe: rough, wild, grim, rethy
finally: lastly, at last
finger joint: fingerlith
finish: end, ending, break off
firm: hard, steadfast, tough
firmly established: rootfast, steadfast
fiscal: gavelly
fix, unite, connect, compose: fay
flexibility: lithebyness
flexible with leeway, open, bendy, litheby
flood barrier/ protection: floodward
flower: bloom
fluctuate: go up and down
fluent, verbose: wordful
fluency, eloquence: toungeness
foetus, embryo: unborn child, birther
font (baptismal): fulloughtbath
for the duration of: while, as long as
for the purpose of: to, so as to
foreign: althedish, outlandish

foreign nation: althede
foreign, alien, strange: fremd
foreignness: althediness
forest: weald, wold
form: shape, shapen, build, make, set up
form, pattern: onlikeness
formation: 1 setting up 2 *creation:* shapeness
fornication: forlayness
fornicator: forlier
fortunate, prosperous: eady
fortunately, prosperously: eadily
fortune: eadiness
forum: mootstow
foundation n. 1 start, setting up, grounding, groundwork, frumth, groundwall 2 *f. stone:* groundstone 3 *position, institution, construction, record:* setness
foundation, base, support, station, position, state, condition: staddle
fount, source: ordfrume
frank: straight, blunt
fratricide: brotherslaying
fraud, deception, deceit: swiking
fraudulent, deceitful: fakeful, swikeful
frequent: often, felefold
frequently: often, many times
frivolity: lightmoodness
from remote place/ time: ferren
frugal, economical: holdsome, thrifty
fruit: ovet , wastum
fruit, product, produce: wastum
fruitfully, productively: wastumly

fruitfulness, productivity, fertility: wastumbearingness, wastumbearness
frustrate: thwart, hinder, beway
frustrated mood/ distressed: angmood
frustration, distress: angmoodness
fuel: firefood
fulfilment, completion: filledness
function, occupation: brooking
functionally, serviceably: brookingly
functionary, attendant, officer: ambighter, wike
furnish: set up with, give, with
future (a.): coming, forthcoming, to be
future (n.): aftertime, time/ days to come/ to be, hereafter, forthshaft

G

generous: big hearted, kind, unmean, givle
generous, virtuous: custy
general, commander: heratower
generation, race, tribe: strind
generosity, liberality: givleness
gentle: smolt
gentleness: 1 smiltness 2 *humility, submission:* edmede
gently: smoltly
genuflection: kneebowing
give a preview: foreshow
glacial: ickly
glade, valley: dale, dene, slade

glorify: wulder
glorious: wulderful, wuldry
gloriously: wulderfully
glory, splendour: wulder
glossary: wordlist
gluttonous: 1. overeattle 2. *to be g.:* overeat, to
gluttony: overeattleness
go on expedition: fird
grace, pleasure, favour, bounty: este
gracefulness: estfulness
gracious: 1 estful, esty 2 *respected, honest:* orefast
graciously: 1 estely 2 *respectfully, honestly:* orefastly
gradually: stepmeal
graciousness: estiness
grandfather: eldfather
grandmother: eldmother
granary: cornhouse
grateful (in advance): forethankful
gratitude: thankfulness
gratitude, deserving g.: thankworthy
gratuitous: uncalled for, needless
great grandfather: third eldfather (*great great g.* = fourth eldfather a.s.f.)
grief: heartsoreness
grieve, vex, afflict: awhene
grievously, severely, cruelly: tharly
group: team, gathering, flock
guard (v.), protect: beward
guardian: ward, holder, holdand
guardian of treasure: hoardward
guidance, discipline: steerness

guide, demonstrator, exhibitor: beshower
guileless: fakeless

H

habit, usage, custom, conduct (n.), disposition, manners: thew
habitable: erdingly
habitation: erdstead, earthbegoingness, woneness
habitual: thewful
habitually: woningly
hall officer: hallthane
handle: arine
harbour, port: hithe
harmonious, united, agreeable: thwear
harmoniously, agreeably: thwearly
harmony, unity, agreement: thwearness
have regard for, provide for: besee
having a stable, settled home: hearthfast
herbivorous: plant eating
heritage: yearve
hero: heleth
hiatus: break, gap
high official, prefect: reeve
high quality: uply
hilarious: laughterful
hindrance: hinderness
honest: truthful

honour, respect, favour: 1 ore, oreworthness
2 *respect, reverence:* oring 3 *dignity:* worthfullness
honouring, valuing: worthing
honourable, dignified: 1 worthful, oreworth 2 *moral, virtuous:* thewfast 3 *reputable:* unforcouth
honourably, with dignity: worthfully, oreworthily
hope, opinion, expectation, supposition: ween
hope (v.), expect, imagine: ween
horrible: loathly, hately
horticulture: earthtilth
horticulturalist: earthtiller
hospitable: comelithe, guestly
hospitality: comelitheness
host at a meal: eatgiver
hostage: yisle
hostage, state of being: yislehood
hostile, odious: hately, loathly, hattle
hostile intentions, with: hatethinkle
hostility: harmheartness, hattleness, loathingness
human race: earthkin
human/ common right, generally accepted: folkright
humane: metheful
humanely, moderately, proportionally: methely
humble: lowly, meek, mild
humility, submission: edmede
humble, to: make low/ meek, bring down

233

honest, respected, gracious: orefast
honestly, respectfully, graciously: orefastly
honesty, respect: orefastness
human: werely
human race: werekin
hydrophobia: waterfrightness
hyphen: dash

I

i.e. (id est): that is, t.i.
ibid (ibidem): in the same work, i.s.w.
if this is not the case: if not
if this is the case: if so
ignite, inflame, incite, consume: anneal
ignobility, humiliation: unathelness
ignominious: bismearful
ignorance: unloredness
ignorance, stupidity: unwisdom
ignorant: unlored
ill mannered, immoral, inconstant: thewless
illegible: can't be read
illiteracy: unreadness
illiterately: unreadly
illuminate, enlighten: inlighten, onlight, onlighten, yondshine
illumination, enlightenment: onlighting, inlightness, onlightness
illuminator: inlightand/ inlighter
imagination: mind's eye, see in the mind

imagine, expect, hope (v.): ween
imitate: evenlatch
imitation: evenlatching, likebusning
imitator: evenlatcher
immature: unriped
immeasurable: unmete
immeasurably: unmetely
immediate: straight away, straight off, from now
immediately, instantly: straight away, right there/ then, thereright
immense, extraordinary: unmete
immersion: drenchness
immodest: unshamely
immoral: unthewfast, unthewful, thewless
immortal: deathless, undying
immovably, unmovingly, motionlessly: unstiringly, steadfastly
impart: tell, let know, give
impatience: unthild
impatient: unthildy
impatiently: unthildly
impenetrably: unthroughshotingly
imperatively: bebidingly
imperfect: unfulfremed
imperfection: unfulfremedness, unfulfreming
impertinence: cheek
impetuous, to be: forthyearn
impractical, redundant: unworkly
implant, introduce into: onsow
implement: do, set about/ to, go ahead with, get started on
implore: beg, beseech

importance: weight
importance, value, estimation: worthliness, worthness
important function: highthaning
important, valuable, distinguished: worthly
impose put upon, onset
impossible, not possible: unmightly
impressive work/ action, deed, miracle: wonderwork
imprison, confine: beclose
impudent, confident: headbold, cheeky
in accordance with: in line with
in addition: as well, also, furthermore, withal *in addition to:* as well as, on top of
in conjunction with: with, together with
in good condition, prosperous: soundful
in lieu of: instead of
in manner of foreigners: altheodily
in my manner: minely
in order/ succession: endbirthly
in perpetuity, perpetually: everly
in prejudicial way, prejudgementally: fordeemedly
in receipt of: get, have
in regard to: about, on
in terms of need: needwise
in the event of: if, when
in the eventuality of: if, when
in view of the fact that: as
in way that marks/ cuts off: sheeringly

inability: unmightiness
inability to injure: unscathefulness
inaccuracy: offsetness
inaccurate, incongruous: unwrast
inaccurately, incongruously: unwrastly
inaccurately, erratically: missly
incantation: galdersong
incarnation: infleshness, fleshness
incidence: how often
incite, consume, ignite, inflame: anneal
incitement, instigation, exhortation: tighting
inclination: want, feeling
inclined to laugh: laughle
including: with, such as, with ...too/ also
incompetence misholdsomeness
incompletion: unfulfreming
incongruous, inaccurate: unwrast
incongruously, inaccurately: unwrastly
inconsideration: unfreming
inconstancy, mutability: whurfulness
inconstant, unreliable: untruefast, whurful
inconstant, ill mannered, immoral: thewless
incontinence: unholdsomeness
incontinent: unholdsome
inconvenience, trouble: uneathliness
inconvenient: awkward
inconvenient, unsuitable: unhaply
incorporate: bring in, take up, embody
incorrect: wrong, not right, unright

incorrect/ wrong education: forlearning
incorrectly: unrightly
incorruptedly: unforrotedly
incorruptibly: unforrotingly
increase (v.): raise, up, swell, broaden
increase (n.), accumulation: upping, rise
incredible: unlieveful, can't be believed, unbeliev*able*
incredibly: unlievefully, unlievedly, unbeliev*ably*
incredulity: unlievefulness
increment: raise, raise up, step
incur: run up, get
incursion: infare
indefatigable: unweary
independence: selfdom
indiscreetly, indiscriminately, irrationally: unshedwisely
indiscretion, indiscrimination, irrationality: unshedwiseness
indiscreet, indiscriminate, irrational: unshedwise
indescribably: untellingly
indescribably, ineffably: unsayingly
indiscrimination, irrationality, indiscretion: unshedwiseness
indiscriminate, indiscreet, irrational: unshedwise
indiscriminately, indiscreetly, irrationally: unshedwisely
index, indicator, discloser: beckonand/ beckoner
indicate: show, mark, mean

indicator, discloser, index:: beckonand/ beckoner
indifferent: neither one way or the other, unyearnful
indigenous, native: inlandish
individual, private, special: onlepy
individuality, privacy, speciality: onlepiness
indolent (v.): idleyearn
industrious: hard working, workful, deedly
ineffable: untellable, cannot be told
ineffably, indescribably: unsayingly
inevitably: unfightingly
inextricably: unbreakingly
inferior: lower, lower/ less than, less, netherly
inferiority: netherness
infirmity, state of not being trim: untrimness
inflame, incite, ignite, consume: anneal
inflame: inheaten
inflammation: walm
inflation: blowness
inflexibly: unbowingly
inflict upon: onbeload
infrequently: unseldom
ingratitude: unthank
inhabit: live/ dwell in, wone
inhabitant: earthbeganger
inhale: breath in
inharmonious, disunited, disagreeable: unthwear
inharmoniously, disagreeably: unthwearly
inherit: yearve

inhospitable: uncomelithe
iniquity, injustice: unrightwiseness, wrongdoing, wickedness
initiate: begin, start
injure: hurt, harm, wrong, scathe
injurious: scatheful, scathy
injurious deed/ crime: scathedeed
injurious person, antagonist: scather
injury, damage: scatheness, scathiness, scathing
injustice, iniquity: unrightwiseness
innocence, simplicity: bilewhitness
innocent: 1 unshildy, unsinny, shildless 2 *simple, sincere:* bilewhit
innumerable: unmete
innumerableness unmeteness
innumerably: unmetely
inoffensive: unharmyearn
inquire: throughseek, frayne
inquirer, investigator: speeriand/ speerer
inquiry: seekness, befrining
inquisitive, curious: frimdy
insane: mad, brainsick
insatiably: unfilledly
insatiably, avariciously: yetsingly
inscription: inwriting
insensitive: unfeeling
insensitivity: feelessness
inseparable: untodealy
inseparably: unsunderedly, unshearingly
inserted: insetted
inspection: inshowing
inspection, examination: onbeshowing

inspiration: onblowness (see note: p. 84)
inspire: inblow (see note: p. 84)
instability: unsteadfulness
instant: handwhile
instantly, immediately: straight away, right there/ then, thereright
instigation, incitement, exhortation: tighting
institute (n.): setness
institute (v.): inset
institute, to: begin, start, set up, lay down, get going
institution, foundation, position, construction, record: setness
institution, regulation: insetness
instruct, command: bebid
instruct by example: beseen
instruction: teaching, learning
instructor: lorethane
insult, derision: hoker
intellect: wit, anget
intelligence: wit, wits, brains
intelligent: angetful
intemperance: unmetefastness
intemperate, immoderate, excessive: unmetefast
intend, purpose (v.), design (v.): underbegin
intense, excessive, severe: swithly
intensity, severity, excess: swithliness, swithness
intention: inthink, inthought
inter alia/ alios: among others/ other things

237

intercept: 1 forfare 2 *i. with vehicle/ horse a.s.f.:* forride
interest (on loan a.s.f.): gavel
interim: meantime, for now
interior, internal: inly, inside, inward
interjection: betwixalayedness
intermission: betweenforletness, forletting
internal disease: inaddle
internal pain: inwark
internal, interior: inly, inside, inward
internally: inside, inwardly, inly
international: worldwide
interpolate: put in, misleadingly put in/ say
interposed: set between, betwixset
interpreter, translator: wender
interrogation, questioning: frayness
interrupt: cut in, break in, break
intolerable: unbearable, can't bear/ stand
intolerably: untholingly, unbearably
introduce: bring/ lead/ let/ put in, spread, inlead
introduce into, implant: onsow
inundate: flood over
invent: : think up, think of, come up with
inventor, originator: frumer
invention, device, discovery: afoundness, findle, withmeetedness
invert: put upsidedown/ the other way up
investigate: underseek, speer

investigate, examine, scrutinise: underseek, ascruten
investigation: 1 speering, scrutning 2 *trail, test, proof:* fanding
investigator, inquirer: speeriand/ speerer
invisible: unseen, can't be seen
invisibly: unseenly
invitation: lathing
invite: inlath
involuntarily: unwilsomely
irrational, indiscreet, indiscriminate: unshedwise
irrationality, indiscretion, indiscrimination: unshedwiseness
irrationally, indiscretionately, indiscriminately: unshedwisely
irreverence, indignity: unoreworthness
irritate: irk, bug
irritate, provoke, enrage: greme
irritating: irksome, bugging
isolate: cut off
issue: give out/ off/ forth
itinerant, widely travelled: widegoing

J

jaundice: yellowaddle
join 1 *associate:* thede 2 *unite, connect, fix, compose:* fay
joined, merged, united, unified: samedfast
joining, joint, composition, diagram: fay

joint: lith
journey: fareing
joy of youth: youthmirth
joy, pleasure: blitheness
joyful: blithe, happy, winsome
judge (v.): deem
judge (n.): deemer/ deemster
jump: leap
junction: wayleet
junior: young, younger
just: rightdoing, fair, right
just: only, but (as in 'all but', 'none but' a.s.f.)
just, in a correct way: rightwise
justice: fairness, rightness, rightwiseness
justice, righteousness: righwiseness
justifiably: rightwisely
justification: rightwising
justify: rightwise, to
juvenile: young, youngster, youthful, youth, child

K

keep vigilant, alert, keep vigil: throughwatch

L

laborious: arvethly
laboriousness: longsomeness, arvethliness
labour: 1 work 2 *trouble, difficulty:* arveth
laceration: slitness
lack of unity, disturbance, discord, disharmony, disagreement: unthwearness
lacking perception: ongetless
lament: beweep
lamentably: beweepingly
lamentation: sorrowword
land force/ army: landhera
language: tongue, speech, rerde
latitude: leeway:
lay foundations (v.): groundwall, to
laziness: slackerness
legal: lawly
legal (in sense not breaking law): lawful
legal right: lawright
legible: can be read, read*able*
lethally: deathbearly
lethalness: deathbearness
lethargic, somnolent: sleeple
lethargy: 1 sleepfulness 2 *somnolence:* sleepleness
liberal: free minded, roop
liberalise: free up, unfetter, unshackle
liberality: roomheartness, roopness
liberality, bountifulness: roomgivleness
liberality, generousness: givleness
liberating: aleasinglike

239

liberator: 1 freeand 2 *deliverer, redeemer:* aleasand/ aleaser
liberty: freedom
library: bookhouse
lifeguard: lifeward
likeable: likeworthy, likeworth
likeably, pleasingly: likeworthly
likeability: well likeworthness, likeworthness
limit: bound, keep down, keep to
liquid emetic: spewdrink
literary: bookly
literature, consideration of l.: readthoughting
literary commentator: readthoughter
live luxuriously: to este
liver complaint: liveraddle
loaning/ security trouble: borrowsorrow
local: stowly
locality, site, position, station: stowe, stow, stead
location, place, position, station: stead, stowe
logic: wordlock
loquacity: speakleness
loyal, noble, brave: 1 thanly 2 *l. to a lord*: lordhold
loyalty, allegiance: holdship
lunar: moonly
lunatic: moonsick

M

magic: galdercraft
magnanimous: great minded
maintain: keep up/ going, hold, uphold, stay on/ with
make fortunate: eady
make noble: to athel
making peace: sibsoming
male, masculine: mannish
maleness, masculinity: manship
malevolent: evilwilling
malice: evilwillingness, evilyearness
malicious: nithy
maliciously: nithfully
manager: dightner, workreeve
mania, zeal, rage: hotheartness
manifest, certain, familiar: couth
manifestation: atewedness, (known root: atew)
manifestly, certainly, familiarly, evidently: couthly
manner: way
manners, usage, custom, habit, conduct (n.), disposition: thew
manual: handbook
manual art: smithcraft
marine, maritime: sealy
maritime, marine: sealy
market: chapstow
married (man): wifefast
marry: wed
marry (a wife): wive
marrying: wiving
martial: heraly

masculine, male: mannish, manly, mannishness
masculinity, maleness: mannishliness, manship
masculinely: mannishly
masonry: wallwork, stonetimber
maternal: motherly, mothren
matter: stuff, thing(s)
mayor, provost: boroughreeve
measure, degree, proportion, rate: methe
mechanics: workings, workcraft
mediator: middliand
mediocre: middling
mediocrity, centrality: midness
meditate: underthink
meditate, ponder, determine: hedge
melancholy: down (hearted), low, heavyhearted
mellifluous: honeysweet
memorandum: minding
menace: threat
menstruation: monthsickness
menstruous: monthsick
mental: mind, of the mind, in the head
mention: talk/ speak of
mercy, compassion, benevolence: milce
merged, unified, absorbed: samed
merged, joined, united, unified: samedfast
message: errandspeech
metropolis: elderborough
militarily: firdwise
military (the) (n.): firdship
military equipment: heriot

military expedition: wyesith
military operations on land: landfirding
military service: firdfare
military, martial: firdly
minister: thane
minister of the church: churchthane
ministerial: thanely
ministry, service, administration: thaning
minority: lessness
miracle: 1 wondertoken 2 *impressive work/ action, deed:* wonderwork
miscarriage: misbirth
miser: feeyetser
miserable, troubled: unblithe, sorrowly, yomer
miserably 1 *pitiably:* armly 2 *destitutely:* tharfingly 3 *with trouble:* yomerly
misery, trouble: 1 woe, yomering 2 *poverty, distress:* ermth
misfortune: mishap, woe, lack of luck
missile: shoting
mitigation, satisfaction: quemeness
model, pattern, example: beseen, beseening
moderate: metefast
moderately: metefastly
moderately, humanely, proportionally: methely
moderation: metefastness
modest: shamefast
modus operandi: way of working

moisture: wetness
monitor (n.): overseer
monitor (v.): oversee, look after
more excessive: swither
moral (a.): thewly, thewfast, thewful
morally, virtuously: thewfastly
mortality: deathliness
most central: midmost
most particularly, most especially: mostlyest
motion, proposition, proposal, purpose: forthsetness, foresetness
motionlessly, immovably: unstiringly
mountain: highberg
move, to; disturb, agitate, excite: onstir
movement 1 *disturbance:* unstillness, onstiredness 2 *power of motion, disturbance, tumult:* stirness
multiple: manifold, many
in multiple ways: manifoldly
multiplicity, abundance, complexity: manifoldness
multiply by: times
multitude: felefoldness
mutability, changeability, inconstancy: wendingliness, whurfulness
mystery, profundity: 1 deepness 2 *secret, secrecy:* roun

N

narration, statement: kithing

nation, community, population, administration, association: 1 thedeship 2 *population, people:* folkship 3 *n., province:* thede 4 *foreign nation:* altheod
national, social, provincial: thedely
national council, parliament: witanmoot
native : inlander
native, of our country: ourlandish
native, indigenous: inlandish
natives: landfolk
nature, quality: suchness
nautical: shiply
naval: fleetly
naval battle: shipfight
navigation: wayfinding
necessarily: needbehovely, needbehovedly, behovely
necessary: needful, needed, needly, needbehove
necessitate: need, have to
necessity: needness, needhood, needwiseness, needbehovedness
necessity, distress: tharf
negative: unfremeful
neglect: lack of care, carelessness
neglect (v.): 1 overlook 2 *disregard, despise:* forhow, misyeme
neglecter, despiser: forhowand/ forhower
negligence: yemelessness
negligent: yemeless
negligently: yemelessly
negotiations: talks
nephew: brother's/ sister's son

newly converted: newwhirved
nobility: 1 athelness 2 *noble class:* athelkind
noble born: athelborn
noble, aristocratic: athel
noble, brave, loyal: thanly
noble class: athelkind
non suffering injury: unscathedness, unscathefulness
not ambiguous: untwoly
not causing suffering/ injury: unscatheful
not contrarily/ discordantly: unwitherwardly
not considered, not expected: unbethought, unforthought
not contrary/ discordant: unwitherward
not dangerous, not injurious: unscathy
not dangerously, not injuriously: unscathily
not described, not planned: unfremed
not desired: unbecraved
not discordant/ contrary: unwitherward
not displayed, not demonstrated: unbeshowed
not injurious, not dangerous: unscathy
not injuriously, not dangerously: unscathily
immoderate, intemperate, excessive: unmetefast
not planned, not described: unfremed
not of noble birth: unathelborn

not possible, impossible: unmightly
not pretty, disfigured, deformed: unwlitty
not useful, unprofitable: unfremeful
notice (v.), perceive: underget, onfind, yeme
noticeable: marked
notion: thought
nourishment: feedness
novelty: newness

O

obedience: 1 hearsomeness 2 *submission:* underthedeness 3 *discipline:* thewfastness
obedient: heedful, hearsome
obediently: heedfully, hearsomely
obey (v.): hearsome
obligation: boundness
obliged: have to
oblique: slanting
oblivion: forgetelness
obscure: thesterly
obscure, to: fordim, thester
observance: 1 holdness 2 *practice, exercise:* begeng
observance, restraint, preservation, devotion: holdsomeness
observation: beholdness
obsolete: out
obstacle: thing on/ in the way, hinderness
obstinacy: onewillness

obstruct: 1 hinder 2 *prevent:* stand in the way of, forstand
obtain: get
occasion: time, chare
occupy: 1 busy, keep busy 2 *posses:* besit
occupying/ established in a house: housefast
occurrence: happening
ocean: sea, high sea, the deep
odiferous: stenchbringing
odious, hostile: hattle
of equal birth: evenborn
of foreign nation: althedy
of harbour/ port: hithely
of no avail, without result: noughtly
of our country, native: ourlandish
of the people, secular: folkish
offence, ruin (n.): fallness
offer, order (v.), proclaim, summon, present (v.), command (v.), direct, announce, declare: abede
office: 1 ambighthouse 2 *prefecture:* reeveship 3 *service, command:* ambight
officer, attendant, functionary: ambighter, wike
old age: oldness, eldness, forolding
omit: leave out/ off, overlook
omnipotence: almightiness, almight
on the contrary: its the other way, there again
op cit (opus citatum):   work quoted
operation: 1 work, working, running
2 *workability:* workness

operationally, practically: workly
opinion, supposition, hope (n.), expectation: ween
opponent, adversary: witherling
opportunity: tideliness, davenliness
oppose, resist: be/ go/ stand/ set against, *oppose*, forstand
opposite: straight over from, over against
opposition: 1 withsetness 2 *adversity:* witherwardness
oppress, trample, afflict, repress: thrutch
order: endbirth
order (v.), proclaim, summon, present (v.), command (v.), direct, announce, declare, offer: abede
order - in o., in succession: endbirthly
ordering, disposition: dightning
orientals: eastleod
origin: 1 from, stem, frume 2 *cause:* frume
3 *foundation:* frumth
original: 1 first, ordfrim 2 *primitive:* frumly
original creation, primeval condition: frumshaft
originate: stem/ start/ begin from
originator, inventor: frumer
ornithology: birdlore
out of control, profligate: steerless
outward passage: outfare
overtalkative: overspeakle
overtalkitiveness: overspeakleness

244

P

pacific, peaceable: frithsome
paganism: heathendom, heathenness
page, chamberlain: bowerthane
pain, suffering: wark; f.e. found in: bladderwark, breastwark, heartwark, liverwark, shoulderwark, sidewark
palate: mouthroof
parable, allegory: onlikeness
park (n.): eddish
parliament, national council: witanmoot
part: share, deal, bit
part, west p.: westdeal; also: eastdeal a.s.f.
participate: take part
pass: go by, spend
passage, passing away: ferness
passing away, passage: ferness
passing, transitory, temporary: whiling
passion, suffering, endurance: tholing
past (n.): time(s)/ days gone by
pastoral: herdly
paternal (ancestral): forthfatheren
paternal: fatherly
patience: thild, longsomeness
patient: thildy
patient, to be: thild
patiently: thildily
pattern, example, model: beseen, beseening

pattern, form: onlikeness
paucity: fewness
pauper, poor/ destitute person: tharver
peaceable: sibsome
peace: frith, sib
peace agreement, treaty: frithwrit
pedestrian: footly
penetrate: get into, throughgo
penitence: deedboteness, deedbote
penultimate: last but one
people: 1 folk(s) 2 *nation, province:* thede
3 *population, nation:* folkship
people's right: folkright
per annum: yearly, a year
per capita: a head, each
per day: daily, a day
per diem: daily, a day
per person: each, a head
per se: as such, by or in itself
per year: yearly, a year
perceive, notice: underget, onfind
perceive, recognise, distinguish: onget
perception, recognition: ongetness
perception, comprehension: understandness, ongetness
perceptive: ongetful
perceptively: ongetfully
perform: 1 bego 2 *proclaim, relate:* kithe
perhaps: maybe
perilous, dangerous: plightly, freckenful
perishable, transient: fallenly
perjury: forswornness, oathbreach

permanent: settled, steady, ongoing, steadfast
permissible: leavedly
permit: let
permit (v.), consent to: thave
perpetually, in perpetuity: everly
perseverance, persistency, tenacity: throughwoning, throughwoningness, throughwoness
persevere: go/ fight on, keep at it
persist: keep on/ up
persistency, perseverance, tenacity: throughwoning, throughwoningness, throughwoness
person who is evil-disposed: unrightwilland/ unrightwiller
personally: for one's self, in one's self
personal power: handweald
persons: folk(s), those (who)
persuade: beswape
perusal: throughlooking
peruse: read, go over/ through, look over/ through
pervade: yondfare
perverse: warped
perversion: warpness, towarpness, towarpedness
pervert (v.): bewarp
philosopher, sage: witter
phobia: fear, fright
phrase, proverb, sentence: quide
physical: bodily

piecemeal: bit by bit, a bit at a time, bitmeal
pierced: holed, throughholed
pilot: 1 shipsteerer, helmward 2 *director:* steerer
pitiably, miserably: armly
pity: armheartness
place 1 *location, position, station:* stead 2 *of death:* deathstead 3 *of demonstration/ exhibition:* showingstowe 4 *of meeting, assembling:* moothouse
place (v.): set, stow
place before, propose: foreset
pleasant, agreeable, acceptable: queme
please (v.) satisfy, comply with: queme
pleasing 1 *likeable:* likeworth 2 *satisfying:* qweming 3 *satisfying, suitable, satisfactorily:* quemely 4 *deserving gratitude:* thankworthy
pleasingly, likeably: likeworthly
pleasure 1 *delight, joy:* blitheness, winsomeness, wellquemness 2 *satisfaction, mitigation:* quemeness 3 *ease:* eathness 4 *favour, grace, bounty:* este
pledge, to: wedfasten
pledged: forwedded
pleurisy: sideaddle
plumb line: wallthread
plunder: herahuth, houth
plural: more than one
plus: and, also
poison, venom: atter
poisonous, venomous: attery, atterly, atterbearing

pollute, dishonour: besnit
pollution, degradation: besnitness
ponder, meditate, determine: hedge
poor/ destitute person, pauper: unhaver, tharver
poor quality: unrightcrafting
poor, destitute, miserable: arm
poorly: 1 *destitutely:* tharvly 2 *miserably, pitiably:* armly
popular: 1 well-liked, folk 2 *public, common:* folkly
popular: in terms of what is p.
population, nation, people: folkship
population, community, nation, administration, association: thedeship
portray: outline, outliken
portent, sign of misfortune: woetoken
position, place, site, locality, station: stowe, stow, stead
position, foundation, institution, construction, record: setness
position, base, foundation, support, station, state, condition: staddle
positive, constructive: fremeful
positively, constructively: fremefully
positive attitude: winsomeness
positively: winly
possible: maybe, could/ might be, mightly
possibility: mighliness
posterity: aftergoingness, afterwardness
poverty, destitution: tharfliness, tharfedness
poverty, misery, distress: ermth

power, authority: 1 onwieldness, might 2 *p. of motion, disturbance, tumult:* stirness
powerful: mightful, mighty
pp (per procurationem): on behalf of, for
practically, operationally: workly
practice, exercise: begeng
practitioner: begenger
pray: bede
preaching: loreboding
preamble: forespeech
precede: go before, forego, foregang, forestep
precedence: forestepping
preceding: foregoing, going before, the last
precentor: foresingand
precious: dearworth
preciously: dearworthly
preciousness: dearworthness
precursor: forerunner, forestepper, foresteppand
predecessor: foreganger
predict: foretell, foresay
prediction: foresaidness
pre-eminence, authority, dominion, seniority: elderdom
pre-eminence, authoritativeness: elderdomliness
pre-eminently, authoritatively: elderdomly
preface: foreword, background
prefecture: reeveship
prefer: would rather/ sooner, like better/ more

prefer, in preference: would rather, forechoose
prejudge: fordeem, foredeem
prejudicial, in p. way: fordeemedly
prejudice (n.): fordeemedness
prejudice (v.), prematurely judge: fordeem
prematurely judge, prejudice: fordeem
premeditate, consider: forethink
premeditated: erebethought
premier: foremost, top
preoccupy (v.): forebusy
preparation: gearing, foregearing, gearingness
prepare: ready, get ready
preponderate: weigh more, be more/ greater
prescription: forewriteness
present (v.), order (v.), proclaim, summon, command (v.), direct, announce, declare, offer: abede
present (n.): gift
present (adj.): right now, now, at this time, here
present, to be p.: instand
presently, in way of being p.: instandingly
preservation, economy, restraint, observance, custody, devotion: holdsomeness
preside: foresit
press, oppress: athrick
presumption: 1 fortrueing 2 *arrogance:* uphaveness
presumptuous, venturesome: daresty
presumptuously, arrogantly: uphavely

prevent: 1 stop, stay, cut off, keep from, forestall, head off 2 *resist, oppose:* forstand
3 *dissuade:* belean 4 *surpass, surprise:* forcome
preview: forelook (as in to see a p.), foreshowing (as in to show a p.)
previewer: foreshower
previous: former, one(s) before
previously: formerly, before, herebefore, last time
pride 1: highmoodness 2 *arrogance:* wlenk
prime: foremost, first
prime minister, ruler: highelder, First Thane
primeval condition, original creation: frumshaft
primeval, primitive: frumthly
primitive: frumly
principal 1 *(a.):* main, foremost, top, highest 2 *capital:* headly
prior to: before
priority: high up, high(er) on the list
prisoner, captive (n.): haftling
privacy, individuality, speciality: onlepiness
private, separate, special, singular: sunderly
private, individual, special: onlepy
privilege: sunderfreedom
pro: for
probability: likelihood
proceed to: go on to

proclaim, announce: 1 forthsay 2 *order (v.), summon, present (v.), command (v.), direct, announce, declare, offer:* abede
proclaim, relate, perform: kithe
produce (v.): come up with, bring forth, forthbear
produce (n.), fruit, product: wastum
product, produce, fruit: wastum
productively, fruitfully: wastumly
productivity, fruitfulness, fertility: wastumbearingness, wastumbearness
profitability, usefulness: fremefulnes
profitable, beneficial: fremeful, fremely
profitably, usefully, beneficially: fremefully
profligate, out of control: steerless
profligately: steerlessly
profound: deep, heartfelt
profundity, mystery: deepness
programme (n.): set/ ongoing plan
programme, to: set to do
progress (n.): headway, forthwardness, forthship
progress (v.), advance: forthgang
progressive forthward
prohibit: forbid
prohibition: forbode
prolific: teamful
prologue: foreword, forewrit
promoter: furtherer, furtherand
promotion: furtheringness
pronounce: say
proof, trail, test: fanding

proper: rightworth
proper ordinance/ appointment: rightsetedness
properly: 1 rightly, aright, right; 2 *properly appointed/ established:* rightset
property: ownness
proportion, measure, degree, rate: methe
proportionally, moderately, humanely: methely
proposal, proposition, motion, purpose: forthsetness, foresetness
propose, place before: foreset
proposition, proposal, motion, purpose: forthsetness, foresetness
proprietor: owner
prospect: outlook
prosperity: 1 soundfulness, weal 2 *fortune:* eadiness 3 *development:* growness
prosperous: doing well, wealthy, wealy
prosperous, fortunate: eady
prosperously: soundfully
prosperously, fortunately: eadily
protect, guard: beward
protection, defence: shieldness, shielding, foreshieldness 2 *covering:* helm 3 *truce, asylum:* grith
protector, defender: 1 shielder 2 *guardian, ruler:* holdand, holder
protracted, tedious: longsome
protractedly, tediously: longsomely
proud: wlonk

prove, try, test: 1 costen   2 show   3 *experience:* afond
provenance: from
proverb, phrase, sentence: quide
provide for, have regard for: besee
province, nation: thede
provincial, social, national: thedely
proving, trial, temptation: costness
provocation: greming
provoke: 1 bring about, set off, get   2 *enrage, irritate:* greme
provost, mayor: boroughreeve
prudence: care, foresight, forethought, forethinkleness, howship
prudent: with forethought, forethinkle, howe
prudently: howly
public meeting: folkmoot
public officer: folkreeve
public place: folkstowe
public, popular, common: folkly
publicly known: folkcouth
pupil (child): learningchild
purchase: buy
purgative: cleansingdrink
purport: reckon, say
purpose (v.), design (v.), intend: underbegin
purpose (n.), proposition, proposal, motion: forthsetness, foresetness
pursue: go/ run after, follow
pursuit: toseekness, toseekening
pursuant to: under
push: shove
pusillanimous: weakminded

put safe, establish, utilise, use: befasten

Q

q.v. (quod vide): see
quadruple: fourfold
quadruply: fourfoldly
quality, nature: suchness
quarrelsome: unsibsome
quarrelsomeness: unsibsomeness
quarry, ravine: crundle
quarter: fourth, one in four
quartered: fitherdealt
question: frayning, frayn
question, to: befrine
questioning: frayning
quiet, silence: swey

R

race, generation, tribe: strind
radiance: shineness/ sheenness
rage, zeal, mania: hotheartness
rapid: fast, swift
rare, extraordinary: seldseen
rare, strange: seldly
rare, unusual, strange: seldcouth
rate, measure, degree, proportion: methe
ratify/ apply fully: fullfasten
rational: rightwittly

rationally, discriminately, discreetly: shedwisely
ravage: forharry, harry
ravine, quarry: crundle
reach: rine
rear: behind, back, endmost
reason: ground, wit
rebel (v.): rise up, rise/ go against
rebellious, disobedient: unhearsome
rebelliousness, disobedience: unhearsomeness
rebellion: uprising
recently: lately, of late, latterly
recognise, distinguish, perceive: onget
recognition, perception: ongetness
recompense, requite: foryield
reconcile: sibsome
reconciliation: eftthinging
record, foundation, position, institution, construction: setness
recover: get better/ over/ back, find again, acover
recovery, salvation: healness
recrimination: backblaming
rectify: put right, straighten out, put to rights
rectitude: rightness
redeemer, liberator, deliverer: aleasand
redemption, remission, release (n.): aleseness, aleasedness, eftleasing
reduce: lessen, lower, cut, bring down
reducing: lessening, lowering, cutting down, smalling
reduction: cut, lessening
reestablishment: edstathling

refer to: talking about, meaning
refrain: not do, hold, stay
refuge, reserve, sanctuary: frithstowe
refute, repel: withshove
regard - to have r. for, provide for: besee
regarding: about, on that
regeneration: eftkenedness
region: landstead, landship
regret: sorryness, rueness
regretful: rueful, ruey
regretting: rueing
regulation, institution: insetness
reimburse: give back
reject (v.): leave, cast aside/ outside, withchoose
rejection, abandonment: forsakeness
rejection, denial: forsaking, withsaking
relate, proclaim, perform: kithe
related: linked, kin
relative(s): kinsman/ woman/ folk, kith and kin
release (v.): let go, let out, alease
release (n.), redemption, remission: aleseness, aleasedness, eftleasing
reliable, trusty: truefast, trueful, wordfast
relieve: soothe, help, lessen
relinquish: forlet
relinquishment: forletness
remember: keep/ bear in mind, not forget, eftmind
remembering: eftmindy
remembrance: 1 mindiliness 2 memorandum: minding

remission, parole: letness
remission, redemption, release (n.): aleseness, aleasedness, eftleasing
remnant, legacy: lave
remorse: swithrueness
remote: slight, small, little, far off/ away, outside, farlen
remotely: outly
removal: taking away/ off, awayleadness, faring
remove: take away/ off, shift
remunerate: edyield
render: send, give, make
renew, restore: ednew, anew
renewal, restoration: anewing
renewer, restorer: ednewand
renounce: give up, do/ go without, not have
renounce, deny: atsake
reparation, atonement: betness
repeat: say/ do again
repel, refute: withshove
repentance: beruesing
replace: go instead, take the stead (of)
report (n.), obedience: hearness
reprehensible: steerworth
repress: keep/ hold down, quell
repress, trample, oppress, afflict: thrutch
reprimand: tell off
reproach (n.): 1 shendle 2 *disgrace, defilement:* besmear 3 *affliction:* shending
reproach (v.), disgrace, defile (v.): besmear

reproof: steerspeech
reptile: slinkand
repudiate: awayen
repulsive, terrible: atel
repulsively, terribly: atelly
reputable, honourable: unforcouth
require: need
requirement, duty: oughting
requisite: needbehoveness
requite, recompense: foryield
rescue, save: aredde
research, to: throughseek
resemblance: likeness
reserve: 1 misgiving 2 *sanctuary,*
refuge: frithstowe
reside: live, stay, dwell
residence: home abode, where one lives
resident, established (in a home): homefast
resist: oppose: withstand, stand it, stand up to, go against, hold oneself, forstand
resources, capability: wherewithal
respect, honour, favour: ore, oreworthness
respect, honesty: orefastness
respect, reverence: oring
respected, honest, gracious: orefast
respectfully, honestly, graciously: orefastly
restitution: edgift
restoration: 1 eftnewing 2 *renewal:* anewing
restore: edstall
restore, renew: ednew, anew

restorer, renewer: ednewand/ ednewer
restrain: hold/ keep back, hold, forhave
restraint: hinderness
restraint, temperance: 1 behavedness 2 *preservation, custody:* holdsomeness
restraint, economy, preservation, observance, devotion: holdsomeness
restrict: keep to/ within, keep down to
result: outcome, upshot
resume: go on, take up again/ once more
resurrection: upariseness, arist
retain: keep, hold, withhold, keep/hold back
retainer: handthane, elderthane
retentive, tenacious: fasthavle
retentiveness, stinginess, economy, tenaciousness: fasthavleness
reticent: keeping quiet, holding back
retinue, society, companionship: fareship
retire: withdraw, leave, go
return: go/ come back, againcome, edwend
revelation: atiwedness
revenge, vengeance: wreckness, wrack
revenue: income
reverence, respect: oring
review, summary: throughlooking
revive: edquicken
revolt (v.): rise up, rise/ go against

revolt: uprising
revolution, change: wharving
revolution, transition, change, conversion: wharveness
revolve, change, transfer, convert: wharve
rewriting: gainwrit
rich: wealthy
ride round: beride
right honourable: oreworthyful
righteousness, justice: righwiseness
rightful establishment/ appointment/ office: rightsetness
riparian: streamly
river bank: staith
rocky hill/ mountain: stoneberg
rotation, change, subversion: wending
row round: berow
ruin (v.), destroy: fordo
ruin (n.), offence: fallness
ruler: ricser, holder, holdand
ruler, prime minister: first thane, highelder

S

safe, secure: holdfast, heldly
sagacious: wiseheedly
sage, philosopher: witter
saint: hallow
salubrious: healthy, wholesome
salvation: 1 *recovery:* healness 2 *deliverance:* aredding
sanctifier: hallowand

sanctuary, refuge, reserve: frithstowe
satisfaction, mitigation: quemeness
satisfactorily, satisfying, suitable: quemely
satisfactory: enoughsome
satisfy, please (v.), comply with: queme
satisfying: qweming
satisfying, suitable, satisfactorily: quemely
saturate: throughdrench, indrench
sauna: stovebath
savage, fierce, cruel: slithe
savagely, fiercely, cruelly: slithely
save (coordinator): but, but not, though not
saviour: healand
scandal, disgrace: shandliness
scandalous, disgraceful: shandful
scandalously, disgracefully: shandly
scar: woundswathe
scare: frighten
school, college, university: learninghouse
sciatica: hipboneache
scrutinise, investigate: underseek
sea voyage: seafare
search: seek, look for
seclusion, separation, separateness, singularity: sunderliness, tweming
secret, secrecy, mystery: roun
secretary: inwriter
section (v.), amputate: offcarve
secular: worldkind
seduce: forlead, forspan
seduction, allurement: forspanning
seizure: gripness

selective: choosy
self-restraint, temperance, abstinence: forhaveness, forhavedness
seminal: seedly
senior: elder, higher
seniority: elderliness, eldership
seniority, authority, dominion, pre-eminence: elderdom
sense (n.): 1 way 2 *conscience:* inheed
sense (v.): feel
senseless: unwitful
senselessness: unwitfulness
sensitive: thinskinned
sentence, phrase, proverb: quide
separate: put asunder, break up
separate in two: tweme
separate, special, private, singular: sunderly
separateness, separation, seclusion, singularity: sunderliness, tweming
separating: betwixgoing
separation, seclusion separateness, singularity: sunderliness, tweming
separation, distinction, discretion: shed
sequel, succession: afterfollowedness
seratim: at one time
series, succession, arrangement: afterfollowingness, endbirthness
servant: 1 ambighter 2 *minister:* thane
serve: 1 *minister (v.):* thane 2 *command:* ambight

service: 1 ambightness 2 *ministry, administration:* thaning 3 *duty, ability, valour:* thaneship
serviceably, functionally: brookingly
severe: 1 hard, rough, tough, over the top 2 *strict:* tharl, stern, hard, tough, rough, tharlwise 3 *cruel, fierce, violent:* rough, wild, grim, rethy
4 *intense, excessive:* swithly
severe disability: crippleness
severity, strictness: tharlwiseness
severity, intensity, excess: swithliness, swithness
severely 1 *cruelly, grievously:* tharly 2 *exceedingly:* swith 3 *strictly:* sternly, roughly, toughly, tharlwisely
ship master: shipward
sic: so spelled!/ said!, thus spelled!/ said!
silence, quiet: swey
silent: soundless, still, unuttered, unspeaking, unspoken
similar: like, alike, akin to, much like
simple: 1 straightforward 2 *single, unique, sincere:* onefold 3 *sincere:* bilewhit
simplicity: 1 onefoldness 2 *innocence:* bilewhitness
sincere: heartfelt, deep, luter
sincere, single, unique: onefold
sincerity: luterness
single, unique, sincere: onefold

singular, separate, special, private: sunderly
singularity, separation, seclusion separateness: sunderliness, tweming
site of a house: housestead
site, position, locality, station: stowe, stow, stead
size, abundance: muchness
slave: theow
slavery: theowdom
sober: undrunk
sobriety: soberness
social, provincial, national: thedely
society, association: fellowship, fareship, thedeness
solar: sunly
soldier: wyeman, heraman
soldiering: ferding, firding
solidarity: steadfastness, oneness with
somnolence: sleepleness
soporific: sleepbear
sort (n.): kind
source, origin: frume, upcome, ord
space: room
spacious, spaciously: wellroomly
special, separate, private, singular: sunderly
special, private, individual: onlepy
special skill: sundercraft
speciality, privacy, individuality: onlepiness
splendour, glory: wulder
sponsor, advocate: forspeaker
squander (v.): forspend
stabilise: make steadfast

255

statement, narration: kithing
state, base, foundation, support, station, position, condition: staddle
state of not being trim, infirmity: untrimness
station, base, foundation, support, position, state, condition: staddle
station, location, place, position: stead
status: standing, standness
steam, vapour: ethem
sterility, unfruitfulness: unwastmbearness
stimulate: get going, raise, up
stipulate: set, set/ lay down, say
strange, foreign, alien: fremd
strange, rare: seldly
strange, unusual, rare: seldcouth
station, site, position, locality: stowe, stow, stead
strenuous, vigorous: cove
strenuously, vigorously, actively: covely
strict, severe: stern, hard, tough, rough, tharl, tharlwise
strictly, severely: sternly, roughly, toughly, tharlwisely
stinginess, retentiveness, economy, tenaciousness: fasthavleness
stupid: daft, dim/ slow witted, silly, sot
stupidity: silliness, daftness, dimness, sotship
subdue, subjugate: underthede
subject, to: 1 put through, make go through
2 *subjugate, subdue:* underthede

subjection, compulsion: 1 underdriveness
2 *submission, obedience:* underthedeness
subjugate, subdue: underthede
submarine (a.): underwater, undersea
submission, obedience: 1 underthedeness
2 *humility:* edmede
substance: stuff
substitute, to: put instead/ in the stead of
subterfuge: underhandedness
subtlety: smalliness
subtract: take, take away/ off
suburb: underborough
succession, series, arrangement: afterfollowingness, endbirthness
succession, sequel: afterfollowedness
succession - in s.: endbirthly
succumb: fall to
suffer, endure: thole
suffering, endurance, passion: tholing
suffering: hardship
suffering, pain: wark; f.e. found in: bladderwark, breastwark, heartwark, liverwark, shoulderwark, sidewark
sufficient: enough
sufficiently: enoughly
suffix: ending
suicide: selfmurdering
suicide - one who commits: selfmurderer, ownslayer
suitable: fitting

suitable, satisfying, satisfactorily: quemely
summon, order (v.), proclaim, present (v.), command (v.), direct, announce, declare, offer: abede
superficial: shallow
superfluity: overflowness
superior: higher, above, haughty, high
superscription: overwrit, overmarking
superstructure: overwork
supervene: overbecome
supervise: oversee, watch over
supplementary: more, further, on top of
support: bolster, fulltum
support, base, foundation, station, position, state, condition: staddle
support (v.), endure: underbear, bolster
supporter: fulltumer
suppose: take it as, guess, think, it seems
supposition, hope, opinion, expectation: ween
supremacy: the upper hand
surfeit: overfill, overfillness
surpass: go over, do better/ more
surpass, surprise: forcome
surprise: take aback
surprise, surpass: forcome
surrender: give in/ up/ over
surround: befare
surroundings: outabstandness
survive: live on, outlive, overlive

sympathise: evenfain
sympathy: evensorrowing
synonym: same meaning as

T

tacit: unspoken, wordless
talkative: felespeakle, felewordness, speakful, speakle, toungeful
tardy: slow, late
taste, to: smatch
tedious, protracted: longsome
tediously, protractedly: longsomely
tediousness: longsomeness
temperance, self-restraint, abstinence: forhaveness, forhavedness
temperance, restraint: behavedness
with temperance: forhavingly
temperate: mild
temporary, passing, transitory: whiling
temporary, transitory: whilewendly
temptation, testing, trial: costning
temptation, proving, trial: costness
tempter: costiand
tenacious, retentive: fasthavle
tenacity, perseverance, persistency: throughwoning, throughwoningness, throughwoness
tenacity, retentiveness, stinginess, economy: fasthavleness
terminate: end, stop

257

terrain: ground
terrible, repulsive: atel
terribly: 1 adreadingly 2 *repulsively:* atelly
terrific: great
test (v.), prove, experience: afond 2 *try, prove:* costen 3 *examine, experience:* fand
test (n.), trail, proof: fanding
testament, testimony: kitheness
tester, trier: fander
testifier: kither
testimony: kithedness
testimony, testament: kitheness
testing, temptation, trial: costning
theatre: playhouse
thorax, chest: forebody
timid: unbold
tolerably: forbearingly
torment (n.): thresting
torment (v.): dretch
totally responsible: fullholden
touch (n.): rining
touch (v.): 1 atrine 2 *handle:* arine 3 *reach:* rine
towards unity: togetherward
town citizen: boroughman
trader: chapman
tradition: eldsay
transgress, traverse: overgo
transient, perishable: fallenly
trial, testing, temptation: costning
trail, test, proof: fanding
trample, oppress, afflict, repress: thrutch
transfer: shift

transfer, revolve, change, convert: wharve
transfix: throughfasten
transform: forshape
transgress, do incorrectly/ wrongly: misdo
transition, change, conversion, revolution: 1 wharveness 2 *passage, passing away:* ferness
transitory, passing, temporary: 1 whiling 2 *temporary:* whilewendly 3 *changing, changeable:* wharvely
translate, change: put into, wend, awend
translator, interpreter: wender
transmit: broadcast, onsend, oversend
transparent: seethrough, showing through
travel: fare
travel over: overfare
travel with trouble: misfare
traverse: 1 overfare 2 *pervade:* yondfare 3 *surround:* befare 4 *transgress:* overgo 5 *perform:* bego
treacherous, false, deceitful: trueless
treachery, falsehood, deceit: truelessness
treachery, deceit: swike, beswike
treasure: goldhoard
treasury: goldhoardhouse
trial, experiment: overfoundness, onfoundness

trial, explanation, experiment, experience: onfoundness
trial, proving, temptation: costness
tribe, race, generation: strind
tribulation: 1 yomerness, threatness, thrutchness 2 *affliction:* dretchedness
tributary: sidestream, feeding into
trier, tester: fander
triple: threefold
triply: threely
triumph (v.): seyfast
triumph, victory (n.): sey, seyfastness
triumphal: seyerly
trouble (n.), difficulty: 1 angsomeness, swenk, swenkedness, arveth 2 *contrition:* threstness 3 *inconvenience:* uneathliness
trouble (v.): 1 swenche 2 *torment (v.):* dretch
trouble, difficulty: hardship, hard time/ thing, uneath, uneathness, heanhood, arvethness
trouble/ disease bearing: addlebearing
troubled, miserable: yomer
troublesome: 1 angsome 2 *laborious:* arvethly
troublesomely, with difficulty: angsomely, uneathly
truce, asylum, protection: grith
trusty, reliable: truefast, trueful, wordfast
try: fand
try, test, prove: costen
tumour: wen

tumult, power of motion, disturbance: stirness
turn (v.), convert: 1 bewend 2 *revolve, change, transfer, convert:* wharve
type: kind

U

ultimate: last, endmost
unabated: unlessened
unanimity: onemoodness
unanimous: sameheart, onemood
unarmed: weaponless, unweaponed
unavoidably: unforbowingly
unbearably: unbearingly
unchangeability: unwendness
unchanging: unwharving
uncle: eme
unconquered: unoverwon
uncontested: unbefought
uncorrected: unright
uncreated, unformed: unshapen
undeserving of gratitude: unthankworthy
   a. *of unthankworthy:* unthankworthily
undivided: untodealed
undividedness: untodealness
unencumbered: unheavied
unexpected: unweened
unexpectedly: unweenedly
unformed, uncreated: unshapen

unfortunate: unlucky, luckless, illstarred
unfruitful, unproductive: wastumless
unfruitfulness, sterility: unwastmbearness
ungracious: unestful
unguent: smearsalve
unification, union: samening
unified, absorbed, merged: samed
unified, joined, merged, united: samedfast
unique, single, sincere: onefold
uninhabited: folkfree
uninvited: unlathed
union: samening
unite, connect, fix, compose: fay
united, joined, merged, unified: samedfast
united, harmonious, agreeable: thwear
unity, harmony, agreement: thwearness
universal: everywhere, ally
university, school, college: learninghouse
unjust: unrightful, unrightwise
unjust judge/ critic: unrightdeemer
unmannered, immoral, disorderly: unthewful, unthewfast
unmarried: unbewedded, wifeless
unmasculinely: unmenishly
unmoving: unstiring, unstill
unmovingly, immovably: unstiringly, steadfastly
unnecessary: needless
unopposed: unbefought

unpleasant: unwinsome
unpleasantness: unwinsomeness
unproductive, unfruitful: wastumless
unprofitable, not useful: unfremeful
unrelated: unsibb
unreliable, inconstant: untruefast, whurful
unrenewingly: unanewingly
unrepproached: besmearless
unseasonable: untidely
unseasonableness: untime
unstable: 1 unsteadful, steadless, not steadfast 2 *perishable, transient:* fallenly
unsuitable, inconvenient: unhaply
unusual, rare, strange: seldcouth
urban: townly
usage, custom, habit, conduct, disposition, manners: thew
use (v.), utilise, put safe, establish: befasten
use (v.), enjoy: brook
use (n.), function: brooking
useful: 1 handy, neat 2 *profitable, beneficial:* fremeful
usefulness, profitability: fremefulnes
usefully, profitably, beneficially: fremefully
usual, customary: wonely
utilise, put safe, establish, use: befasten

V

v.s. (vide supra): see above
vain: empty, idle
vain desire: idlelust
vain joy: idlebliss
valid: true, good, worthwhile
valley, glade: dale, dene, slade
valour, duty: thaneship
valuable, important, distinguished: worthly
value, importance, estimation: worthness, worthliness
vanish, disappear: go, fordwine
vapour: smitch, smeech
vapour, steam: ethem
variety, diversity: mislikeness, missenliness
various: sundry, missenly
vehicle: fering
venomous, poisonous: attery, atterly, atterbearing
vengeance, revenge: wreckness, wrack
venturesome, presumptuous: daresty
verbose: wordy
verbose, fluent: wordful
verification: ground truthing
versus/ vs: against, playing
very: 1 highly, right, downright, most, fele
2 *exceedingly, severely:* swith
very likeable: well likeworthy
vex, grieve, afflict: awhene
via: go through/ by way of
vibrate: shake

vice, fault: unthew
victorious: seyerfast, seyfast, seyly
victory: seyer, seyerfastness
victory, triumph: sey, seyfastness
view (n.): outlook, thoughts, thinking
view (v.): look at/ on watch; think, deem as
vigil: nightwatch
vigilant: watchful, keep eyes peeled
vigorous: 1 strong, healthy, cove 2 *severe, strict:* tharl
vigorously, actively, strenuously: covely
villain: nithing
violent, severe, cruel, fierce: rough, wild, grim, rethy
virgin soil: maidenearth
virginity: maidhood
virtuous: 1 *generous:* custy
2 *moral:* thewfast, thewful
virtuously, morally: thewfastly
vis-à-vis: on, about
visible: seen, see*able*, seenly, eyeseen
vision: sight, sightness
visitor: comer, guest, ingenger, ingoer
viz (videlicet): namely
vocabulary: wordhoard, wordstock/ list
vocation: calling
voice: 1 steven 2 *language:* rerde, speech, tongue
volition: will
voluntarily: 1 wilfully, wilsomely
2 *arbitrarily:* selfwillingly

voluntary: wilful, selfwilling, wilsome
vomit: spew, be sick, sick/ throw up
voracious: greedy
vulgar: low, dirty, lowminded

W

war, combat: 1 hild 2 *battle:* guth 3 *contest:* wye
warrant officer, herald, preacher: beadle
warrior, soldier: wyeman
well demonstrated: wellbeshowed
well pleasing: wellquemedly
widely travelled, itinerant: widegoing
with a solid, firm roof: rooffast
with difficulty, troublesomely: angsomely, uneathly
with reference to: about
with regard to: about
with respect to: for, about
with temperance: forhavingly
without deceit, guileless: fakeless
without duplicity: untwofold
without necessity/ distress/ trouble: tharfless
without support: fulltumless
with trouble, miserably: yomerly
worth remembering, mentioning/ minding: mindworth
wound inflicting, dangerous: woundly

wrong/ incorrect education: forlearning

Y

yearly commemoration: yearmind

Z

zeal, rage, mania: hotheartness
zero: nought, nothing

Updated Words related to current words, but generally without obvious modern loanword equivalents (many of these are in Step 1):

Key: Updated words in **bold**.

awe: **aweless, awelessness, awely**
bear: **unbearing, wellborn**
bind: **unbindingly**
birth: **misbirth**
bliss: **blissy**
blithe: **unblithe**
blossom: **blossomy**
book: **booklore**
careful: **carefulness**

Christian: **Christianness**
cleanse: **uncleansed**
cliff: **cliffy**
craft: **craftless, craftly, songcraft, uncraft, uncrafty**
day: **middaily**
deadly: **undeadliness, undeadly**
deal: **dealtly**
dizzy: **dizzydom**
do: **misdo, ondoing, underdo**
drink: **overdrink**
earl: **earlish**
end: **endlessness, unended**
evil: **evilful, evilness, evily**
fake: **fakedeed, fakely**
fen: **fenny**
field: **fieldly**
fiend: **fiendship**
flood: **floodly**
forgive: **forgivenly**
forlorn: **forlornness**
friend: **friendlore**
frost: **frostly**
glad: **gladding/ glading, unglad, ungladly, ungladness**
good: **goodless, ungood**
grim: **grimful, grimness**
groundless: **groundlessly**
guest: **guesty**
harvest: **harvestly**
health: **unhealth**
heed: **unheedly, unheedy**
here: **hereonamong**
hither: **hithercome, hitherward**
hold: **mishold**
hue: **hueless, manyhuely**

in: **inwise**
inland: **inlandishness**
kin: **kinly**
late: **latemost, latesome**
laughter: **unlaughterworthy**
law: **lawbreach**
less: **lessly**
like: **likeworthily, likeworthiness, likingly**
little: **littleheedy, littleness, smally, unlittle**
loathe: **loathless**
live: **mislive**
lore: **loredom, lorely, loresome, lorewriter**
love: **lovesome, lovesomely, lovesomeness**
lust: **lustfulness, unrightlust**
manifold: **manifoldly**
man: **manless**
marred: **unmarred**
meat: **meatless**
might: **unmight, unmightily, unmightiness, unmighty**
mild: **mildheartness**
mind: **mindily, mindy**
mood: **hardmoodness, heavymood, moodful, moodless, moodsick, moodsickness, moodthought, sorrymood, starkmood, unmoodiness, weakmoodness**
much: **muchly**
narrow: **narrowness**
nether: **netherward**
nought: **noughtness**

old: **oldly**
overseas: **overseaish**
qualm: **qualmbearingly, qualmbearness, qualmful, qualmness**
room: **roomly**
rough: **roughful**
right: **rightwilling, unrightdeed, unrightdoand/ unrightdoer**
scathe: **scathingly**
seek: **foreseek**
set: **overset, underset**
shame: **unshamefulness**
show: **overshow, overshowand, overshower**
shrink: **misshrunk, unshrunken**
sin: **sinny**
sorrow: **sorrowless**
sound: **unsoundly**
speak: **misspeak, overspeak, unspeaking**
speech: **overspeech**
still: **unstillness**
tame: **handtame, untamedly**
teach: **misteach**
tear (n.): **teary** (a.)
thence: **thenceward**
think: **misthink**
thus: **thusly**
tight: **tightness**
token: **foretoken**

towardly, **towardness**
trim: **untrim, untrimly, untrimness**
true: **untruly**
uncouth: **uncouthly, uncouthness**
underneath: **underneathmost**
wrought: **unwrought**
upland: **uplandish**
spring: **upspring**
way: **wayless**
whole: **unwhole**
wife: **wifehood, wifely**
will: **wilsomness**
winsome: **winsomely**
wise: **wiseness, unwiseness**
wish: **wishedness, wishingly**
wit: **unwittily, unwitty, witlessness, wittyness**
womb: **wombaddle, wombhoard**
wonder: **wonderly**
worse: **worsely**
wrath: **wrathly**
write: **miswrite**
youth: **youthly**

Endword

The book has looked at some key areas of how English might look today had the English won at Hastings in 1066. We have seen that there would be lots of words which don't really look strange, or only a little so, and yet they haven't been part of how we talk for a long time. There would be other words which really do look strange. If we now come back to the questions asked in Note 8, under *what difference would it have made anyway?*, are we any closer to answering this now than we were at the start of the book? I think yes - but we can only go some way on this! Here are the questions from Note 8 again, with some suggested answers:

i) Would less educated people have felt such a gap between their own speech and that of the ruling classes right down to today?
Answer: This has really got to be 'no, they wouldn't have'. This would be true both in the times when French was the elite language (particularly 1066 to the mid 1300s or so), and also in terms of the posher words and phrases (of the kinds William Barnes noted) which are often *still* being pushed as 'higher' alternatives (for example, recall the needless use of *received* instead of *had* or *got* in the Lead-in, before Step 1).

ii) Would there have been less social friction and stress as a result?
Answer: If the answer to i) is basically clear, then there would surely have been less stress, and thus quite likely to have been less social friction too. But in exactly what ways is hard to tell.

iii) Might England have had a less class-ridden history, and generally been a fairer place to those who might appear to be underlings?
Answer: In as far as there may have been less stress and friction, then some negative effects of such a class-ridden society in history *could* have been less; exactly how is something which we cannot tell. On being a *fairer place* or not, in as far as words got and get one access to jobs and power, less class difference in speech would have meant at least one less barrier to those at the bottom.

iv) Could the history of fighting, colonial conquest and invasion, which ran through many aspects of England's dealings with the rest of Britain, Europe and the world - could this have been different?
Answer: We can say very little here. Might we at least dare to say that it seems unlikely that it would have been *worse*?

v) In light of question iv), how would we talk in Wales, Scotland, Ireland and elsewhere if the English had won in 1066?
Answer: Very hard to tell! But if there hadn't been so many English nobility and other settlers fleeing to Scotland, then Gaelic could have been stronger there. If Wales and Ireland had not each been hit by a scramble of Norman land-grabbers, they might have developed with Welsh and Irish being stronger languages. For elsewhere its harder to tell, but we can at least say that where English would have been spoken, it would have been more like the English in this book.

Do we leave it here, as a 'fun' look at what might have been - but was lost - or can we go further? Its up to you, speakers of English! We have seen many words that can give English even greater expression. It would only take the use of a word in a popular newspaper or TV/ radio show, or in novels and poetry for it to become noted as a current word. So drop one in an e-mail or slip it into a conversation! You may arouse positive interest and comment. Brand new words are always coming into the language - isn't it now about time that we 'wake up' some of these amazing words from the earlier wealth of English itself?

OUTGANG

Lightning Source UK Ltd.
Milton Keynes UK
04 November 2009

145775UK00002B/97/P

9 780755 211678